VISHWA
SHASTRA

future-oriented, interpreting India to a world that increasingly needs to understand this complex country as it becomes a leading power on the international stage'—**Nirupama Rao, former Indian foreign secretary and ambassador to the United States and China**

'Does the old international order get new India? Dhruva Jaishankar's tome traces the past and the future of India's place in the world. He calls out the outdated boxes and cliches still used for India—a stubborn inability to reflect changing realities. India is the face of a new kind of contestation in global affairs. It is pushing to reset flailing multilateral institutions even as it builds new coalitions in the Middle East, Indian Ocean and the Bay of Bengal. India is the change agent nobody saw coming'— **Shekhar Gupta, editor-in-chief and chairman, ThePrint**

'India's rise as a global power hasn't yet generated a body of literature that looks at the world through distinctly Indian lens. Dhruva Jaishankar has attempted to fill this gap with a study of India's strategic impulses over the ages. It is an invaluable guide to the possible choices that India could make in the twenty-first century. This book is rich in scholarship and shaped by original thinking'—**Swapan Dasgupta, former member of Parliament (Rajya Sabha)**

VISHWA SHASTRA

INDIA AND THE WORLD

DHRUVA JAISHANKAR

PENGUIN
VIKING
An imprint of Penguin Random House

VIKING

Viking is an imprint of the Penguin Random House group of companies
whose addresses can be found at global.penguinrandomhouse.com

Published by Penguin Random House India Pvt. Ltd
4th Floor, Capital Tower 1, MG Road,
Gurugram 122 002, Haryana, India

Penguin
Random House
India

First published in Viking by Penguin Random House India 2024

ISBN 9780670091058

Typeset in Adobe Caslon Pro by Manipal Technologies Limited, Manipal
Printed at Thomson Press India Ltd, New Delhi

www.penguin.co.in

MIX
Paper | Supporting
responsible forestry
FSC® C010615

Dedicated to the youth of India

उत्तिष्ठत जाग्रत प्राप्य वरान्निबोधत।
क्षुरस्य धारा निशिता दुरत्यया दुर्गं पथस्तत्कवयो वदन्ति ॥

—*Katha Upanishad 1.3.14*

Contents

Introduction | प्रस्तावना

Why India Matters, Why the World Matters

In 2008, the Tata Group, which originated as a trading company in nineteenth-century Bombay, purchased Jaguar Land Rover, and assumed ownership of a pair of venerated British brands famous for luxury sports cars and off-road vehicles. Seven years later, in 2015, the US Embassy in Yemen, concerned about the deteriorating security situation in that country, advised American citizens to seek assistance from the Indian government. Over ten days, using resources available to its military, India evacuated citizens of more than thirty countries from a contested war zone. Eight years after that, in 2023, a three-metre-long spacecraft designed in Gujarat, developed in Karnataka, and launched from Andhra Pradesh became the first man-made object to make a successful soft landing near the moon's southern pole.

These three separate events—demonstrations of India's growing international role in the corporate, military, and technological realms—generated considerable pride in India and a degree of surprise elsewhere. Taken together, they signified India's growing role in international affairs. But what is appreciated less often is that India has a rich legacy of international exchange and influence, one that has altered both India and the world in some unexpected ways.

As India rises, it is increasingly clear that the world matters for its future. It has one of the world's largest diasporas, the second-largest number of overseas students, and is among the largest recipients of remittances. It is a major trader and market, with among the largest current account deficits of any economy. It is the world's third-largest energy importer and, in recent years, has been among the world's largest arms buyers and recipients of greenfield foreign direct investment, signalling new corporate operations in the country.[1] Whether for its territorial defence or overall economy, its knowledge or power, its food or human security, India's future will be shaped in large part by its foreign interactions. It is therefore crucial that India understands the world better.

India also increasingly matters to the rest of the world. It is the world's most populous country; indeed, it is the most populous country in human history. India is, as of 2024, the fifth-largest economy by gross domestic product (GDP) and will soon be the world's third largest. It has the second-largest number of people online and is expected to have the world's largest working-age population. India is also third in energy and electricity consumption and greenhouse gas emissions. It boasts the largest active-duty military, it has in recent years been the third- or fourth-largest military spender, and it possesses nuclear weapons.[2] India will therefore play a critical role in determining the future of the international order, the global economy, the digital realm, and the earth's climate. The rest of the world must understand India better.

Why This Book

The understanding of India's engagements with the world—past, present, and future—remains limited. There is a rich body of literature on many aspects of India's foreign policy: many significant works are included in the references at the end of this book. They encompass diplomatic, military, and political histories, numerous personal memoirs, polemical works and essays, intellectual and cultural studies, and edited volumes. Most focus on specific relationships, periods, individuals, or themes. This book draws on various strands of existing scholarship and other materials to tell a concise history of India and the world, one that helps provide important context and a framework for thinking about its national objectives and global priorities today. It tells the story of an India that witnessed complex discussions about its place in international affairs, made tough decisions, endured daunting challenges, and played a more active global role than is often understood. In doing so, this volume also attempts to channel an inherently Indian perspective on some issues, overturn some conventional wisdom, and contribute to India's strategic vocabulary.

Capturing a particularly Indian perspective on international affairs is intrinsically difficult. Outsiders have often sought to interpret India, but with rare exceptions such works often impose their own lenses. The task of presenting a singular Indian perspective is, of course, complicated by the diverse and sometimes sharp debates and differences of opinion within India on almost any given issue. But while acknowledging that difficulty, I have attempted to channel the vantage point of policymakers and leaders in India, past and present. If it sometimes strikes an overly sympathetic note, it is primarily to offset the inevitability of hindsight.

While this book is not strictly an academic work, it does attempt to address and engage academic discourse on India's foreign relations. For many reasons, scholarship on India in international politics has not always kept pace with developments. Indeed, academic studies frequently fall back on outdated clichés and enduring myths that do not necessarily reflect the new realities and impulses guiding India's relations with the world. These include the notions that India's world view remains grounded in Non-Alignment, that it lacks the capacity to be a great power, that it seeks prestige or status rather than power or influence, and that it must sort out its internal or regional challenges before it can move on to global aspirations. The historical narrative and analysis presented here should hopefully disabuse readers of some of these questionable notions.

A further motivation, therefore, is to update India's strategic vocabulary. It is evident that India has gradually transitioned from the Non-Alignment of India's first prime minister, Jawaharlal Nehru, to something quite different after 1991. The contours of India's post-Cold War foreign policy are clearly discernible, and include an emergence from relative economic isolationism, a refocus on a more dynamic Asia and Indo–Pacific, closer and more comprehensive relations with the United States and its allies (such as Japan, Australia, Europe, and Israel), and the dedicated pursuit of nuclear security. Subsequently, after its nuclear tests of 1998, India's changing foreign policy also saw it gradually distinguish (or 'dehyphenate') itself from Pakistan and become less hesitant about projecting itself as a rising global power. Non-Alignment—at least as it was originally envisioned—was a product of another era and very different international circumstances. India's recent realignments are instead about positioning itself as a stronger and more capable actor in a more contested and interdependent world.

This book is meant as a basic introduction to India and the world, one that remedies some of the shortcomings of the existing literature. It is intended to encompass some big ideas and themes in a concise and serviceable manner. The title—which might be loosely translated from the classical Sanskrit as 'a treatise on the world'—hopefully connotes the necessary degree of ambition, scope, and timelessness. For it to be India's world, a Vishwa Shastra is necessary.

The Arguments

This book, particularly Part I: 'History', is meant to be more descriptive than polemical. Readers are invited to draw their own conclusions about events and developments. But the more discerning might notice a few underlying but consistent themes. In the spirit of self-awareness, these are worth highlighting explicitly at the outset.

The first is that India has long had a national strategy. Indeed, it has a rich strategic culture and tradition of statecraft. In some sense, this should not be surprising. However, the belief that India lacks either a strategic culture or the capacity for strategic thought remains an unfortunately prevalent notion in many quarters, including in India. To be sure, strategies often change and adjust, even when fundamental interests do not.

The narrative arc therefore underscores changing international circumstances and New Delhi's shifting responses. The opportunities and challenges confronting India in 2024 look very different from those in, say, 1994, 1974, or 1954, and it would be foolish to expect India to think and act in exactly the same way.

Second, this strategy has for the most part had decidedly realist underpinnings. Ultimately, India, like all sovereign states, has had to look out for its own interests. Contested outcomes were often shaped by the balance of power. Mutually beneficial economic exchanges, effective international institutions, deeper social interactions, and cultural affinities were certainly desirable but proved ultimately subordinate to more powerful interest-driven forces. Both the longer historical narrative and the outline of India's policy priorities appear to support this idea and run counter to the belief, popular in some academic circles, that India is driven primarily by post-colonial resentment or by prestige or status in international affairs.

Third, India's foreign policy has long been connected to domestic objectives. India has since Independence sought to use foreign relations to accelerate its domestic economic, social, and technological development while leveraging its domestic strengths internationally. But while the goal of a 'self-reliant India' is a worthy one, particularly in critical sectors where India can be exposed to vulnerabilities by adversaries, that goal will often require greater international cooperation rather than isolationism. In fact, as several examples from India's own experience in higher education, agriculture, public health, telecommunications, and infrastructure reveal, India has often prospered most when it has benefited instrumentally from foreign partnerships. Other countries, not least Japan and

China, also offer useful lessons for India. Equating self-reliance with isolationism has often proved detrimental to Indian interests in the long run.

Fourth, readers of Part II: Strategy might notice the degree to which China's rise and behaviour today inform almost all aspects of India's external interactions. As the historical overview makes clear, China is not a new factor in India's foreign policy. But it is an increasingly dominant one. Whether India's trade, industrial, or technology policy; its engagement with the neighbourhood, Pakistan, Indian Ocean, and Indo–Pacific; its partnerships with the United States, Europe, Russia, and Japan; or its approach to global governance and multilateral institutions, China looms increasingly large in India's strategic consciousness. Indeed, China's rise is likely the primary factor influencing India's grand strategy today. Understanding that will be vital to students, observers, and practitioners of India's foreign policy.

The Audiences

I seek to reach several different audiences through this book. The first and most important readership is the average Indian, particularly Indian youth. The hunger among a rising generation of Indians for knowledge and perspectives about India's place in the world is immense. One need only interact with university audiences or civil service aspirants in a given Indian city. I hope that students in college classrooms; lifelong students in bookstores, cafes and living rooms; and civil service and military trainees in places like Mussoorie and Mhow derive the most out of it.

I also, in part, wrote this for those new to India, whether foreign diplomats, journalists, or businesspeople, or simply those living abroad, with a particular interest in the country. This should provide an accessible introduction to at least one important element of India's complexity. Visitors' first impressions of India do not always consider the historical background—in some cases, how far India has travelled or the occasionally unprecedented nature of new developments. In other cases, they may be unfamiliar with important historical or cultural contexts, or past precedents for contemporary Indian actions or policies.

While it is not its primary purpose, the book can also serve as a rough guide for Indian policymakers. In an era of more fractious political rhetoric and social media polarization, it tries to offer a plain and concise road map for India's international dealings. This is an attempt to connect the dots and make evident the contours of India's policies and strategies. Part II: Strategy, in particular, is meant to give a sense of broad objectives and priorities that can help guide contemporary policymakers.

Finally, while not strictly an academic volume, it does engage with contemporary academic debates about India in international relations. The book has benefited from considerable scholarship done by others, particularly historians and diplomatic practitioners, and can hopefully serve as an introductory text in classrooms. The numerous citations, multiple references, and catalogue for further reading can also possibly serve as a gateway for additional exploration in a field primed for deeper study and analysis in the years to come.

A Synopsis

This book seeks to introduce readers to the interactions—past, present, and future—between India and the rest of the world.

Part I: History describes India's interactions with the world in five phases, from prehistoric times to 2024. Chapter 1: Before Independence summarizes India's long tradition of statecraft captured in Vedic texts, epics, Ashoka's edicts, codes such as the *Manusmriti*, and prescriptive treatises such as the *Arthashastra* and *Nitisara*. It also tells the story of ancient India's trade and cultural links with West Asia and the Mediterranean, including the Persian and Hellenistic worlds to the West. In addition, India was deeply connected via Buddhist and Hindu religious and trade networks with Southeast Asia and China, and had varied engagements with Central Asia and Africa. The portions of the world with direct or indirect contact with India—what might be considered the 'Indianate world'—were much wider than many realize. Medieval India saw the arrival and imprint of Islamic rule in various ways. This included Mughal rivalries with the Ottomans and Safavids as well as continuing trade, commerce, and military exchanges in the Deccan. Early modern Indian international engagements involved the Marathas, Sikhs, Dogras, and Tai-Ahoms, including their military contact and conflict with modern Afghanistan, Tibet, and Myanmar. This chapter also describes the arrival of Europeans as colonists and traders, including the East India Company. Under Company rule and the British Raj, India's interactions with the world both intensified and were disrupted. This period—marked by extractive colonialism—left a lasting imprint on India's borders, diaspora, industry, governance, and politics. The Indian Army was also deployed over extended regions around the world. The chapter concludes with historical lessons for contemporary India on the importance of military power, commercial exchanges, and contested ideas.

India became independent from Britain in the context of the Cold War and, as described in Chapter 2: 1947–1971, had to immediately deal with questions of territoriality and development. India's attempts at incorporating the princely states (as well as French and Portuguese possessions) and creating buffer zones required both diplomacy and the use of military force. India also made efforts to manage its economy through state planning in the 1940s and 1950s. By being Non-Aligned, it attempted to benefit from economic and technical assistance from both the United States and the Soviet Union, along with their allies. The post-Independence period also saw India initiate its nuclear programme and attempt to position itself as a leader in the post-colonial world, including at the Bandung conference in 1955. But these developments were overtaken by growing tensions with China after its annexation of Tibet in 1950 and intensifying disputes along the contested border, culminating in a short but decisive border war in 1962. India's defeat in part contributed to Pakistan's adventurism and another war in 1965 which, while inconclusive, significantly altered dynamics in the Indian subcontinent. The period between 1965 and 1971 was marked by political and economic transitions, including a skirmish with China and the Green Revolution.

Chapter 3: 1971–1991 describes the last two decades of the Cold War. During this period, India aligned more closely with the Soviet Union out of concern for the US–China–Pakistan partnership. The victory over Pakistan in the Bangladesh Liberation War in 1971 proved decisive and defined relations between the two countries for decades. India conducted a peaceful nuclear explosion in 1974, but despite its success, India's nuclear weapons programme stalled until the early 1980s, when it began to revive following Pakistan's nuclear progress. This period was also marked by a slow and tentative re-engagement with China until 1985, when Beijing reasserted its claims. After India's response to a military stand-off in the late 1980s, a visit by Rajiv Gandhi to China began to normalize ties with Beijing. The latter years of the Cold War also witnessed Indian military and political interventions in its immediate region, including in Sri Lanka and the Indian Ocean. But a lasting legacy was India's continued economic isolationism at a time when many other Asian economies opened up and grew. In hindsight, the 1970s and 1980s were difficult decades for India, when it was often on the defensive in international affairs.

In and around 1991, several things changed, including in terms of India's politics, security, international relations, and economy. Chapter 4: 1991–2008 describes how the assassination of Rajiv Gandhi, the Kashmir insurgency and Bombay blasts, the collapse of the Soviet Union, and a balance of payments crisis in 1991 contributed to a new phase in India's international relations. Under P.V. Narasimha Rao, India established diplomatic relations with Israel and the Association of Southeast Asian Nations (ASEAN), initiated a Look East Policy, attempted to normalize relations with China and the United States, and explored the possibility of nuclear tests. In 1998, under Atal Bihari Vajpayee, India tested its nuclear weapons but swiftly engaged the United States and its allies, China, and Pakistan. Despite these efforts, the period after 1999 was marked by successive crises with Pakistan, including the Kargil War and a rise in cross-border terrorist activity. After 2004, under Manmohan Singh, India worked to normalize its nuclear programme and improve relations with the United States in a period of American unipolarity. This period also saw important developments in India's neighbourhood, including the end of civil conflicts in Nepal and Sri Lanka.

Despite various strides taken after 1998, the global financial crisis and other domestic and international developments in and around 2008 resulted in something of a pause, described in Chapter 5: 2008–2024. In the first five years or so after the global financial crisis, ties with the US and Europe were marked by irritants and instead India attempted to work constructively with other rising powers, such as China, as in the BRICS grouping (along with Brazil, Russia, and later South Africa). But continued diplomatic dialogue with Pakistan proved frustrating, and differences persisted with Beijing. After 2014, under Narendra Modi, India made a concerted attempt to reengage its neighbourhood and the Indian Ocean. Motivated by growing divergences with China, India consolidated its partnership with the United States and the Quad (Australia, India, Japan, and the United States) in the Indo–Pacific. It also attempted to reach out to new constituencies, including in business, technology, and new geographies. Various domestic Indian policies had international implications after Modi's reelection in 2019 but were overtaken by three major crises: the Covid-19 pandemic, India–China border clashes, and Russia's war in Ukraine. India's extended region also saw significant turmoil, including in Afghanistan, Sri Lanka, Myanmar Bangladesh, and West Asia (the Middle East). Despite these complications, India continued to invest in closer relations with the United States and its allies and partners in Europe, Asia, the Gulf, and Israel, while attempting to preserve ties with Russia and Iran. India's trade, technology, defence, and industrial policies also transformed in response to growing competition with China. Finally, India renewed its attempts at reaching out to the Global South and sought to lead multilateral negotiating efforts at the G20.

The period after 1991, therefore, witnessed some major changes to India's interactions with the world: from a closed economy to a more open, integrated, and competitive one; from deep distrust of the United States and its allies and partners to a closer and more cooperative set of partnerships; from a narrow conception of its region as South Asia to a wider role in the Indo–Pacific balance of power; from the rhetoric of third-worldism to that of a rising power; and from a preoccupation with Pakistan to a greater priority on the long-term and structural challenges posed by China's rise and assertiveness. This, in summary, represents India's realignment in international affairs in the post-Cold War world.

Part II: Strategy is more prescriptive than descriptive. It is intended to highlight the main strategic challenges facing India today and offer policy priorities to address them. India's five major objectives are: (i) accelerating its domestic development and thereby improving the fundamentals of its power, (ii) ensuring a stable periphery in its neighbourhood, (iii) balancing China in the Indo–Pacific, (iv) reshaping West Asia despite continuing problems emanating from Pakistan and (v) restructuring international institutions and organizations to advance Indian interests.

Chapter 6: Atmanirbhar Bharat describes how India can develop its domestic capabilities by investing in military preparedness (including defence indigenization) and an industrial policy (with a focus on critical and emerging technologies). It can also better leverage international partnerships to accelerate domestic development, drawing both from its own prior experiences in agriculture, education, health, telecommunications, and transportation, and by reflecting upon the historical experiences of other rising powers, including the United States, Russia, and especially Japan and China. Ultimately, India cannot afford to mistake self-reliance for isolationism.

The near neighbourhood also remains a priority, as described in Chapter 7: Neighbourhood First. India has five privileged partnerships in its immediate periphery—Bhutan, Nepal, Bangladesh, Sri Lanka, and the Maldives—which deserve a priority in its international outlook, in addition to regional partners such as Myanmar, Afghanistan, Mauritius, and Seychelles, where India is less omnipresent. In its near neighbourhood, India confronts rising democratization, populism, concerns about sovereignty, and a growing Chinese presence. To address these complex dynamics, India must offer greater diplomatic priority and attention to these neighbours, including further investments by the strategic and scholarly community. It must also recast regional cooperation in a more constructive light; increase aid, lending, and humanitarian assistance; and improve connectivity to enhance trade, investment, energy flows, and people-to-people exchanges. These steps—which are encapsulated in a policy of 'Neighbourhood First'—can help mitigate volatility in relations with neighbours.

India confronts a much greater challenge in China's rise and assertiveness, as described in Chapter 8: Act East. Maintaining a balance of power has required India to place a greater emphasis on security, imagine a wider region, and increase the urgency of delivery in its Look East Policy. This has resulted in a new name and approach: the Act East Policy. The new geographical scope, in turn, has required conceiving of the Indo–Pacific, which envisions the Indian and Pacific oceans as a single strategic continuum. In practice, 'Acting East' in the Indo–Pacific requires India to take steps to secure the Indian Ocean, using its naval capabilities, strategic investments, and leadership at regional organizations. It also involves India connecting further—whether diplomatically, economically, or strategically—with Southeast Asia. To maintain the balance of power in the region, India must improve its partnerships with the United States, Japan, and Australia: the Quad. It must also explore other Indo–Pacific partnerships, as with South Korea, Taiwan, and Europe, while striving to preserve its strategic relationship with Russia. Finally, India can try to find ways to manage its ties with China, while remaining mindful of structural competition. For India, preserving a favourable balance of power in the Indo–Pacific is critical to maintaining a global balance of power.

Major developments are also underway in India's west, including generational leadership transitions, a post-'Arab Spring' environment, the Taliban's takeover of Afghanistan, and Pakistan's political and economic woes. These developments, as described in Chapter 9: Think West, present opportunities for India to try to compel Pakistan to abandon its policy of using terrorist proxies against India. This will require making use of positive and negative incentives. India must also try to continue engaging Afghanistan to ensure favourable outcomes to its north-west. More ambitiously, New Delhi will have to work with a variety of partners to reshape West Asia (the Middle East) and connect further with Europe, while remaining mindful of its diversity of regional partnerships (including with the Gulf Cooperation Council, Israel, and Iran) and interests (including energy, the diaspora, security, investment, trade, connectivity, and technology).

Finally, Chapter 10: A Leading Power describes the erosion and growing ineffectiveness of global governance structures and institutions. International institutions are important for managing matters of war and peace, governing the global commons, and facilitating economic exchange and development. But a combination of vested interests among the established powers and revisionism among certain rising powers is making these institutions less effective. As a reformist power, India can work to try to revitalize multilateral organizations (including by making them more representative), build new issue-specific international coalitions, and reach out to the Global South to widen stakeholders. This involves taking steps to have a bigger global footprint, including diplomatically, economically, and perhaps even militarily. In this way, India can advance its own national interests at international forums while positioning itself increasingly as a leading power.

Part I

History | इतिहास

1

Before Independence: Anarchy and Power

Understanding the Past

India's international relations before it gained independence in 1947 are often overlooked today.[1] But that history still matters, for it continues to shape India's identity and outlook in meaningful ways. The legacy of India's pre-independent history still influences the nature of the country's economy, the composition of its military, its networks of trade, the spread of its diaspora, its boundaries and unresolved conflicts, its religions, and its peoples' daily lifestyles.

The long view of India's international engagement also dispels some widely held misconceptions. One, easily refutable, is of India as a relatively novel political entity. In fact, an understanding of India by outsiders has been documented for well over 2500 years. Terms such as India, Shendu, and al-Hind (all of which derive from the same root, the river Indus or Sindhu) were long used by Europeans, Chinese,

and Arabs respectively to refer to the region east of the Indus
and between the Himalayas and the Indian Ocean. Indians,
of course, referred to their own country by several different
names: Jambudvipa, Bharat, and Hindustan. Although the
exact geographical definition of India evolved, it constituted a
region that had certain shared attributes, including the imprint
of a common cultural and linguistic heritage. While the 'core'
areas of India were never in doubt, a broad cultural definition
potentially extended 'India' to a wider region, including at times
parts of Central Asia and Southeast Asia. The idea of a Greater
India has periodically captured the imagination, most notably
in the context of India's independence movement during the
early twentieth century, but it did not necessarily reflect a long
or lasting political cohesiveness.[2]

Another misleading notion is of India traditionally being
a strategic backwater, 'a world apart' as a prominent American
statesman once mischaracterized the subcontinent.[3] Instead,
the history of India's international relations shows lengthy
and—in some cases—extensive links with West Asia (the
Middle East), the Mediterranean, Central Asia, Southeast Asia,
China, Europe, Africa, and subsequently even the Americas.
Over the centuries, India was of great interest to outsiders,
whether travellers, conquerors, traders, or missionaries—from
Alexander of Macedon and Faxian to Ibn Battuta and Vasco da
Gama. Additionally, India, in turn, was shaped by competing
international orders, and perhaps just as importantly left strong
imprints around the world that are not always appreciated
today. At times, India straddled various global systems, such as
between East Africa and Southeast Asia in the Indian Ocean
basin or between the Islamic world and China across Central
Asia along what was later termed the Silk Road. In fact,

international politics were a persistent feature of Indian history from its earliest days.

This seemingly ancient history remains important for a few reasons. One, it reinforces the timelessness of international politics as an ultimately competitive enterprise, in which outcomes are determined by power and security. Two, it shows the wide extent of international commerce and the perils of isolationism. The rest of the world has taken an interest in India, even during periods when India has chosen to retreat into itself. In turn, questions of power and trade hold important lessons for the security of the Indian Ocean, as India's colonial experience in the eighteenth and nineteenth centuries made clear. Finally, the long view of history reminds contemporary readers of the importance of defining and shaping international norms. The ideological crosscurrents throughout Indian history—whether Hindu, Persian, Hellenistic, Buddhist, Islamic, Chinese, or European—are relevant to defining and contesting contemporary international values and ideas.

West by North-West: Ancient India until 700 CE

India has been continuously inhabited since pre-historic times, first by early human relatives (hominids) and later by *homo sapiens*. Hominid remains have been discovered in the Narmada Valley and Tamil Nadu. Plentiful Palaeolithic tools associated with early human populations have been found throughout the country, and petroglyphs (rock art) have been preserved in places like Bhimbetka. Around 12,000 years ago, early Indian villages and settlements emerged in what is now Rajasthan, Ladakh, Madhya Pradesh, the Ganga River Valley, and the Deccan, with evidence of agriculture and domestication of animals.

From nomadic life and early villages, human communities
in India began to witness growth into cities. The earliest
evidence of urban developments in India is associated with
the Harappan culture, which peaked between about 2600
and 1900 BCE. Prominent examples include sites such as
Lothal, Rakhigarhi, and Dholavira in today's India as well
as in Mohenjo-Daro and Harappa in what is today Pakistan.
The Harappan culture provides some of the earliest evidence
of trade between India and other regions. Harappan artefacts
such as seal inscriptions, ivory, and carnelian beads have been
found in modern Oman, the United Arab Emirates, Bahrain,
Iraq, and Iran, indicating maritime trade networks up to
Mesopotamia. By land, Harappan exports extended to present-
day Turkmenistan, while commodities such as jade, tin, and
lapis lazuli were imported. Trading posts were established in
places like Shortughai in northern Afghanistan.[4]

The Vedic cultures that followed after around 1500 BCE
provide us with the earliest decipherable Indian historical
records, including religious, mythological and political texts
in Sanskrit, Pali, vernacular Prakrits and Tamil, among other
languages. These were often recounted orally or written on
palm leaves (*talapatra*) and are complemented by archaeological
finds, inscriptions, coins, and other such materials. A common
theme in much of the surviving literature involves matters of
governance, war, and peace. The Rig Veda, for example, details
warring tribes, victorious kings, and battles. Politics and warfare
are, of course, central to the Ramayana and Mahabharata.
Later Buddhist texts, such as the *Mahavastu*, refer to Gandhara
and Kamboja—approximating today's Khyber-Pakhtunkhwa
and parts of Afghanistan—as among the *mahajanapadas* or
'great states' of India. Other early Buddhist scriptures recount

maritime voyages, coinciding with evidence of early trade with both West and Southeast Asia.[5]

Taken together, the Vedic texts, Puranas, and Buddhist and Jain literature offer a rich illustration of statecraft in the period from roughly the ninth to the third centuries BCE. The *mahajanapadas* included both *rajyas* (kingdoms) and *ganas* (oligarchies or republics in which power was shared). This period saw the rise of cities like Kashi and Mathura as political centres, Ujjain as a trading hub between the Gangetic plain and the Arabian Sea, and to the north-west the celebrated locus of learning Taxila, described in later Roman and Chinese sources. Magadha—around modern-day Bihar—eventually rose to be the most powerful state in north-central India between the sixth and fourth centuries BCE, first under Bimbisara and his successors and later under the Nandas. Subsequent accounts by foreigners describe reports of the Nandas ruling over massive, powerful armies.

The north-western Indian regions, or at least parts of them, were conquered by Persia in the sixth century. Persian records at Persepolis and Hamadan mention Gandhara and Hidus (possibly referring to Hindus of the Indus Valley) as subjects and tributaries. For Persia's leaders, parts of India remained important sources of mercenaries and highly sought-after war elephants during the fifth and fourth centuries BCE. Despite some cultural legacies, such as the introduction of the Kharoshti script, Persian influence appears to have waned in north-western India by the time of Alexander of Macedon's invasion of Punjab in 327–26 BCE.[6]

After spending a considerable period subjugating Central Asia and Afghanistan, Alexander decided to move beyond traditional Persian lands and invade India, a land associated

in Greek minds with mystery and wonder—the edge of the
known world. His armies moved through the Khyber and
Swat to Taxila, laying siege to several cities and Alexander
encountered new experiences, both human (philosophers) and
natural (elephants), which seemed to deeply impress him. At
the River Hydaspes (Jhelum), he faced the local king Porus in
battle under torrential weather conditions. Alexander's plans,
Porus's counters, and their tactical ingenuity were described
by Greek chroniclers, who add that Porus surrendered, and
Alexander claimed suzerainty over his realm. The Macedonian
leader then proceeded east, although the exact route was
difficult to determine. At a point believed to be the banks of
the Beas River, his forces refused to advance further. Struggling
with heat and disease, Alexander's armies marched south down
the Indus and retreated west.[7]

Alexander's invasion of Punjab was relatively brief, but
it resulted in a long-term Greek cultural presence around
what is today Afghanistan and north-western India under the
Seleucids. As a consequence, India came into direct contact
with the Hellenistic (Greek-speaking) world. From the third
to the first century BCE, Bactrian Greek kingdoms maintained
a Greek cultural, artistic, and linguistic heritage in and around
northwest India, as evident in surviving statuary and coinage.
The Greeks Ctesias and Megasthenes wrote works titled *Indica*,
although neither survives in their entirety. Ctesias, writing
before Alexander's conquests, reflected Persian views of India,
with frequently fantastical and absurd descriptions. Megasthenes
was a Greek ambassador of Seleucus Nicator to the court of
Chandragupta, and while his characterization of India heavily
informed later Hellenistic and Roman writers, many ancient
writers also cast severe doubts on the accuracy of his accounts.[8]

It was also in the aftermath of Alexander's invasion in the late fourth century BCE that the Mauryas rose to power in north-central India. The Emperor Ashoka—grandson of the dynastic founder Chandragupta—built a legacy as a patron and proselytizer of Buddhism. The life of Ashoka, often referred to in inscriptions as Piyadasi Devanampiya, is rather poorly recorded in historical literature. Surviving texts associated with Mauryan rule such as the *Ashokavadana* were likely written much later. However, Ashoka's plentiful edicts—engraved across India on rocks or pillars—leave a remarkable and direct legacy of his governance philosophy. They were written in Prakrit, a dominant political language in north India, as well as in Greek and Aramaic in north-west India. Inscriptions have been found as far afield as Kandahar in today's Afghanistan, Lumbini in today's Nepal, and in Gujarat, Odisha, and Karnataka. It is from these locations that an outline of the extent of Mauryan influence has emerged.[9] While they touched on issues of administration and justice, Ashoka's edicts were primarily focused on *dhamma*, Prakrit for *dharma*.

Contrary to popular lore, Ashoka was not simply a pacifist. While his rock edicts do recount his remorse at seeing widespread death and destruction during his victory over the Kalingas (in present-day Odisha), he did not reject the use of force against tribal chiefs or in future conflicts. Instead, Ashoka argued that his descendants must be merciful and moderate in their use of force.[10] Rather than a demonstration of hegemony or pacifism, Ashoka's edicts can perhaps best be thought of as an attempt to establish a rules-based international order in his extended region, perhaps among the first such attempts in history. Ashoka's edicts demonstrate a considerable degree of contact with the world at large, with references to contemporary rulers in Syria, Egypt, Macedonia, Cyrenaica (modern-day Libya) and Greece.[11]

In religious tradition and popular lore, Ashoka has developed a powerful reputation as a Buddhist evangelist and patron as far afield as today's Sri Lanka, Myanmar, and Thailand, where he is credited with sending Buddhist missions. (Mauryan and Shungan artefacts, such as ringstones, have been found as far as peninsular Thailand.) By the second century BCE, Buddhism had found patrons among the rulers Dutthagamini in Sri Lanka and Menander in Bactria. Ashoka's legacy lives on in the symbolism of the Republic of India, including the chakra on the national flag and the Sarnath Lion Capital as the state emblem.

It was in the Mauryan period (third and second centuries BCE) or shortly thereafter that a significant work called the *Arthashastra* was composed. The *Arthashastra* is a practical guide to statecraft in fifteen books of prose. It prescribes ideals for ruling a hypothetical state, which lends it a timeless quality, and offers lessons in realpolitik and maximizing power in ruthless and almost paranoid terms, but not without a degree of morality. Indeed, it suggests practical reasons for the moderate use of force, engages questions of dharma, and emphasizes the economic aspects of governance. The *Arthashastra* also offers detailed descriptions of a sophisticated state apparatus—including taxation, judicial processes, resource extraction, trade networks, and private enterprise—as well as a rich and complex society featuring spies, slaves, courtesans, and tribal leaders. At the same time, the treatise offers few contemporary historical examples, some references appear anachronistic and its authorship remains questionable. Although the author is identified in the text as both Kautilya and Vishnugupta, the *Arthashastra* has come to be associated with the popular figure of Chanakya. After being lost for centuries, it was rediscovered only in 1905 in Mysuru by R. Shamasastry, who came by the Sanskrit document written in the South Indian *Grantha* script. Later manuscript discoveries have further contributed to our present-day understanding of the text.[12]

The Shungas, who succeeded the Mauryas in the second century BCE continued some of their predecessors' international engagement. This is evidenced by a remarkable inscription in Besnagar in today's Madhya Pradesh from about 100 BCE, in which Heliodorus, the ambassador of the Greek king in Takshashila (Taxila), dedicates an inscribed pillar to the Shunga king Bhagabadhra; it is a potent symbol of early Indian diplomacy. This period also sees evidence of trade in Bengal with Southeast Asia (Java) and several other regions, especially through the port of Tamralipti.

Somewhat later, in the first century CE, the Kushans came to India from Central Asia, often depicting themselves in Central Asian attire, and reflecting religious iconography from India, Persia, and Greece in their coinage. Kushan rule at times covered much of Afghanistan and parts of Central Asia and Xinjiang. The dynasty reached its apex under Kanishka, who like Ashoka was a major patron of Buddhism and who sent missionaries to Kashgar and Yunnan, among other places. Meanwhile, the roughly contemporaneous Satavahana rulers in peninsular India minted coins showing double-masted ships, suggesting a seafaring tradition.[13] It was in this broad period also that numerous *Dharmashastras* were compiled, including the famous *Manusmriti* (or Laws of Manu). In addition to spiritual laws and codes of conduct, the *Manusmriti* devotes considerable attention—indeed an entire chapter—to guidance on statecraft, including norms of warfare.[14]

Indian commercial contacts with the Roman Empire, roughly contemporaneous with the Kushans, were extensive. Indeed, the Kushans may have risen to power on the back of trade with Rome, given their control over important trade routes. Roman-era traders—often described as *yavanas*, the same word used for Greeks—imported rare metals, pepper, gemstones, textiles, indigo, and ivory from India in exchange for glass, coral, frankincense, wine, and especially coins. The writer Pliny the Elder describes Roman imports from the east worth about half the Roman empire's annual coin production and Roman coins from the reigns of Augustus and Tiberius have been found across south-eastern India and in such unlikely places as near Nagpur in central India.[15] A papyrus housed at the Austrian National Library in Vienna records an agreement between a Roman-era merchant in Alexandria, Egypt and a counterpart in Muchiri (Muziris) in Kerala, an early example of a recorded and decipherable trade agreement with India. The importance of the spice trade is highlighted in Tamil Sangam literature, which describes warfare between local Indian rulers to control commercial flows. Medieval European copies of ancient maps suggest a Roman presence on the Malabar coast to manage and secure spice exports, including concerns about pirates.[16] It is little surprise that these links also saw the exchange of people, including the arrival over successive centuries of Jews and Syrian Christians on Indian shores. By tradition, St Thomas the Apostle went on a mission to India in the first century; he died and was buried in present-day Chennai.

Roman-era perspectives of India were documented by writers such as Arrian, Strabo, and Philostratus, who—based on the travels of Alexander, the admiral Nearchus, and the philosopher Apollonius—wrote of India as a source of special knowledge and luxury goods, as well as the edge of the known world.[17] Embassies from India are recorded as having visited Rome or Constantinople during the reigns of the emperors Trajan, Constantine, and Julian. The Indian Ocean is the subject of a fascinating work of geography, *The Periplus of the Erythraean Sea*, written by a Greek-speaking Egyptian, which dates from around the first century. Among many other places, the Periplus describes the rich trading port of Broach (in Gujarat), the former royal capital of Ozene (Ujjain) and the rule of the Pandyan in Damirica (Tamil country).[18] There was also an exchange of art between India and Rome: Indian statuary has been recovered from first-century Pompeii in Italy.

The Gupta Period of the fourth to the seventh centuries CE was marked by a flourishing of classical Hindu literature and culture. In inscriptions, Gupta rulers mention the people of Simhala (Sri Lanka) as subordinates, with other sources recalling that Sri Lankan rulers sought the Guptas' permission to build a monastery in Bodh Gaya. Although the literature of the Gupta era is associated with the celebrated playwright Kalidasa and the Panchatantra fables, it also produced political texts such as the *Nitisara* of Kamandaka (also known as Kamandaki). The Guptas, after all, had to contend with feudal politics and foreign invasions, specifically by the Huna who invaded from the north-west. Like its predecessor, Kautilya's *Arthashastra*, the *Nitisara* is a treatise on governance, but differs in a narrower scientific focus on power, on the constraints of governance and ethics, among other areas.[19]

Northern India was, of course, not the only area which interacted with the international arena. In some sense, the ancient coastal states of the Deccan and peninsular India were as much—if not more—involved in trade and cultural exchanges with the world at large. These include the Pallavas in south-eastern India and the Chalukyas in south-western India in the first millennium. The Chalukyas were eventually succeeded by the Rashtrakutas. Throughout this period the export of cloths, precious stones, woods, and oils and the import of such commodities as gold, wines, and horses were productive enterprises, requiring systems of taxation and customs in the ports of the Deccan and Gujarat. Further south, the Cholas, Cheras, and Pandyas—whose histories were captured in classical Tamil literature—jostled for political control and trading routes and privileges.

Indo–Pacific Antecedents: India and Asia, c. 100–1300 CE

While many documented interactions in early India were with the north and west, significant Indian engagements were underway to India's east and south, both across the Himalayas by land and south by sea to Southeast Asia. One aberration, in that it involved military engagement, concerns the Chola Empire, ancient India's most significant maritime power, sometimes described as a thalassocracy (seaborne empire). A family claiming the old Chola name and its heroic associations rose to power in present-day Tamil Nadu in the ninth century and established prominence over significant parts of southern India. They sent military expeditions and raiding parties by land as far as Bengal, as well as by sea. Chola inscriptions describe raids over locations identified as the Kra Isthmus, Malay peninsula, and Sumatra. Anuradhapura in today's Sri Lanka was attacked and the northern part of the island was ruled directly for a while by the Cholas. (They were not the first Indian rulers to militarily venture into Sri Lanka. In the ninth century, Pandya King Srimara Srivallabha invaded the island and took a golden Buddha image back to his capital Madurai.)[20] More famously, although for reasons that can only be surmised, a Chola armada during the reign of Rajendra Chola sailed to Srivijaya in Southeast Asia and sacked several cities in Sumatra and the Malay Peninsula.[21]

The Indian cultural footprint in Southeast Asia was certainly wider than the area of direct Chola military intervention. Tamil, which was the Chola courtly language along with Sanskrit, appears in inscriptions in Burma, Thailand, Sumatra, and southern China. Kingdoms in Burma and Cambodia sent ambassadors to the Chola court, and a Buddhist *vihara* (monastery) was established by the king of Srivijaya in Nagapattinam.[22] This period in India also includes among the earliest references to navigation charts, such as in the fifth century *Brihat-katha-shloka-samgraha*, an abridged retelling by Budhaswami of an epic adventure story. Given the breadth and frequency of contacts between India and Southeast Asia, it can be presumed that such charts—of which none survive today— were commonly used.[23] Additionally, the *Manusmriti* and other *Dharmashastras* had considerable influence overseas, including in parts of Southeast Asia.[24]

The imprint of Indian culture is still discernible in the origins of most Southeast Asian scripts and writing systems and the exchange of folktales. The impact of Hinduism is evident in such places as Cambodia, Java, and Bali and in the littoral of the South China Sea. Trading links were strong: records from the third-century point to a thriving exchange of commodities (including horses) between India and today's Vietnam. The references in Indian writings to *Ratnadvipa*, *Agadvipa*, *Yamadvipa*, and *Suvarnadvipa* are associated with Sri Lanka, Malaya, Sumatra and Southeast Asia respectively.[25] The massive Hindu temple complex at Angkor Wat in today's Cambodia was constructed in the twelfth century. Similarly, the Champa culture in central and southern Vietnam showed the sustained influence of Hinduism throughout much of the first millennium and up to the thirteenth century. The imprint of Indian literature and mythology on Indonesian and Thai art, architecture, language, and folklore is strongly evident. Hindu iconography can still be found in the remains of temples in southern China on the Taiwan Strait.

If Hinduism and Buddhism spread in a south-eastern direction, the influence was no less to the north-east. Under the Pala Dynasty in what is present-day Bihar and Bengal, perhaps the last major flourishing of political Buddhism took place in India south of the Himalayas, which saw the establishment of universities at Nalanda, Vikramashila and Odantapuri. From these centres of learning, Buddhist art, icons, texts and ideas sometimes escaped destruction, reaching Kathmandu and Tibet. The influence of Indian Buddhism on Tibet cannot be overstated, including the large-scale import and translation of Sanskrit texts. The great Tibetan ruler-benefactor Trisong Detsen invited prominent Buddhist philosophers from India such as Santarakshita of Nalanda.[26] Via China and Southeast Asia, there were early associations of India with Korea and Japan, such as the legendary Korean queen Heo Hwang-ok who was said to have come from Ayodhya. According to Japanese chronicles, the South Indian Bodhisena travelled to China in the eighth century, where he met a delegation from Japan, journeyed on to the Kansai region and consecrated a Buddhist temple in Nara.[27]

Trade and social interactions also took place in the first and early second millennium between India and its west. Trading networks that followed the seasonal monsoon winds linked India not just with the Arabian Peninsula and Red Sea, but with eastern and southern Africa. This included trade with east African ports such as Mogadishu, the Lamu archipelago, and Zanzibar.[28] The late first millennium saw East African exports of ivory, gold, and slaves to the Arabian Peninsula, Indian subcontinent, and further east.[29] Recent studies point to Indian women contributing to the gene pool of the Swahili coast in East Africa a thousand years ago, along with Persian men.[30] The same monsoon networks also brought trading and travelling communities from West Asia to India, including Christian, Jewish, Zoroastrian (Parsi), Armenian, and Arab communities to the Konkan, Malabar, and Coromandel coasts.

The Other Middle Kingdom: India and China, c. 200 BCE–1300 CE

An important part of these early Indo–Pacific trade networks was China. China was both a source of valuable commodities—especially silk—and a destination for traders, missionaries, and travellers. Ancient interactions between India and China are particularly well documented by Chinese sources but these must be considered carefully, for they often represent their own biases and worldviews.

An early impetus for initial China–India contacts was trade. The trade of cowrie shells, camphor, and silk via intermediaries dates back over 2500 years to the Shang period in China and the Vedic period in India. The Sanxingdui culture in today's Sichuan appears to have links with the Indian Ocean. Other early but indirect historical contacts date from the Han period, when the diplomat and explorer Zhang Qian, while in the

vicinity of present-day Tajikistan or Afghanistan, found goods
coming from a land called Shendu to the south, corresponding
to one of the early Chinese names for India. Indian diplomats,
possibly from the Gupta Empire, appeared in Chinese courts
in the fifth and sixth centuries.[31] Buddhism also spread to
China from India. During the Han period, two Indian monks,
Kasyapa Matanga and Dharmaratna, travelled to Luoyang in
today's Henan province carrying Buddhist texts and icons.[32]
Other Indian monks such as Kumarajiva, Paramartha, and
Bodhidharma also journeyed to China in the fifth and sixth
centuries. This diffusion of Buddhism from India to China was
not seamless: some ideas struggled with translation ('dharma'
was translated by the Chinese as 'fa', suggesting a more rigid
law or code) while other Buddhists concepts (e.g. renunciation)
were seen to contradict Confucian notions of filial piety.[33]

These early contacts paved the way for further Chinese
visitors to India. The most detailed surviving early Chinese
account of India is by Faxian, who travelled in the early
fifth century via Dunhuang and the Pamirs to the Indus and
returned from Bengal to China by sea. Faxian provided detailed
geographical and cultural descriptions of India to Chinese
audiences for the first time.[34] Similarly, motivated by religious
education, Chinese translators such an Xuanzang visited
the capital of king Harsha in Kannauj (in present day Uttar
Pradesh) and Nalanda (in today's Bihar) in the seventh century.
Later, while based in Chang'an (today's Xi'an), Xuanzang
was able to maintain correspondence through travellers with
his Indian teachers. Drawing upon Xuanzang, the geographer
Daoxuan argued that India—not China—should be considered
the geographical centre of the world. Other Chinese travellers
to India included the diplomat Wang Xuance who journeyed

via Tibet and whose disastrous mission assumed some kind of military dimension, most likely an armed intervention in a local civil conflict.[35]

Trade between India and East Asia accelerated after the tenth century, with improvements in seafaring technologies in India, China, and Southeast Asia. Trade routes linked southern China with Sumatra and Java, Malacca to Sri Lanka and the Malabar coast, and Gujarat to Hormuz and Baghdad. Traders and merchants who were Tamil, Sumatran, Chinese, and Muslims of various ethnicities all participated in these exchanges. The cosmopolitanism of these interactions is nicely captured by the experience of the Buddhist monk Vajrabodhi who, in the eighth century, travelled from the Tamil-speaking Coromandel coast on a Persian vessel to Java and then on to Guangzhou in southern China. The variety of tradable goods was diverse, and included Arabian horses, Indian spices, and Chinese silk. Thriving Muslim and Tamil-speaking communities emerged in Chinese port towns like Quanzhou. The exchange of goods and religion was also accompanied by other interactions. The spread of Buddhism facilitated the diffusion of painting and musical methods, medicinal and astronomical knowledge, and sugar production from India to China. At the same time, India imported such things as gunpowder and paper-making technologies from China.[36]

Gunpowder Empires: Medieval India, 637–1707

Some major political and technological developments resulted in a transition from ancient to medieval India. Notably, the Islamic invasions of India eventually resulted in political rule or dominance over large parts of north India by Muslim rulers. In

637, an Arab naval expedition reached the west coast of India. But such early forays only translated into a permanent political presence in 712, when Muhammad bin Qasim, a kinsman of the ambitious governor of Iraq, defeated Raja Dahir of Sindh. Later, Mahmud of Ghazni (in what is now Afghanistan) started raiding the Gangetic plains and Gujarat and extended Islamic rule to Punjab. Soon after that, another Afghan-based warrior now popularly known as Muhammad Ghori invaded India at the head of an army that included Turkic and Tajik slaves. The institution of military or elite slavery was a Turkic and Persianate import; rulers in Baghdad recruited Turks in this manner from Central Asia. Both Mahmud of Ghazni and Muhammad Ghori were primarily raiders rather than state-builders, who sought to bolster their armies and derive revenue through plunder. These invasions also brought travellers such as al-Biruni, born in what is today Uzbekistan, whose initial interests in astronomy and the natural sciences led to detailed descriptions of Indian society in the eleventh century.[37]

After Muhammad Ghori's death, Qutb ud-Din Aibak declared independence and established himself in Delhi and Lahore. Having successfully resisted rival forces before his death, he was succeeded by the head of his bodyguard, a slave named Shamsuddin Iltutmish (whose coinage, incidentally, featured a Sanskritized version of his name: Suratana Sri Samsadina).[38] This period witnessed an aborted invasion of India in 1222 by Genghis Khan, whose forces stopped at Multan, unable to deal with the heat and damp of India.[39] In 1229, just a few years before the sack of Baghdad by the Mongols devastated the institution of the Caliphate, Iltutmish received a deed of investiture (*manshur*) from the Caliph that recognized his autonomy as a Sultan. The Delhi Sultanate—led by a succession of dynasties including the Khiljis, Tughlaqs, Sayyids, and Lodis—witnessed a variety of international exchanges.[40] This included the visit of the famed Morocco-born traveller Ibn Battuta, who spent considerable time in India, with detours to the Maldives and Sri Lanka, before travelling on to China. The invasion and sacking of Delhi by Timur in 1398–99—which included the capture of stone masons to build monuments in Samarkand—left the Sultanate weakened and strengthened the claims of later arrivals from Central Asia.[41]

A major transition occurred with the establishment of the Mughal dynasty following the invasion of Babur. Babur was an heir to Ferghana in present-day Uzbekistan, but after suffering military setbacks in Central Asia, he managed to establish himself as a ruler in Kabul. Fifteen years later, he began conducting a series of invasions against India culminating in a decisive battle at Panipat in 1525, where his cavalry and canons were used to great effect against Ibrahim Lodi's elephants and mercenaries. Under Babur's grandson Akbar, the Mughal Empire extended its rule to Kashmir and Balochistan and subjugated the rebellious Afghan tribes. But after the death of Akbar's great-grandson Aurangzeb, the Empire experienced a decline, a combination of succession crises, Maratha ascendancy, financial overextension, and secessionism, especially after 1720.[42]

The five centuries of dominance in north-central India by the Delhi Sultanate and Mughal Emperors saw intensified Indian interactions with the Islamicate world—a region stretching from Spain and Morocco to Southeast Asia—where Islam was an influential, if not always the dominant, religion. With its large population and considerable wealth, India was at the centre of the exchange of goods and people within this system, until the arrival of Europeans as missionaries, merchants, diplomats, and soldiers of fortune. In addition to goods and people, there was a vibrant exchange of ideas. For example, the Islamic world saw debates on whether religious, executive, and judicial authority should be derived from Caliphs or directly through kingly right. Among those arguing for the latter was the Spanish-born Abu Bakr al-Turtushi in his 1122 tract *Sirajulmuluk*, where he references among others the Indian author Shanaq (Chanakya).[43]

One remarkable aspect of international exchange during the era of Mughal supremacy in the subcontinent involved Africa. Starting in the fifteenth century, Indian cotton and textiles were traded with the East African coast and Ethiopia for gold, ivory, and slaves. These Habshi slaves (the term referred originally to Abyssinians but was, along with Siddi, used for Africans more broadly) were removed from their families, converted to Islam and sometimes given military training. Many found their way to the Deccan in India. One such Ethiopian-born slave, Malik Ambar, rose to become *peshwa* and army commander to the Sultan of Ahmednagar. His army of 50,000 included 10,000 Africans as well as large numbers of Maratha cavalry, and they harassed the armies and supply lines of the Mughal Empire. Such was Ambar's reputation that he appears in a 1616 painting as a severed head being shot by a bow-wielding Emperor Jehangir perched astride the world.[44]

The medieval and early modern period therefore witnessed direct and indirect Indian material contacts with an astonishingly broad geographical expanse, ranging from North Africa and the Mediterranean to Central Asia and Tibet, the South China Sea to Southeast Asia and across the Indian Ocean to East Africa. These preceded colonial-era networks that both disrupted and accelerated India's international links. For example, to the west from the tenth to twelfth centuries, India was part of Fatimid and Mamluk trading networks centred in Egypt, and from there to Tunis and beyond.[45] Commercial and cultural contacts—including religion and writing systems—extended east as far as the Philippines.[46] To the north, between the sixteenth and eighteenth centuries, Indian traders and moneylenders plied their trade between Persia and Astrakhan in Russia.[47]

Yet the medieval and early modern period also saw a certain inwardness on the part of Indian rulers and the Mughals in particular. Indeed, a common view is that the Mughals had no real interest in overseas matters. For example, an anecdote recounted by the English ambassador to the Mughal Court, Thomas Roe, suggests that Emperor Jehangir was uninterested in European maps that were presented to him. This may be an overly simplistic conclusion, as Mughal courtiers would often request European maps and incorporate some of that knowledge into their own cartography.[48] At the same time, it is true that despite sometimes considering Sri Lanka, Aceh, and Malacca as parts of 'Hindustan', the Mughals did not develop an ocean-faring navy in an attempt to politically subjugate these regions.[49] For this reason, the Mughals' means of retaliation to piracy by the Dutch and English was to restrict their access to trade on land rather than fight back at sea, an approach that initially proved effective.

But a further puzzle is that despite steady trade and the import of mercenaries, the Mughal Empire made little attempt at claiming primacy within the Islamicate world. This was despite their being by far the largest polity and economy in this system, dwarfing even the Ottoman Caliphate and Safavids in Persia. Rivalries between these three 'gunpowder empires' certainly did exist. Akbar attempted to highlight his Empire's relative wealth by, for example, subsidizing the Hajj pilgrimage for his subjects, sending gift-laden delegations and making donations to Mecca and Medina. While giving themselves universal titles (Jahangir and Shah Jahan mean 'World Conqueror' and 'Lord of the World' respectively), the Mughals referred to the Ottomans only as Sultans rather than Caliphs. There were other forms of more direct competition, including between the Mughals and Safavids over control of Kandahar. The Mughals remained concerned about Persian relations with the Deccan Sultanates and Ottoman naval encroachment around Gujarat. But despite this rivalry and the power disparity in the Mughals' favour, the rulers of India ultimately accepted the Ottomans and Safavids as peers.[50]

The Delhi Sultanate and Mughal Empire were, of course, not the only medieval Indian entities to have extensive interactions with the outside world before the era of European colonial dominance. In the Deccan, a booming trade across the Arabian Sea continued through the fourteenth and fifteenth centuries, with the export of rice, sugar, textiles, jewels, and luxury foods, in exchange for horses, slaves, gold, pearls, and silk from Arabia, Africa, the Caucasus, and China. The Vijayanagara Empire that dominated south India from the fourteenth to sixteenth centuries likely received tribute from overseas, including from what is today Myanmar and Sri Lanka. It was central to trading networks linking Europe and the Middle East to China and Southeast Asia.[51] The cosmopolitanism of the Vijayanagara Empire is reflected in the architecture of its ruined capital Hampi. There were curious military associations as well. In the fifteenth century, Vijayanagara ruler Deva Raya I reorganized his military with a focus on cavalry and mounted archers. These were imported from Persia and Arabia, while Turkish bowmen were hired during a period of remarkable political expansion.[52] After initial European contacts were established, Krishna Deva Raya used Portuguese mercenaries and their matchlock guns to great effect in battles against Bijapur, although he inexplicably did not invest further in gunpowder technologies.[53] In decline by the late sixteenth and seventeenth centuries, the rulers of Vijayanagara also had early interactions with Portuguese, Dutch, and English traders and explorers, permitting European trading stations along the Indian coast.[54]

Confederacies and Generals: Early Modern India, c. 1600–1862

The period after 1707 saw the gradual dissolution of the Mughal Empire. Governors in Punjab, Awadh, and Bengal became functionally independent, Gujarat experienced political strife, the Nizam in Hyderabad defeated two Mughal armies, and Rajputs, Afghans, and Jats took over new areas. The vacuum was partly filled by the Maratha Confederacy, which expanded rapidly into Gujarat and Malwa under Peshwa Bajirao I. In 1739, the Persian king Nadir Shah invaded India and sacked Delhi, leading to the Mughals' effective loss of Punjab and the north-west frontiers. Maratha hegemony expanded further, with Raghuji Bhonsle of Nagpur campaigning to Bengal, Bihar, and Odisha. But this period invited further intervention: for example, a succession crisis in Golconda following the Nizam's death in 1748 resulted in a rare French overland expedition into Maharashtra.

But after a period of Maratha primacy, during which their armies reached Delhi in 1752–55, the battle of Panipat on 14 January 1761, saw a devastating defeat to the Afghan army of

Ahmed Shah Abdali. Even before the battle, the Marathas had trouble securing some allies and their camp suffered from disease and shortages of money and food. Once the battle started, the coordination of forces and artillery proved ineffective against more heavily armed Afghan cavalry. The third battle of Panipat featured perhaps the most battle deaths in a single day in Indian history. Still, Maratha power did not fade immediately, and during a brief renaissance, they were still to inflict some defeats against the British. Among many other developments during the resurrection of Maratha power, this period saw the extraordinary regency of Ahilyabai Holkar of Indore between the 1760s and 1790s, the rare female leader who was both literate and actively engaged in military and diplomatic affairs. (In fact, she could perhaps lay claim to being one of India's first female diplomats.[55]) A combination, however, of factionalism and steady British advances led to the decline of Maratha power between 1803 and 1818.

The Marathas were the last Indian power to develop significant naval capabilities before the dominance of the British. Beginning in the seventeenth century under Shivaji, the Marathas built ships capable of helping in amphibious operations, as against Sidi Yakub's stronghold at Danda Rajapur.[56] The early Maratha navy also benefited from recruiting Portuguese mercenaries. Later, Kanhoji Angre—who governed portions of the Konkan coast after playing a critical role in dynastic negotiations—managed to use maritime forces to successfully defend coastal forts from the Siddis, Portuguese, English, and Dutch between 1710 and 1729.[57] The Marathas were not the only Indian rulers to operate at sea. For example, the famed British Admiral Horatio Nelson's first ever battle experience was against 'armed cruisers' from Mysore, then ruled by Hyder Ali, which the British initially mistook for 'Marratta' vessels.[58]

Another empire that played an important role in shaping India's interactions with external powers was that of the Sikhs. The Sikhs ruled a sizeable territory that extended directly or indirectly into modern-day Afghanistan and parts of Tibet. The rise of the Sikh Empire under Maharaja Ranjit Singh was itself a product of conflict with outsiders. His military successes against the Afghan Durrani dynasty briefly ensured Sikh dominance in the Punjab from Amritsar to Lahore to Peshawar. Allying with British forces, Sikh soldiers marched in Kabul in 1839.[59] Under Sikh suzerainty, the Dogras led by Gulab Singh established themselves as leaders in Jammu and after 1834 Ladakh. In 1841, in a bid to dominate the wool trade, Gulab Singh's ablest general Zorawar Singh led a force of 6000 soldiers into western Tibet. Among other things, this led to fears among British officials of an alliance between the Sikhs and Nepal. While Zorawar made initial advances, his forces were defeated near Missar in Tibet and Zorawar himself was killed. A counter-invasion by Tibetan forces into Ladakh resulted in their defeat in 1842, and a signing of a treaty that recognized Dogra rule of Ladakh but not of Tibet.[60] (This did not prevent future Dogra leaders from sometimes including Tibet in their claims.)

The political history of India is often dominated by North India with detours to the Deccan and South. But North-East India had its own extraordinary legacy, including engagement and conflict with what is today Myanmar, Southeast Asia, and Southwest China. At the centre of much of this engagement during the second millennium was the Tai Ahom dynasty based in present-day Assam. After developing a militia system that helped withstand the Mughal Empire, Ahom rule peaked in the seventeenth century before a combination of popular rebellions in the late eighteenth century, repeated Burmese invasions in the 1820s, and British intervention resulted in the region's colonization.[61] Indeed, colonization by European powers of the entire Indian subcontinent represented a transition to a new phase in India's international history.

Guns and Ships: European Arrivals, 1498–1857

In the medieval period, visitors to India from Europe were few and far between. They included the celebrated Venetian traveller Marco Polo, followed by his compatriot Niccolò de' Conti who stayed in Vijayanagara. In the late fifteenth century, the Russian Afanasy Nikitin came to Bidar and western India for some years. There was an indirect exchange of material culture: for example, a first-millennium CE bronze Buddha statue, possibly from Kashmir, has been found in a Viking hoard in the trading town of Helgö in today's Sweden. But direct interactions between India, on the one hand, and Western and Northern Europe on the other, were virtually non-existent before the arrival in 1498 of Vasco da Gama in Calicut on the Malabar coast.

The arrival of the Portuguese significantly accelerated contacts between India and Europe. Europeans interacted with Indians originally in Arabic, but also quickly learned to communicate in Persian, Malayalam, Konkani, and Tamil. Their early interests in India extended to medicine, botany, navigation, and religion.[62] In 1505, Francisco de Almeida was dispatched as the first Portuguese viceroy of the Estado da Índia, marking the start of European colonialism in India.

The military superiority of Europeans was not immediately apparent, at least not in every respect. For example, the Portuguese military leader Afonso de Albuquerque wrote in 1513 that Indian gunsmiths—who had adopted Ottoman technologies—were producing higher quality firearms than their German counterparts and promptly dispatched some of these gunsmiths to Lisbon.[63] At the same time, after 1520, the Portuguese engaged in piracy against Indian vessels and tried to preserve a monopoly in European trade in the Indian Ocean. This even necessitated an agreement in the Indian Ocean with the Ottomans, who had threatened Portuguese stations in Muscat and Hormuz (including in cooperation with the Zamorin of Calicut).[64] But Portuguese maritime dominance was eventually undermined by the gradual entry into the Indian Ocean of the Dutch, English, French, and Danes.

Except for the Portuguese, who early on claimed imperial rights in India, other Europeans arrived primarily as traders. By the mid-1600s, the English, Portuguese, Dutch, Danes, and French were competing for favour in the Mughal court. It would be 'a good thing to try to remove from the mind of Aurangzeb and the ministers every ground for fearing that we would one day be too powerful in these regions', the French traveller and physician Francois Bernier wrote from India, adding ominously, 'It is not yet the time.'[65] But while various Indian kingdoms and empires—the Marathas, Sikhs, Rajputs, and Mysore—jostled for control of India during the vacuum left by the Mughals in the eighteenth century, so did the Europeans. In was in this environment that the East India Company—a private but state-backed corporation—arose as the leading colonial power in India, paving the way for British rule.

The East India Company was established in 1600 by royal charter and private financing, initially with an eye on the spice trade in today's Indonesia. Its first flotilla of four ships set sail from England in 1601, and next year after stops in South Africa, Madagascar, and the Nicobar Islands, it arrived in Aceh, where it found 'Gujeratis', people of 'Bengal', and 'Malibaris' already engaged in trading activities. Trading posts called 'factories' (led by 'factors') were soon established with a regional base in Bantam in Java in 1617. Despite the company's charter initially making no mention of territorial control, they focused on Pulo Ai and Pulo Run, two tiny islands in the Moluccas covered in nutmeg trees. (King James I later even styled himself the King of 'Puloway and Puloroon', marking some of the first British imperial claims in Asia.[66]) It was only after failures in present-day Indonesia, where the English were eventually ousted by the Dutch—as well as in Japan and Siam—that the Company turned its attention to today's India.

The English commercial presence in India had two rather separate origins. On the east coast, factories emerged as an outgrowth of the Southeast Asian spice trade. In 1611, the English had established a foothold at the Golconda port of Masulipatnam, but natural and political circumstances proved adverse. In 1639, a small plot was negotiated in the village of Madraspatnam (later Madras, present-day Chennai) next to a Portuguese establishment at San Thome, and in the 1630s, Company representatives were sent to Bengal to secure food and raw materials. Initially, European trade with the eastern coast of India was the responsibility of centres in Southeast Asia—the Portuguese in Malacca, the Dutch in Jakarta, and the English at Bantam—because textiles from India helped service the spice trade. Only later did the English consolidate their presence in Madras and Bengal. This included the foundation under somewhat chaotic circumstances of a fort near the village of Kalighat (Calcutta) by an idiosyncratic Company agent named Job Charnock.[67]

On the west coast of India, the English arrived in Surat in 1607 in a bid to diversify trade by tapping the Arabian Sea network. It also became a point of interaction with the Mughal court in Agra. In 1612, the Company won a small but decisive naval victory over the Portuguese off the Gujarat coast, and Emperor Jehangir eventually allowed the English to establish a trading post at Surat. Bombay came into English hands as part of a dowry and defence treaty with Portugal in 1661, as alliances shifted. The complete defeat of the English to a Mughal naval force led by Sidi Yaqub in Bombay in 1689 led to a temporary shift of their operations back to Surat. But Emperor Aurangzeb allowed the English to remain in Bombay under 'humiliating' conditions.[68]

As late as 1750, the British political and military presence in India was still quite modest. It consisted of several factories—major ones in Madras, Bombay and Calcutta, which were the bases of three 'Presidencies'—and a few hundred English soldiers. The industrial revolution had not yet occurred and, economically, India still dwarfed England. However, the Company managed to establish its dominance among Europeans in the Indian Ocean by marginalizing the Portuguese and Dutch in a series of conflicts and establishing an effective monopoly on trade in several goods. By the eighteenth century, their primary European rivals for influence in India were the French, who had a presence in Pondicherry on the Coromandel Coast and Chandernagore in Bengal. The British gained the upper hand following a series of Carnatic Wars in the mid- to late-eighteenth century.[69] Such was the significance of this prize that the Comte de Lally, defeated commander of the French forces in 1760, was tried and executed for treason upon his return to France.

The mid-eighteenth century marks a major turning point for the East India Company. As retaliation against the seizure of Calcutta by the Nawab of Bengal Siraj ud-Daulah, an expeditionary force under Colonel Robert Clive was dispatched from Madras. Using a good deal of deception and bribery, Clive won the Battle of Plassey in 1757 and installed a proxy ruler, Mir Jafar. Company control of Bengal and Bihar was consolidated after the Battle of Buxar in 1764. A year later, Clive and the Mughal Emperor Shah Alam II signed the Treaty of Allahabad. This gave the Company *diwani* rights, that is the rights to collect taxes in Bengal and Bihar in exchange for tribute to the Mughal court. Two other developments further deepened Company Rule. In 1774, Warren Hastings was appointed the first British governor-general, consolidating control across the three presidencies from a capital in Calcutta. Additionally, the East India Company Act of 1784 also brought Company Rule in India under the British Government. In just a few decades in the mid-eighteenth century, the East India Company went from traders to colonial administrators.[70]

The military employment and structure of the Company is important to keep in mind when considering British expansion in India in the eighteenth and early nineteenth centuries. Each East India Company Presidency—Madras, Bombay and Calcutta—initially had its own army, which started as guard forces for their outposts. Over time, regiments of local Indian soldiers (sepoys, from the word *sipahi* for soldier) led by British officers were established, and they benefited from European drilling and training techniques. At times, these forces were supplemented by Royal regiments of the British Army, such as the 33rd Regiment, which came to be associated with the Duke of Wellington. In the century after Plassey, the Company, along with Crown forces, waged a series of wars against Indian powers that had splintered from or supplanted the declining Mughal Empire: Mysore, the Marathas, Nepal, Burma, the Afghans, and the Sikhs. In 1803, British forces reached Delhi. Furthermore, the Doctrine of Lapse promoted by Governor-General Lord Dalhousie was used to annex Indian states where succession was in question. These efforts at Company expansion were not all unmitigated successes. In fact, the Mughals, Mysore, Marathas, and Afghans all imposed military defeats on the British, in a few cases with French assistance.[71] But none of these defeats of the British military were decisive enough to be completely irreversible.

An Extractive Enterprise: The British Raj, 1857–1947

The rebellion of 1857 against Company rule—which spread rapidly across many parts of India—marked a major turning point. It resulted in the Government of India Act of 1858, which made India a colony of the British Crown. The Mughal Empire came to a formal end with the trial and exile to Rangoon of the last Mughal Emperor Bahadur Shah Zafar II. For the next ninety years, Britain ruled most of India directly or claimed suzerainty over a large number of princely states. An India Office under a secretary of state for India was established in London to manage India policy, while the governor-general of India was now considered a viceroy. India was now under the rule of the British Raj.

Under both Company and Raj rule, India's contact with
the world altered in various ways. First, the prior religious,
economic, and cultural links with Southeast, Northeast,
Central and West Asia were fundamentally disrupted. Instead,
India's international economic and social exchanges evolved
into interactions within colonial networks. These extended to
Europe and Britain's other colonies—from the Caribbean to
Africa and Malaya—as well as other areas where Britain had
commercial interests such as China, the Arab world, and the
United States. With China, at first, Indian cotton was sold
for tea, and proceeds from this trade paid for British supplies
and military expenditure in India. However, declining demand
for Indian cotton in Qing China as a result of an economic
downturn and import substitution led to its replacement with
opium.[72] With opium from India to China and tea from China
to Europe, the Opium Wars that resulted could just as easily
have been called the 'Tea Wars'.[73] Beyond the triangular trade
with China, Indian raw materials were shipped to Britain, where
the industrial revolution resulted in the export of manufactured
goods. The world of finance also shifted: Indian financiers
played a role in Hong Kong and Shanghai, just as Baghdadi
Jews sought opportunities in Bombay.

The colonial exchange of goods and capital also extended to
people. Indentured labourers were taken from India, including
convicts or otherwise coerced individuals, to such places as
Guyana, Trinidad and Tobago, Fiji, and Mauritius where their
descendants now account for over 30 per cent of the population,
and about 70 per cent in the case of Mauritius. An Anglo–
Dutch Treaty of 1870 led to similar indentured labour being
sent from India to Suriname, where people of Indian origin
still constitute over a quarter of the population. While not quite

chattel slavery, such Indian labour was often transported under abysmal conditions with high death rates.[74] Indian workers were also employed elsewhere, whether on tea plantations in Ceylon or as professional workers in Burma, resulting in populations in today's Sri Lanka and Myanmar. Beyond labour, Indians also migrated as traders to other British colonies, establishing sizeable communities in today's Kenya, Tanzania, Uganda, South Africa, Malaysia, Singapore, and Hong Kong.

The colonial period also shaped India's relations with the American colonies that would become the United States. After his decisive defeat at Yorktown contributed to American independence, General Charles Cornwallis was dispatched as the British commander in India, where he oversaw the war with Mysore that resulted in the defeat of Tipu Sultan. Several American-born individuals played critical roles in India, such as Elihu Yale, who became the East India Company's chief representative in Madras. He later donated some of his substantial riches to a prestigious college in Connecticut that would later be named after him. Massachusetts-born David Ochterlony was a commander in the Anglo–Nepalese War and became Britain's resident in the Mughal court. The United States' third vice president, Aaron Burr, fathered two unacknowledged children with a woman believed to have been born in Calcutta, making his descendants among the earliest Indian-Americans.[75]

After American independence, one of the United States' first diplomatic missions in Asia was dispatched to Calcutta, although the first consul Benjamin Joy was not recognized by the East India Company. In the nineteenth century, ice farmed in the United States was shipped to India (the ice house in Chennai built by the American magnate Frederic Tudor later became associated with Swami Vivekananda, who briefly stayed there). Economic links between India and the United States also took some unexpected turns: the suspension of the cotton trade during the American Civil War resulted in a boom in Indian textile exports. India was certainly viewed with disdain by many prominent Americans, some of whom approved of aspects of British colonialism (such as former US president Ulysses Grant who visited in 1879). But the country and its culture also positively inspired such disparate characters as Henry David Thoreau, Mark Twain, and Robert Oppenheimer in the nineteenth and early twentieth centuries.[76]

For their part, many leading Indians ventured abroad during this period, including political leaders, lawyers, scientists, writers, and religious figures. Swami Vivekananda famously took part in the Parliament of the World's Religions in Chicago and travelled across the United States, Europe, and Asia. India's first Nobel Laureate Rabindranath Tagore also travelled widely on account of his celebrity, including to the United States, Argentina, Italy, Hungary, China, Indonesia, Japan, Germany, the Soviet Union, and Iran.

The growing Indian Independence movement also had strong international associations. Many Indian political elites—including those belonging to the first generation of post-Independence national leaders such as Mahatma Gandhi, Pandit Jawaharlal Nehru, and Sardar Vallabhbhai Patel—studied in the United Kingdom. Gandhi, of course, gained initial fame for his protests and organization in South Africa. (The anniversary of his return to India in 1915 is still commemorated in Pravasi Bharatiya Divas or the Day of the Overseas Indian.) Veer Savarkar, after travelling to the UK for law studies, sought asylum in France before his arrest by British authorities.[77] B.R. Ambedkar was educated in the United States in addition to the UK, which in turn influenced his worldview. Somewhat more unusually, the Indian communist M.N. Roy founded what became the Mexican Communist Party before returning to India.

Beyond economic and cultural exchanges, there were direct consequences of British colonialism for India's role in international politics and security. At various points in time, Burma, Sri Lanka, Malaya (including Singapore), Yemen, Somaliland, the Trucial States (United Arab Emirates), Bahrain, Oman, Kuwait, and Qatar were governed or administered from today's India, although sometimes only for brief periods or indirectly. Meanwhile, the British Indian Army was deployed widely overseas. In China, Indian soldiers were involved in the sack of the Old Summer Palace outside Beijing in 1860 during the Second Opium War and in the suppression of the Boxer Rebellion in 1900–1901. (Both episodes are still remembered as national humiliations in China today.[78]) In the nineteenth century, Indian forces were deployed frequently in North and East Africa and in India's extended neighbourhood: from Burma to Ceylon and Malaya. In Tibet, Indian forces took part in the Younghusband Expedition in 1903–04 to Lhasa meant to extend Britain's economic influence across the Himalayas and pre-empt Russian advances as part of the 'Great Game'.[79]

During World War I, the Indian Army saw action in Mesopotamia, Africa, Gallipoli, and the Western front in Europe. Over 70,000 Indian soldiers perished. Troops from the princely states contributed in significant ways to, among other things, the capture of Haifa (now in Israel), an occasion commemorated in New Delhi's Teen Murti Memorial. During World War II, a volunteer Indian force of 2,500,000 was raised, trained, and deployed. It served in Singapore, Burma, Iraq, Iran, North Africa, and Italy, and suffered nearly 90,000 fatalities. In both World Wars, Indian revenues contributed significantly to the British-led war effort, including from the princely states.[80]

A further Indian involvement in World War II concerned the Indian National Army (INA). In 1941, Netaji Subhas Chandra Bose sought assistance first from the Soviet Union, then Nazi Germany, before reviving the INA with Japanese assistance in Southeast Asia. The INA, made up of prisoners of war from Malaya and Singapore, among others, fought alongside Japanese forces in the Burma theatre. As Japanese forces retreated, Bose died in a plane crash in Formosa (today's Taiwan) in 1945.[81] The divided Indian approach to World War II revealed itself in criticism within the Congress and among some of its political opponents of the Quit India Movement, during which Gandhi urged the Congress to call for British withdrawal from India even as the war was underway.[82] The defence by Congress leaders—including specifically Jawaharlal Nehru—of INA officers in high-profile trials highlights the complex attitudes in India to World War II.

Beyond the military, the employment of Indian manpower by the British Empire in a variety of overseas conditions was immense and varied. As the Viceroy Lord Curzon boasted in a speech in 1904, '[I]f you are fighting the Mad Mullah in Somaliland, you soon discover that Indian troops and an Indian general are best qualified for the task, and you ask the Government of India to send them; if you desire to defend any of your extreme outposts or coaling stations of the Empire, Aden, Mauritius, Singapore, Hong-kong, even Tien-tsin or Shan-hai-kwan, it is to the Indian Army that you turn . . . It is with . . . Indian trained officers that you irrigate Egypt and dam the Nile; with Indian forest officers that you tap the resources of Central Africa and Siam; with Indian surveyors that you explore all the hidden places of the earth.'[83]

The colonial period also directly influenced India's state structures and physical boundaries. To the north and west, British competition with the Russian Empire—the so-called 'Great Game'—played an important role. (Russia was viewed by Indian nationalists as no less an imperial power; many Indians celebrated Russia's defeat in the Russo–Japanese War.) As a process of British expansion and frontier competition, a series of legal treaties were established between British India and its neighbours that continue to influence borders. These include agreements with Nepal, Bhutan, China, Tibet, Afghanistan, and Myanmar. But British agreements were often problematic, vague, error-strewn, and repeatedly revised, contributing to many of the boundary disputes that India still faces. India's western boundary with Pakistan—the Radcliffe Line—was marked in a rather haphazard and rushed manner by British civil servants, adding to the trauma of Partition. Similarly, the Durand Line separating Afghanistan from British India and the McMahon Line separating what is now Arunachal Pradesh from Tibet both remain politically relevant today.[84] Beyond borders, it was during the British colonial period that India developed its current military and bureaucratic structures. Due to the belated addition of Indians to the civil service and officer cadre of the military, India inherited a bureaucracy and military from the British. India still retains many of these organizational features, including its regimental traditions and a generalized civil service.[85]

Much of the British colonial legacy had a lasting effect on independent India: from the judicial system and civil service to the army and infrastructure. But for the most part, these institutions were meant for extractive purposes, a consequence of which was the immense transfer of wealth from India to Britain during the period of the Raj. The extensive Indian railway network, for example, was designed primarily to transport raw materials and troops and was heavily subsidized by Indian taxation. Under British rule, agricultural policies in India were often disastrous and industrialization was suppressed, resulting in almost no per capita economic growth in India between 1900 and 1947.[86] The struggle for Independence from British rule was therefore both a moral and practical necessity for Indians.

Power, Trade and Ideas: Lessons from Pre-Independent India

The history of India's interactions with the world before Independence makes it possible to derive several lessons relevant to the present day. At least three stand out. First, India's long history shows the persistence of power politics. It is politics, after all, that creates nations, borders, leaders, laws, and ideologies. Politics in turn is shaped by power, whether military, economic, cultural, or ideological. In contrast to national politics, international politics is defined by anarchy: the absence of an overarching central authority that can enforce recognized laws such as a world government or global police force. The international stage is thus a naturally competitive place, whether due to a human urge to dominate or due to persistent mistrust.

Many other 'realist' lessons find ready examples from Indian history.[87] The constant competition and regular warfare among Indian states are indicative of the security dilemma, whereby states seeking security for themselves contribute to the insecurity of others. Threat perceptions constantly changed because of geography, resources, ideology, and technology, reflected in India's experiences with Greek, Huna, Arab, Afghan, Turkic, Mongol, and Persian invaders from the north-west. Throughout this history, rapid changes caused leaders to misperceive intentions and miscalculate. This was sometimes the result of technological breakthroughs, changes in political leadership, or organizational developments; perhaps the most dramatic of these transformations involved the arrival of European colonial powers. In early modern India, various actors—Sikhs, Marathas, Afghans, Nepalis, British, French, Portuguese, and Ottomans—understood the importance and value of instrumental coalitions and alliances. India today can draw lessons from these and other experiences. Ultimately, modern India will have to act decisively to protect its national interests and should thus remain conscious of the inherently competitive nature of international politics, the sources of threat at any given point in time, the need to enhance its comprehensive national power, and the necessity at times to enter partnerships or coalitions to preserve a stable balance of power.

A second set of lessons involves the constancy of commerce. Trade is a consistent characteristic of India's interactions with the world throughout history, often playing a major role in eliciting interest from others, or otherwise shaping India's interactions with the outside world. Even if India were to choose isolationism, the rest of the world is likely to come knocking for resources or markets. Well before India settled into large kingdoms and empires, it engaged naturally in trade with far-flung regions of the world. Even before the arrival of Europeans, the direct material contact with India could be felt as far away as Alexandria and Astrakhan, Samarkand and Xinjiang, Luoyang and Lombok, Axum and Zanzibar. Commercial considerations invited interest from parties across the Afro–Eurasian landmass, from the European colonial powers after Vasco da Gama's voyage in 1498, and from much of the modern world after the nineteenth and twentieth centuries. The nature of Indian commercial exchange also changed over time, from rare commodities, to manufactured goods such as textiles, to services provided by Indian labour.

Taken together, power politics and international commerce have particular implications for India in the maritime domain. Until the Mughal Empire, India could afford to be focused on terrestrial preoccupations as the Indian Ocean was never dominated by any one party. Chola expansionism into maritime south and southeast Asia represented an aberration in Indian maritime history, which was otherwise characterized primarily by commercial activity and coastal defence. However, the effective British monopoly in the Indian Ocean after the Carnatic Wars turned the tables, enabling almost two centuries of British dominance on the subcontinent. India must therefore take pains to ensure that the Indian Ocean is not similarly dominated by a single actor in the future. A failure to do so could have incredibly damaging consequences for Indian security and sovereignty.

Third, the long history of India's external interactions shows the importance of establishing, shaping, and enforcing international norms that advance Indian interests. In any competitive enterprise, such as a sport, it is always advantageous for a player to also define the rules and act as a referee. This explains why all major powers have attempted to establish norms, even if they were only partially enforceable or selectively enforced. In the pre-modern world, such norms were almost always more of an ideal than an actual practice. Major historical empires, such as the Umayyad and Abbasid Caliphates, the Spanish and Portuguese Empires, and successive Chinese dynasties attempted to establish hierarchical international orders that often drew legitimacy from religion: the Caliph in the Islamic world, the Pope in Western Christendom, or the 'Son of Heaven' in Imperial China. By contrast, the modern international order is grounded in the notion of sovereignty— that a state has supreme domestic power, freedom from foreign interference, and equality with other states—confirmed at the Treaties of Westphalia in 1648. Today, the idea of Westphalian sovereignty sits uneasily with notions of universal ideals or normative values. Even when attempts were made to articulate and enforce universal norms—as after the American, French, and Russian Revolutions—notions such as a balance of power and colonial control took precedence in practice.

India has often felt the impact of norms defined by others, but its pre-colonial history also shows glimpses of an ability to establish normative standards for itself and the world. There are good reasons, then, for India to articulate and implement its own vision of international norms, at times in conjunction with like-minded partners. For India today, this will require drawing broader lessons from the Indian experience. Indeed, why should the lived experience of the most populated country in human history not have wider—perhaps even universal—applications? But it will also require investments in scholarship, which would benefit from more assiduous recordkeeping, the preservation of relevant documentary and material evidence, and their greater accessibility. Ultimately, the articulation and enforcement of norms and values will require aligning words with deeds and power with persuasion. In fact, some of these challenges were already apparent as India emerged as an independent republic in the middle of the twentieth century.

2

1947–1971: Independence and Non-Alignment

The Cold War: US and Soviet Bipolarity

India became independent two years after the end of World War II and under very specific geopolitical circumstances. The World War had caused considerable devastation in Europe and East Asia, while the decolonization movement had gained momentum in Africa and Asia, with India at the vanguard. But even by 1947, when an indebted and war-weary Britain hastily partitioned and left India, it was clear a Cold War was already underway between one bloc led by the United States and another led by the Union of Soviet Socialist Republics (USSR). Both the US and the Soviet Union had booming war economies and they had partitioned Europe and Korea. This was now a bipolar world.

The USSR was founded after the Russian Revolution of 1917. Led by Vladimir Lenin, the revolution was inspired by the ideas of Karl Marx, a nineteenth-century German intellectual who lived much of his later life in Britain. Marx argued that history was a class struggle that would conclude with the rise of the working classes and society's eventual organization into ideal self-governing communes. The Communist Revolution in Russia inspired revolutionaries in China, Europe, Southeast Asia, Africa, India, the United States, and Latin America. Communist International (or Comintern) held its first congress in 1919 and promised to create an 'international Soviet republic as a transition stage to the complete abolition of the State'.[1]

Meanwhile, the United States under President Franklin D. Roosevelt was emerging from the Great Depression and decades of relative isolationism. In January 1941, almost a year before the United States entered the World War II, Roosevelt laid out an ambitious vision of 'a world founded upon four essential human freedoms' that would form a 'definite basis for a kind of world attainable in our own time and generation'. These were the freedom of speech and expression, freedom to worship, freedom from want, and freedom from fear, and as Roosevelt repeatedly emphasized, these were possible 'everywhere in the world'.[2] Roosevelt's neo-liberal vision was very much at odds with the then-dominant notions of colonialism, communism and fascism.

The Cold War era that followed World War II was a dangerous time. In direct dealings between the Soviet Union and the United States—such as in Europe—an unstable peace was preserved. This was in large part due to the presence of nuclear weapons and strong alliances on both sides. The United States had demonstrated the terrible, destructive power of nuclear weapons by using them on Hiroshima and Nagasaki in 1945. After the Soviet Union acquired and tested its own nuclear weapons in 1949, a massive arms race ensued between the United States and the Soviet Union during which thousands of nuclear weapons were aimed by the superpowers at each other, including in close proximity to one another in Europe. As the two sides deterred each other—not wanting to fire the first shot of what could result in mutually assured destruction—their competition took other forms. Spy games driven by intelligence concerns and matters of prestige (such as the 'space race') featured prominently. Both sides also advanced their economic models. The United States unveiled the ambitious Marshall Plan, a massive aid project that saved Western Europe from famine in the late 1940s, but also deliberately checked the advance of communism.[3] It also established the North Atlantic Treaty Organization (NATO), a mutual defence treaty of European and North American countries to defend against the Soviet Union. The USSR, meanwhile, promoted its own state-led industrial model among its Warsaw Pact allies in Central and Eastern Europe.

While the international system was being primarily defined and shaped by the superpower rivalry, another major development was unfolding. This was the decolonization of much of the world, from South and Southeast Asia to Africa and from the Caribbean to the South Pacific and West Asia. (South and Central America had mostly decolonized in the nineteenth century.) Using membership of the United Nations as a criterion, there were just fifty-one recognized sovereign states in 1945, 117 by 1965, and 154 by 1980. In other words, over 100 new sovereign states arose in just thirty-five years.

Both the United States and the Soviet Union made efforts to attract and influence these newly independent states, including through foreign aid, military support, and technical assistance.

For the United States, the focus of reconstruction efforts was initially on Europe and Japan. For the Soviet Union, actual communism initially flourished only in Central and Eastern Europe and parts of East Asia. Other areas remained contested, and the Cold War played out brutally across the world, from Cuba and Chile to Angola and Yemen. For the Soviet Union, preserving or advancing the 'people's revolution' required heavy-handed military interventions, including in Hungary, Czechoslovakia, and later Afghanistan. For the United States and the West, upholding a liberal international order involved supporting some very brutal and illiberal regimes if it meant countering the challenge of the Soviet Union. This applied to Guatemala, Iran, South Africa, Pakistan, Indonesia, and the Philippines; Washington was even hesitant about some efforts to stop genocide and ethnic cleansing, as in Bangladesh or Cambodia. Those who romantically recall the Cold War as a simpler time—or, worse, a period of international peace (which applied, if at all, only to Europe)—ignore this tragic and messy global story.[4]

Debating the Foundations: After Independence in 1947

Although a freedom movement had been gaining steam for some time in India, it was in the context of the early Cold War that Independence occurred suddenly on 15 August 1947. As one British historian would write decades later, 'The British Empire did not decline, it simply fell.'[5] The rashness with which the Indian Subcontinent's future was decided was, in hindsight, shocking. A provisional government for India was announced in August 1946, the status of the semi-autonomous princely states was only seriously addressed after January 1947, and an

Independence plan was hastily drafted in May and announced on 3 June. In late June, barely six weeks before India and Pakistan became independent, Sir Cyril Radcliffe—a lawyer who had never been to India—was tasked with drawing a line that would partition the two countries.

The Partition of British India into India and Pakistan was itself a product of complex circumstances. The Pakistan movement gained traction between 1906 and 1947, although proposals for separate homelands for Indian Hindus and Muslims go back to the late nineteenth century. (The term PAKSTAN, proposed as a Muslim homeland by a Cambridge student named Rahmat Ali in 1933, was originally an acronym for Punjab, Afghan, Kashmir, Sind and BalochisTAN.)[6] The Muslim League under Muhammad Ali Jinnah was not initially the most popular political representative of the subcontinent's Muslims. Others, including the Jamaat-e-Islami under Abul A'la al-Maududi and various Shia leaders, offered alternatives. The Muslim League gained ground after the 1930s and especially after the Congress initiated the Quit India Movement during World War II. After the war, suspicions abounded in London about the orientation of an independent India in the nascent Cold War. But as late as 1946, the prospect of a unified but federated independent India was seriously considered.[7]

At Independence in 1947, India found itself in an inhospitable international environment, quite apart from the frightful trauma of a violent Partition. India's leaders during and immediately after Independence included Mahatma Gandhi, Prime Minister Jawaharlal Nehru, Deputy Prime Minister and Home Minister Sardar Vallabhbhai Patel, Chairman of the Constitution Drafting Committee and later Minister of Law and Justice B.R. Ambedkar, the second Governor-General

C. Rajagopalachari (known as Rajaji), the first President Rajendra Prasad, Minister of Education Maulana Abul Kalam Azad, Minister of Railways (and later finance) John Matthai, Minister of Commerce and Industry Syama Prasad Mookerjee and even the last British Viceroy and first Governor-General Lord Mountbatten. These were among the individuals who deliberated and shaped India's approach to domestic, economic, and foreign policies.[8] As vice president of the Executive Council of the Interim Government of India and later as the country's first Prime Minister and External Affairs Minister, Nehru played a significant role in shaping the eventual outcomes. But it is important to note that there was not always consensus among leaders within his Indian National Congress (such as Patel, Prasad, or Rajaji), let alone among its political opponents such as Ambedkar and Mookerjee, about the direction that a newly independent India should take.

The balance of consensus initially rested on a three-fold approach. First, and least controversially, the country would be governed as a Westminster-style democratic republic. This was an ambitious vision, given that the majority of voting-age Indians were then illiterate, and few countries had offered full women's suffrage at the outset. But a parliamentary democracy appeared to be the only practical way to manage a country of India's diversity. India also had an experience and tradition of democracy within the framework of the Indian National Congress (which would regularly elect presidents) and of governance in British-administered territory due to the Government of India Acts of 1861, 1909, and 1919. The last Indian provincial elections held before Independence were in 1946. After 1947, a democratic Constitution was drafted, deliberated, and amended by India's Constituent Assembly, as part of a process led by Ambedkar. The Constitution came into force in 1950.[9]

The second element of India's policy orientation after Independence involved a significant degree of state direction over the economy and industry. It was informed heavily by the Fabian Socialist leanings of Nehru and other Congress leaders—supportive of gradualist social democratic reforms— and were consistent with many of the economic orthodoxies of that time, including in Britain. State-led economic planning gained further credence due to the successes at that point of Soviet industrialization and of the New Deal in the United States, which saw government spending and employment to stimulate recovery following the Great Depression. To various degrees, the idea of state planning was contested by other leaders (Rajaji eventually founded the Swatantra Party which advocated an alternate approach). The likes of Matthai, India's second finance minister, and Patel, the first deputy prime minister and home minister, protested the growing power of the Planning Commission—responsible for Five Year Plans— in the years immediately following Independence, believing that the body's efforts were not accountable and marginalized the elected government.[10] While these debates progressed, India's per capita incomes increased about 2 per cent annually throughout the 1950s after almost no per capita growth in the first forty-seven years of the twentieth century under British colonial rule.

The third element of independent India's initial policy orientation—concerning foreign policy—was informed primarily by Non-Alignment, a notion articulated by Nehru before Independence, including in an address to All India Radio on 7 September 1946.

We [the Interim National Government] shall take full part in international conferences as a free nation with our own policy and not merely as a satellite of another nation. We hope to develop close and direct contacts with other nations and to cooperate with them in the furtherance of world peace and freedom. We propose, as far as possible, to keep away from the power politics of groups, aligned against each other, which have led in the past to world wars and which may again lead to disasters on an even vaster scale. We believe that peace and freedom are indivisible and the denial of freedom anywhere must endanger freedom everywhere and lead to conflict and war. We are particularly interested in the emancipation of colonial and dependent countries and peoples, and in the recognition in theory and practice of equal opportunities for all races . . . We seek no dominion over others and we claim no privileged position over other peoples. But we do claim equal and honourable treatment for our people wherever they may go, and we cannot accept any discrimination against them.[11]

In that same speech, Nehru went on to call for 'friendly and co-operative relations' with Britain and the Commonwealth, recognized the 'major role in international affairs' played by the United States and warned that India would have 'to undertake many common tasks' with the Soviet Union. He highlighted that Indians were 'of Asia and the peoples of Asia are nearer and closer to us than others' and that India was 'the pivot of Western, Southern and South-East Asia'. Finally, he hoped that China 'that mighty country with a mighty past' would emerge as 'a united and democratic China'.[12] China was then in the midst of a civil war but was led by the Chinese Nationalist Party or Kuomintang (KMT) under Chiang Kai-Shek.

Non-Alignment was premised on the belief that formal alliances were destabilizing, and that Indian independence and autonomy would not benefit from allying with either the United States or the Soviet Union. Instead, a 'third way' was possible, particularly among newly decolonizing states. Other post-colonial states, including Burma, Ceylon, and Indonesia, initially shared this assessment and cooperated with India in this respect. In theory, Non-Alignment enabled India to derive benefits from both the US-led and Soviet-led blocs and gave India a natural leadership perch in the post-colonial world. Nehru did not intend it to be equated with isolationism and wanted it to be flexible, as he himself argued in the Constituent Assembly on 4 December 1947:

We have proclaimed during the past year that we will not attach ourselves to any particular group. That has nothing to do with neutrality or passivity or anything else. If there is a big war there is no particular reason why we should jump into it. Nevertheless, it is a little difficult nowadays in world wars to be neutral. Any person with any knowledge of international affairs knows that. The point is not what will happen when there is a war. Are we going to proclaim to the world . . . that when war comes, we stand by Russia? . . . That shows to me an amazing ignorance of how foreign affairs can be conducted. We are not going to join a war if we can help it; and we are going to join the side which is to our interest when the time comes to make the choice. There the matter ends.

But talking about foreign policies, the House must remember that these are not just empty struggles on a chessboard. Behind them lie all manner of things. Ultimately, foreign policy is the outcome of economic policy, and until India has properly evolved her economic policy, her foreign policy will be rather vague, rather inchoate, and will be groping.[13]

Nonetheless, as with state planning, there was criticism and debate within the Indian government about Non-Alignment as it played out in practice. In 1950, Patel—concerned about Nehru advocating for better relations with Beijing after the Communist Revolution and invasion of Tibet—argued that 'even though we regard ourselves as friends of China, the Chinese do not regard us as their friends'.[14] In a 1951 speech explaining his resignation from the cabinet, Ambedkar worried that Non-Alignment had unduly distanced India from potential partners: 'The third matter which has given me cause . . . for actual anxiety and even worry, is the foreign policy of the country . . . Today, after four years, all our friends have deserted us. We have no friends left. We have alienated ourselves.'[15] Other opponents of Nehru—from Acharya Kripalani to the Jan Sangh—espoused still different views on international affairs in the 1940s and 1950s.[16] But before India's leaders had an opportunity to engage in big debates about India's place in the world, there were some urgent problems that had to be negotiated in the first few weeks and months after Independence.

Imperfect Unity: Territorial Consolidation, 1947–1961

The most immediate and important set of foreign policy challenges related to how India would address the consequences of Britain's departure and the Partition of India into two countries: India and Pakistan. These were existential problems in nature, as they would determine the physical contours and demographic constitution of independent India. The process was complicated enough given that Pakistan would be constituted of a geographically separate West Pakistan and East Pakistan, requiring divisions in Punjab and Bengal. But the status of the almost 600 'princely states' that recognized British paramountcy was vague when the plans for Independence and Partition were finalized in 1946 and 1947. Several states flirted with autonomy or accession to Pakistan, including Jodhpur and Travancore, while others such as Bhopal, Indore, and Mysore expressed reservations about acceding to India. Secretary of the Ministry of States V.P. Menon and Deputy Prime Minister and Home Minister Sardar Vallabhbhai Patel led the effort to offer states accession to India. An Instrument of Accession was drafted whereby such states would retain some autonomy, but transfer responsibility for external relations, defence, and communications to the Dominion of India. By April 1947, several major states such as Baroda, Jaipur, Cochin, and Patiala joined the Constituent Assembly. By 15 August 1947, the status of all but a handful of states contiguous to India had been determined in India's favour, including some such as Travancore, Indore and Bhopal that had previously proved reluctant.[17]

One of the exceptions was the coastal state of Junagadh in Gujarat. It was led by a Muslim Nawab but populated by a Hindu majority. While Junagadh indicated initially that it would accede to India, the acting *dewan* Shah Nawaz Bhutto (father of Pakistan's future prime minister Zulfikar Ali Bhutto), persuaded the leadership to announce an accession to Pakistan on 15 August. Local leaders in several portions of the state

disagreed, and Junagadh used its military resources to impose
its control over these breakaway regions. Over the following
months, both Bhutto in Junagadh and Pakistani leaders in
Karachi realized that Pakistan was unable to provide sufficient
military assistance, despite prior assurances to the contrary. On
1 November, Indian troops took over some of the disputed
territory and, under pressure, the Junagadh State Council
reversed its earlier decision on 5 November.[18]

Hyderabad, a much larger and wealthier state in the centre
of India, proved a bigger test. Like Junagadh, it was led by a
Muslim ruler, the Nizam, but had a mostly Hindu population.
With the encouragement of Pakistan's leader Muhammad Ali
Jinnah, Hyderabad initially sought independence from both
India and Pakistan, including 'full sovereignty and autonomy'.
Throughout the subsequent months, negotiations took place over
the terms of accession to India, with the Nizam's government
seeking greater autonomy. At the same time, the Nizam took
steps to secure greater financial independence, enhance arms
stockpiles (with the assistance of an enterprising Australian),
and further centralize rule. Many of these steps went against
the terms of a standstill agreement that had been negotiated
with India. Meanwhile, violence by militias, the detention of
transiting Indian officials by Hyderabad, and mob attacks on
Indian trains added to the tensions. Hyderabad also made an
unsuccessful attempt at reaching out to the United Nations.
On 13 September 1948, India launched Operation Polo, widely
referred to as a 'police action' in Indian officialdom. Five days
later, Hyderabadi forces surrendered.[19]

The third territorial crisis of Partition—and one that
proved the longest lasting—related to Jammu and Kashmir, a
strategically important princely state ruled by a Hindu Maharaja

Hari Singh, who governed a majority Muslim population. While Pakistani leaders were confident that Kashmir would fall into their laps, the Maharaja and the popular National Conference political party of Sheikh Abdullah were disinclined to join Pakistan. As the Maharaja considered holding out for independence, local leaders in Poonch who wished to join Pakistan rebelled, and they soon began to receive support from Pakistan. In late October 1947, Pakistani tribal militia or *lashkars*—backed by the state—seized towns in western Kashmir. The Maharaja panicked, signed the Instrument of Accession with India, and sought military assistance. Air lifted Indian forces arrived in Srinagar just in time to stop the advancing irregular forces from Pakistan, and thereby saved the Kashmir Valley for India.[20]

As fighting continued, Jinnah initially expressed opposition to a plebiscite, a public referendum on the fate of Jammu and Kashmir. He may have believed that the tribal invasion into Kashmir would succeed, or that it would weaken Hyderabad's case for independence, and possibly that a vote would not go in Pakistan's favour given the looting and rape by the Pakistani *lashkars*. After an escalation in fighting, the situation had stabilized by January 1948, when India made a fateful decision to approach the United Nations. Although Nehru had been confident that India could make a strong case in its favour, Britain's delegation supported a plebiscite in the presence of Pakistani troops and a 'neutral' administration (i.e. not led by Sheikh Abdullah), a position that was mostly in line with Pakistan. These moves were compounded by measures advanced by Belgium and Canada that did not prevent Pakistan from assisting the invaders and widened the dispute to one between India and Pakistan. Meanwhile, in response to concerns that

the Indian Army would advance beyond the Uri–Poonch–
Naushera line, the Pakistan Army became directly involved in
the conflict in Kashmir in April 1948.[21]

In August 1948, a UN Commission concluded a three-part
resolution that called for a ceasefire; the removal of Pakistani
troops and thereafter a staged withdrawal of the bulk of Indian
forces, with only a residual presence to maintain law and order;
and consultations to determine conditions for settling Kashmir
based on 'the will of the people'. Pakistan expressed reservations
about this plan. Nehru and Patel contemplated a settlement
based on the 'existing military situation', which would have
meant the effective partitioning of Jammu and Kashmir, an
option that was also rejected by Pakistan.[22] With India receiving
assurances that a plebiscite would only be carried out if Pakistan
kept its end of the bargain (i.e. the removal of Pakistani forces),
a ceasefire was agreed in December 1948. The end of the
first India–Pakistan War resulted in an open-ended and less-
than-satisfactory situation: the continued presence of irregular
forces in Pakistan-Occupied Kashmir (PoK), nascent calls for
Kashmiri independence by Sheikh Abdullah as a compromise,
the attempted shifting of the goalposts for demilitarization by
UN mediators, and a special status for Jammu and Kashmir in
the Indian Constitution.[23]

Beyond these three princely states, the process of
Independence and Partition threw up some other ambiguities.
One example was the state of Kalat, in today's Pakistani
province of Balochistan, whose status in British India was
slightly more autonomous than that of most princely states.
Under pressure to join Pakistan, the Khan of Kalat wrote to
India to discuss the possibility of accession in January 1948,
but his entreaties were refused. India lacked a strong legal or

practical basis to stake a claim.[24] The status of the Andaman and Nicobar Islands—which the British had used as a penal colony, and which had been occupied by Japan during World War II—was also in question. Pakistan pressed claims to this territory based on its proximity to East Bengal. The islands only became a part of India in 1950 and are now of considerable strategic significance.[25]

With the Communist Party coming to power in China in 1949 and its annexation of Tibet in 1950–1951, India also felt the need to reinforce relations with buffer states in the Himalayas. With Nepal, Bhutan, and Sikkim, India negotiated new treaties. Nepal, the most autonomous of the three, agreed to a Treaty of Peace and Friendship in 1950 that facilitated the flow of people and goods and allowed for close cooperation on defence, and foreign relations. After signing a standstill agreement upon Indian independence, Bhutan negotiated a Treaty of Peace and Friendship in 1949 that allowed India to guide the country's external relations. Meanwhile, a 1950 treaty made Sikkim an Indian protectorate, with India responsible for external affairs, defence and strategic communications.[26]

There was also the matter of non-British colonial possessions in India. These included two French colonies, Chandernagore and Pondicherry (which also encompassed three other enclaves: Karaikal surrounded by today's Tamil Nadu, Yanam abutting Andhra Pradesh, and Mahé next to Kerala). In 1949, Chandernagore voted overwhelmingly to join India, which it did de facto, and by the early 1950s Pondicherry saw protests in favour of a merger with India. In 1954, Chandernagore officially became a part of West Bengal and Pondicherry became a Union Territory, with the transition of power in the former French colonies completed following treaty ratification by the French Parliament in 1962.[27]

Additionally, Portugal had the colonies of Goa, Daman and Diu, and Dadra and Nagar Haveli. The latter was taken over by pro-India groups in 1954, but Goa, Daman, and Diu remained in Portuguese hands until 1961. India faced mounting criticism both at home and abroad for tolerating continued colonialism at its doorstep. Portugal, for its part, felt that its presence in the North Atlantic Treaty Organization (NATO) alliance would deter Indian military force. On 18 December 1961, amid considerable diplomatic wrangling, support from across the Indian political spectrum, and a looming General Election, Operation Vijay was launched. This involved coordinated Indian army, air force, and navy operations against Goa, Daman and Diu and resulted in a Portuguese surrender on 19 December. The liberation of Goa was not a peaceful one: both sides suffered military fatalities. Portugal only accepted their former colonial possessions—including Dadra and Nagar Haveli—as belonging to India after a 1974 coup (the Carnation Revolution) that transitioned that country into a democracy and accelerated decolonization efforts.[28]

Clever Calf: The Economy and the Cold War, 1947–1965

Beyond the immediate question of the territoriality and unity of the country, independent India's leaders had to grapple with pressing questions concerning economic development and modernization. By extension, this required navigating relations with the advanced industrial economies—the United States, Soviet Union, and their European allies—which would be the most likely partners for economic assistance, trade, and technology. How India navigated Non-Alignment in practice would have important implications for India's development and economic objectives.

India initially attempted to establish closer ties with the Western bloc between 1947 and 1955. India was a founding member of the United Nations, then an international institution established by the victors of World War II. It also participated in the Bretton Woods conference in 1944 to manage the post-war economic order and joined Western-led organizations such as the General Agreement on Tariffs and Trade (GATT) as early as 1948.[29] Nehru and Patel were also concerned about the spread of violent communist movements in India, of a kind that the Soviet Union had been known to sponsor. Although Nehru had expressed strong support for the Soviet Union as a prospective anti-colonial ally—including at the Brussels Congress of 1927—and visited the USSR that year, his views on the Soviets moderated somewhat after the excesses of Stalinism had started to come to light in the 1930s.[30] In fact, Nehru assured US Ambassador Loy Henderson in 1950 that 'in the event of a World War . . . [India] would not side with the Communists'.[31]

Still, independent India's relations with Washington began on a cautious note: despite commonalities, there were a fair number of frictions related to Western backing for Pakistan, US priorities in Europe, different assessments of Communist China, and India's decolonization agenda. Moreover, despite India's need for economic and agricultural aid, there were clear cultural and ideological differences between Nehru's government and Harry Truman's administration in the United States.[32] Future US Secretary of State John Foster Dulles—then representing the US government in the United Nations—

had already expressed scepticism of India's leadership before Indian independence when he declared that 'In India, Soviet Communism exercises a strong influence through the interim Hindu government.'[33]

But the gap in perceptions played out in various practical ways. In 1947, for example, US Ambassador to New Delhi Henry Grady proposed American assistance in dam-building in India. To his surprise, Nehru wanted to limit the use of machines in order to employ more manual workers.[34] A few months later, Grady proposed a 'Treaty of Friendship, Navigation, and Commerce' to deepen the economic relationship, but the Indian side did not take him up on the offer.[35] Yet other initiatives did take off, including assistance from the Tennessee Valley Authority in the United States for the establishment of the Damodar Valley Corporation to manage flooding, navigation, irrigation, and electricity generation and transmission in West Bengal and present-day Jharkhand.[36]

Amid this backdrop, Nehru visited the United States in late 1949 to significant fanfare, although it did little to consolidate relations with the Truman administration. Despite some shared concerns about China, and India's attempt to leverage these concerns to receive aid and economic benefits, the US and India initially had different assessments of China's motivations and security environment, Beijing's relation with Moscow, and the role of Pakistan. Despite significant attention, the visit achieved little that was concrete and may even have contributed to mutual disillusionment.[37] The United States also tended in these early years to defer to the United Kingdom on matters related to South Asia and only began to become more wary of London's agenda after 1951.[38] Relations with the United States were not entirely non-cooperative. With the outbreak of the

Korean War in 1950—during which a US-led United Nations force backed South Korea against a Chinese- and Soviet-backed North Korea—New Delhi did send a small military medical mission in support of US, UN, and South Korean forces. (An Indian flag still flies in front of the Korean War Memorial in Seoul.) India was also involved in the repatriation of prisoners of war during that conflict.[39] But overall, while India did receive some aid from the United States in the early 1950s, it was far less than Europe, Japan and Taiwan, and less per capita than Pakistan.

In Europe too, India tilted more to the West at first. It was quick to recognize West Germany and refrained from establishing diplomatic relations with East Germany until the 1970s. Independent India's defence equipment was initially sourced more from Britain and West Germany (which licensed Dornier aircraft production to India and whose engineers helped India develop its first indigenous combat aircraft, the HF-24 Marut).[40] Despite the colonial experience and the justifiable consternation about Britain's support for Pakistani positions at the United Nations, India also opted to remain a part of the Commonwealth. This enabled India to become a major beneficiary of funds from the Colombo Plan established by the Commonwealth after 1950. This programme helped accelerate investments in agricultural production, medical sciences, urban planning, and technological development.[41]

It was only in the mid-1950s onwards that India began to establish economic and technological relations with the Soviet bloc. Economically, the opportunities for collaboration with the Soviet Union increased after the death of Joseph Stalin in 1953. Until that time, Soviet leaders in Moscow had shunned Indian diplomats, but they began meeting the Indian ambassador to

Moscow S. Radhakrishnan, later India's vice president and president. Soviet propaganda efforts in India became less forceful. In 1955, new Soviet leader Nikita Khrushchev signed an agreement with India to provide economic and technical assistance for a major steel plant in Bhilai in central India. This was the first major example of Soviet economic and technical assistance outside the avowedly communist countries, and it was swiftly accompanied by other projects. That year, Khrushchev and Soviet Premier Nikolai Bulganin made a triumphal visit to India, where they were greeted warmly. Along with Nehru's visit to the Soviet Union, these signals reaffirmed Moscow's commitment to 'co-existence' with non-communist countries. The material consequences of this rapprochement were immediately apparent: Indo–Soviet trade tripled between 1956 and 1959. In 1957, the USSR vetoed a resolution on Jammu and Kashmir that the United States and the United Kingdom had supported, which would have disadvantaged India. India also started sourcing defence equipment from the Soviet bloc, initially transport aircraft, such as An-12 in 1960. In the early 1960s, the Soviets began to provide combat systems such as MiG-21 fighter aircraft.[42]

For its part, the United States during President Dwight D. Eisenhower's second term, while concerned by India's improved relationship with Moscow, was also more reconciled to New Delhi's Non-Alignment than previous administrations. During and after Nehru's 1956 visit to the United States and improved rapport with Eisenhower, both the United States and India tried to downplay their many differences and work toward advancing India's economic prospects as a bulwark against Chinese Communism. This contributed to a substantial increase in US aid to India in the late 1950s and early 1960s.[43]

For a brief period, in practice, India's Non-Alignment truly made it, in the words of Polish economist Michal Kalecki, one of 'the proverbial clever calves that suck two cows'.[44] An enduring and illustrative manifestation of this involved the establishment of the Indian Institutes of Technology (IIT), now a pride of Indian higher education, having produced generations of world-class talent. The first IITs at Kharagpur, Bombay, Madras, Delhi, and Kanpur were established between 1950 and 1961 with assistance from a consortium of leading American universities, the Soviet Union, the United Nations, West Germany, and the United Kingdom.[45]

But even in the 1950s itself, India's balancing act began to look precarious. India did not vociferously criticize the Soviet Union's actions during the Hungarian Revolution, which contrasted with its denunciation of Britain, France, and Israel during the Suez Crisis in 1956. In private, the United States agreed with India on Britain's recklessness in the Suez but was less happy about its stance on Hungary. Nevertheless, its contrasting approaches to the two situations lost New Delhi some of the credibility that it had developed in the first half of the decade. Some of the criticism was domestic in nature: 'By kowtowing to Russia we have abdicated our moral pretensions,' argued one Indian journalist at the time.[46] Other domestic critics of India's double standards included the activist and political leader Jayaprakash Narayan.[47] Moreover, India's efforts at mediation in Korea, Indochina (modern Vietnam, Laos, and Cambodia), the Taiwan Strait, or Lebanon in the 1950s were not perceived favourably by many of the parties involved.[48] Additionally, Pakistan's entry into US- and UK-led defence arrangements such as the Central Treaty Organization (CENTO) and Southeast Asia Treaty Organization (SEATO)

in 1954 and 1955—as well as a bilateral US—Pakistan Mutual
Defense Assistance Agreement—raised questions in New
Delhi about Washington's reliability.[49] But India's position
on international issues was also not decisive enough to secure
sufficient support from the Soviet Union, which would only
come later.

Furthermore, although India managed to navigate some of
this treacherous landscape, it was not always able to capitalize
on economic progress domestically. Some of the reasons had
to do with domestic economic policy. After India's second
Five Year Plan in 1956, its economy started to face some
headwinds. The 1950s had seen the ascendance of the Planning
Commission and P.C. Mahalanobis. Mahalanobis—who was
not an economist by training but a statistician of considerable
renown—became enamoured by the Soviet Union's central
planning after visiting Moscow in 1951. But India's focus on
central economic planning of national economies was also in
line with trends in Western Europe, including the United
Kingdom. Immediately after India adopted the second Five
Year Plan in 1956—the first such plan of consequence—the
country experienced a sharp drop in foreign exchange reserves.[50]

The plan focused on productive capital and technology,
domestic savings and state-led industrialization, but remained
sceptical of trade, focusing on import substitution over
exports. (As one historian recalled later, it was 'more Lenin
than Laski', referring to the radical Soviet leader and the
Marxist academic.[51]) Seven years later, a thirty-year-old Indian
economist named Manmohan Singh wrote a sharp critique
of the plan's disregard for exports in the *Economic Weekly*,
arguing that 'the task of increasing export earnings here and
now assumes a new urgency'.[52] Yet other critics—including in

the Planning Commission—blamed consumers for the balance of payments crisis and called for greater austerity. By January 1957, curbs were placed on foreign exchange spending and the Five Year Plan was revised. A few years later, in 1959, C. Rajagopalachari—who worried that the second Five Year Plan would 'wither the private sector' and should instead have been conceived 'as a supplement to rather than a substitute for the market economy'—launched the Swatantra Party, whose founding statement called for the 'decentralised distribution of industry', promotion of 'competitive enterprise' and rejection of 'so-called socialism' and '"Statism"'.[53] For various other reasons, India was also unable to take full advantage of the technological access and benefits it had accrued diplomatically. In the early 1960s, a high-profile review under Nobel Prize-winning British scientist Patrick Blackett presented a bleak picture of the state of scientific progress in India. In his assessment, the administration of India's research laboratories, brain drain, and lack of applied research were contributing to scientific and technological failure.[54]

Atomic Infancy: The Nuclear Programme, 1947–1971

One area of scientific and technical progress that assumed immediate interest upon independence involved nuclear technologies, which held significant potential both for electricity generation and military applications. The origins of India's atomic energy programme can be traced to the initial efforts of Homi Bhabha. In 1944, Cambridge-educated Bhabha convinced the Tata Trust to fund the Tata Institute of Fundamental Research, which opened the next year and marked the beginnings of established nuclear research in India. Shortly after Independence in 1948, Nehru created the Atomic Energy Commission with Bhabha at its helm. Bhabha understood that an Indian nuclear energy programme was impossible without foreign support in the form of reactor designs, financing, and fuel. This required India to enter into commitments to use foreign-supplied material only for peaceful purposes.

From the 1950s onwards, India benefited from US, Canadian, British, and French nuclear assistance and interest from Soviet nuclear scientists. In 1955, the Apsara research reactor began construction and was supplied with uranium from the United Kingdom. The same year, Canada agreed to help build a larger reactor, eventually called the Canadian–Indian Reactor, US (CIRUS), given that the United States supplied heavy water, containing heavier isotopes of hydrogen and used in nuclear reactors. The resulting fissile material was not placed under safeguards, but India agreed to use it for peaceful purposes. After 1960, India developed a nuclear power station at Tarapur, that would be supplied and financed with assistance from the United States. Although the financial terms for Tarapur were generous, the agreement was criticized in India for being unduly reliant on the Americans, for it required enriched uranium rather than natural uranium, on the grounds that it would produce cheaper electricity. Furthermore, the deal was criticized for being intrusive because of international safeguards, which would ensure that material was not diverted for other uses (non-US fuel used at the facility could be used for other purposes). By the late 1950s, nuclear energy accounted for over a quarter of India's research and development investment and the Atomic Energy Establishment at Trombay (later the Bhabha Atomic Research Centre or BARC) had over 1000 scientists and engineers.[55]

While publicly disavowing the possibility of using atomic energy for 'evil purposes', Nehru and Bhabha kept open the option of nuclear weapons.[56] In 1958, Bhabha built a plant, named Phoenix, to extract plutonium from spent fuel, and with CIRUS this produced India's first weapon-grade plutonium by the mid-1960s. During this period of the early Cold War, the strong international taboo against nuclear weapons that exists today was absent. Most countries that had the ability to acquire nuclear weapons did so, or at least tried to do so. Moreover, in the 1950s there was acceptability, even enthusiasm, about the use of 'peaceful nuclear explosions' (PNEs, sometimes called Plowshare devices), including for excavation, mining, and other such civilian purposes. Both the United States and the Soviet Union engaged in their development. But in reality, there was little meaningful technological difference between a PNE and an explosive device that could be weaponized and used for military purposes.[57]

As early as 1959, amid deteriorating relations with Beijing, concerns began to be raised in India about China's nuclear programme. Nehru authorized an expert group to look into a nuclear explosion in early 1962 and Bhabha promised that it would take him only eighteen months. Immediately after China's test in 1964, Prime Minister Lal Bahadur Shastri reportedly authorized Bhabha to estimate what would be required for a peaceful nuclear explosion. An overt military option risked jeopardizing India's civil nuclear programme, which still benefited from US and Canadian assistance, and so a PNE was the only real option. But this proved more difficult than promised. Bhabha sought assistance—specifically blueprints—from the United States, which independently considered the possibility of conducting nuclear tests on behalf of non-Communist countries in Asia, including India.[58] After Bhabha died in a plane crash in 1966, his successor Vikram Sarabhai expressed much greater reservations about the PNE programme and slowed down its authorized development.

But by the mid-1960s, another important development had occurred: the advent of a nuclear Non-Proliferation Treaty (NPT). In 1965, in multilateral negotiations, India laid out its parameters for agreeing to such a treaty. They included the non-transfer of nuclear weapon technology, a no-first-use commitment against non-nuclear states, a UN security guarantee, a commitment to disarmament, and only in these circumstances a commitment by non-nuclear powers to not acquire weapons. From India's standpoint, these criteria would have blunted China's nuclear advantage. On the other end of the spectrum, the US and Soviet Union envisioned a much narrower treaty that prohibited the transfer of weapons and technology to non-weapon states, the acquisition of nuclear weapons by non-weapon states, and verification that fuel, equipment, and technology would not be diverted for military use. Their suggestion would essentially have closed off the possibility of India acquiring nuclear weapons, or even conducting a peaceful nuclear explosion. India, along with several other countries, also felt that the US proposal downplayed disarmament obligations and was morally questionable, in that it created nuclear haves and have-nots. In the context of its security problems with China and the existing Indian programme, this was enormously problematic.[59]

Despite New Delhi's objections, a draft NPT was presented by the United States and the Soviet Union in August 1967 that largely adhered to their objectives and a final treaty was concluded and opened for signature in 1968. This recognized and effectively legalized only five nuclear weapon states: the United States, the Soviet Union, China, France, and the United Kingdom. In October 1967, India made it clear that it would not sign the NPT. As George Perkovich later noted, 'India may have had logic, principle, and the 1965 negotiating mandate on its side, but the United States and the other nuclear weapon states had power on their side.'[60]

The Third Way: The Post-Colonial World, 1947–1962

Beyond its territorial integrity and its economic and technological development, another set of foreign policy questions that occupied India's foreign policy during the early Cold War related to its relations with the rest of the decolonizing world. This included some significant engagements with Africa. In 1960, when Congo became independent, the mineral-rich province of Katanga broke away with financial and military support from the departing colonial power Belgium. Rajeshwar Dayal, India's high commissioner to Pakistan and later foreign secretary, became the United Nations special envoy as India was seen as a neutral arbiter between competing Western and Soviet interests during the crisis. Between 1961 and 1963, India sent more troops to Congo under a United Nations flag than any other country and helped to put down secessionist forces despite resistance from the country's new pro-Western leader Mobutu Sese Seko. This intervention resulted in the deaths of thirty-nine Indian soldiers and saw the first award of a Param Vir Chakra—independent India's highest military honour—in an overseas conflict.[61] Beyond Congo, India played a role in supporting the development and security of other African states. For example, the newly independent country of

Ghana—which was sceptical of erstwhile colonists in Britain and both superpowers—sought Indian support in establishing its intelligence agency.[62]

India's larger leadership role in Asia, against the backdrop of decolonization, is often overlooked today. It began before Independence. In early 1947, Nehru hosted a major Asian Relations Conference in Delhi, having previously discussed the idea with Burmese leader Aung San. India made considerable efforts to secure participation from Southeast Asia. 'Asia is again finding itself,' Nehru declared while greeting the 300-plus delegates present from China, Korea, Turkey, Egypt, Iran, Afghanistan, Mongolia, Tibet and across Southeast Asia, among other places.[63] 'If the Indians played a leading role in the Asian Conference, it was partly because theirs was the host country, and partly because they believe they have a big destiny in Asia,' an American journalist reported from the venue.[64]

In the 1950s, India was actively involved in diplomacy to settle disputes and facilitate resolutions related to China, Korea, Japan, and Indochina. After the Korean War broke out, India facilitated communications between the United States and Communist China, in their absence of diplomatic relations. Famously, India's Ambassador to Beijing K.M. Panikkar warned Western diplomats that China intended to enter the Korean War if American forces crossed the thirty-eighth parallel on the Korean peninsula. His warning went unheeded, and China entered the war on North Korea's side.[65] As the war progressed, and India provided a medical mission to UN forces, it was also involved in the Neutral Nations Repatriation Commission (NNRC) that exchanged prisoners of war between the North and South.

India was also diplomatically engaged in Indochina as the region decolonized from France. India's role included negotiations to ensure Laotian neutrality and efforts in the International Control Commission to implement the first Geneva Accords that ended the First Indochina War.[66] These negotiations, along with Indian involvement in the Taiwan Strait Crisis and in Lebanon, were seen positively in India, but less favourably in other countries. In fact, it often led to greater suspicions about Indian intentions in Washington, London, Moscow, Beijing, and other capitals.[67]

Perhaps the high point of independent India's early leadership role in Asia was the 1955 Asian-African Conference in Bandung in Indonesia. Despite concerns from several participating countries, including the hosts, India insisted on China's participation. Beijing was at the time still viewed with great suspicion in Asia, including in Southeast Asia. (In an apparent assassination attempt on Chinese Premier Zhou Enlai, an Air India plane transporting Chinese delegates to the conference experienced an explosion and crashed.)[68] Despite concerns among some participants that the Bandung conference was dominated by India and Nehru's star power, the conference itself resulted in a set of principles that condemned colonialism and established principles of peaceful coexistence.[69] As an American newspaper noted about Bandung, '[A]t last the destiny of Asia is being determined in Asia, and not Geneva, or Paris, or London, and Washington. Colonialism was out and hands off is the word. Asia is free. This is perhaps the historic event of our century.'[70] But given the prominence of Zhou Enlai's presence, the conference also helped facilitate the People's Republic of China's entry onto the international stage, to India's eventual detriment.

Bandung was a high-water mark for Non-Alignment, but the idea for a middle course between the two superpower-led blocs found resonance, including with Josip Broz Tito's Yugoslavia and Gamal Abdel Nasser's Egypt. Tito's visit to India in 1954 was a grand success, with Indians relieved to find a European leader whose views on global affairs mirrored their own. Meeting in July 1956 in the Brioni Islands in Yugoslavia, Nehru, Tito and Nasser had practical and ideological reasons to advance the notion of Non-Alignment and maintain some distance from Washington and Moscow. Nehru, however, expressed scepticism about a bloc or coalition, which was formalized with the inaugural Non-Aligned Movement (NAM) Summit in Belgrade in 1961. Unlike Bandung, the Belgrade Summit included participants not just from Asia and Africa, but also from Latin America and Europe. The political orientation of participating regimes was also more varied from conservative monarchies to avowed communist states like Cuba. Overall, the agenda deviated in several ways from Nehru's earlier preferences and risked becoming more rigid and less flexible.[71]

It is often overlooked today that India also helped facilitate Japan's re-entry into the international community after World War II. New Delhi refused to sign the San Francisco Peace Treaty of 1951 between Japan and the victorious allies of World War II. India deemed the agreement unfair and instead negotiated a separate agreement a year later, thus restoring ties with Tokyo.[72] Following visits by the Indian and Japanese prime ministers to each other's countries in 1957, India became the first recipient of yen-denominated loans from Japan. At the time, many countries, still recalling Japan's wartime atrocities, had refused the normalization of economic engagement with

Tokyo. Japanese Prime Minister Nobusuke Kishi's grandson Shinzo Abe, who would become Japan's prime minister in 2006 and again in 2012, would later warmly recount 'As a young boy seated on his knee, I would hear [my grandfather] telling me that Prime Minister Nehru introduced him to the biggest audience he had ever seen in his lifetime.'[73]

Despite India's activism in a wider Asia during the 1950s and early 1960s, a number of political challenges in its near abroad presaged difficulties that were to make themselves felt later. The 1950s witnessed the government in Ceylon (today's Sri Lanka) adopt policies favouring the Sinhalese majority and fan anti-Tamil riots. After political unrest in its nascent democracy, Nepal saw a coup d'état in 1960 by King Mahendra and the restitution of an absolute monarchy. In 1962, a military coup occurred in Myanmar. In these cases, despite domestic debates about how to manage these situations, India by and large opted pragmatically to engage the new regimes.[74]

Himalayan Setback: India and China, 1950–1962

Many of India's initial objectives—the security of its territory, its economic and technological rise and its leadership in the decolonizing world—suffered significant setbacks with the 1962 Sino–Indian border war. The events that led up to that conflict continue to be hotly debated. Although India was early in recognizing the People's Republic of China and worked to involve it in international efforts, notably at the Bandung Conference in 1955, relations took a turn for the worse in the late 1950s. The reasons were many but related primarily to the disputed boundary and the question of China's annexation of Tibet. Chinese domestic politics and international factors involving the Soviet Union and the United States also played a role in precipitating the 1962 Sino–Indian border war. But it ultimately centred on the unresolved boundary.

The India–China border consists of three sectors: the western sector in Ladakh, the middle sector abutting the Indian states of Himachal Pradesh and Uttarakhand (previously part of Uttar Pradesh) and the eastern sector in Sikkim and Arunachal Pradesh (formerly known as the North East Frontier Agency or NEFA). The boundaries of the western and middle sectors between British India and Tibet were undefined prior to Independence. Differences over the middle sector are relatively minor and include areas around the Shipki-La Pass in Himachal Pradesh, as well as Nilang-Jadhang, Lapthal-Sangchamalla, and grazing grounds known as Barahoti north of the Nanda Devi range in Uttarakhand.[75]

Differences in the western sector are more significant. British-era maps variously showed the sparsely populated Aksai Chin as part of India and as part of Tibet. An 1865 British survey and an 1897 modification both placed Aksai Chin within India, and the rulers of Hunza and Kashmir did at times have jurisdiction over this area. The imperial Chinese government did not formally confirm any alignments in the western sector, although an 1893 Chinese proposal placed Aksai Chin as a part of China.[76] Later, in 1956 and in 1960, China advanced two different claim lines that both encompassed Aksai Chin. The 1960 line ran slightly west of the 1956 one, and also encompassed parts of the Chip Chap River and Galwan River valleys and some areas around Pangong Tso (lake). Some areas around the Kongka-la pass and parts of the Chang Chenmo River valley, as well as areas in the vicinity of Demchok and Chumur in the south-east corner of Ladakh, are also still disputed by China.[77]

The eastern sector was traditionally more defined, but even then poorly so. In 1890, Britain and China ratified the Tibet–Sikkim Convention, which defined the alignment of the boundary from the watershed of the Teesta river to the border with Nepal.[78] The boundary was redefined between Britain and Tibet in 1904 and confirmed in an agreement at the 1906 Anglo-Chinese Convention.[79] Following differences, particularly those that resulted in violent clashes in 1967, India and the People's Republic of China subsequently agreed on the alignment of the boundary in Sikkim, and China finally acknowledged India's sovereignty over Sikkim in 2003.

The boundary in today's Arunachal Pradesh was formalized at the Simla Conference of 1914 by British India, Tibet and China, creating the so-called McMahon Line. The basis of the McMahon Line was the Himalayan watershed, but there were a few points of difference between the actual watershed and official treaty maps—such as near Tawang (specifically, the Namkachu and Sumdorongchu rivers and the Thagla Ridge between them) and areas such as Longju to the east—all of which were to be flashpoints between India and China in the years to come. However, imperial China did not ratify the Shimla treaty and the People's Republic of China later claimed that the entire McMahon Line was invalid because it was a colonial legacy and Tibet was in any case not an independent party. Tawang in NEFA was of particular strategic value for China. Various other quirks—vague names, poor surveying by the British, even the thickness of the pen nibs used when drawing maps—have contributed to the layers of complications surrounding the boundary situation between India and China.[80]

The poorly demarcated boundary was also linked to the question of Tibet's status. Culturally and historically, China's claim on Tibet is weaker than on Vietnam, Korea, or Mongolia. Chinese military involvement in Tibet prior to the Qing Dynasty was, in fact, very rare. The difference is that unlike the other states, there was never a clear acceptance by China of Tibet's independence and other powers—notably Britain and the United States—were not necessarily dissatisfied with this arrangement. In 1904, Britain recognized Chinese suzerainty— but not sovereignty—over Tibet, mostly to prevent Russian encroachment there. (For its part, Beijing has dismissed suzerainty—which recognizes control of foreign policy but refrains from domestic involvement in a tributary state—as a colonial-era invention and interpreted its rule over Tibet as sovereign.) The United States was also supportive of China's Tibet claims in the early twentieth century out of concern for Japan's rise.[81]

After the conclusion of the Chinese Civil War in 1949, the People's Republic of China made clear its intent of spreading the revolution to 'all the territory of China' including Tibet. By then, however, the Chinese Nationalist mission in Lhasa had been expelled by Tibetan authorities, seeming to strengthen the case for Tibetan independence. That did not prevent the PLA from invading Tibet in 1950 to reverse what it saw as national humiliation, access Tibetan natural resources, and consolidate its precarious hold on the western province of Xinjiang. In the 1951 agreement in which Tibet ceded its independence to China, Beijing agreed to respect Tibet's cultural and religious autonomy.[82]

Thus, beginning in 1950–1951, for the first time, India and China shared a direct border as independent and sovereign states. Although Indian leaders expressed initial concern and hesitation about recognizing Chinese control of Tibet, India's ambassador K.M. Panikkar appeared to have conceded the reality when he presented credentials to the new Chinese government. In New Delhi, it was generally felt that India did not have the military resources to help Tibet retain its status as a buffer state.[83] But concerns grew about securing the border from the new potential threat. A little over a month before his death, Sardar Patel wrote to Nehru on 7 November 1950 cautioning about Chinese intentions: 'The Chinese Government has tried to delude us by professions of peaceful intention . . . even though we regard ourselves as the friends of China, the Chinese do not regard us as their friends . . . In my judgement the situation is one which we cannot afford either to be complacent or to be vacillating.'[84] A few days later, on 18 November, Nehru—while acknowledging the new realities—issued a note suggesting a different view of Beijing's predisposition: '[T]here is, in my opinion, practically no chance of a major attack on India by China . . . The idea that . . . Chinese communism means inevitably an expansion towards India, is rather naive.'[85]

Meanwhile, concerns also grew in Indian military and intelligence circles. The Himmatsinhji Committee—composed of military, intelligence, diplomatic, and defence officials— examined the consequences of China's invasion of Tibet on the frontier regions, producing reports in April and September of 1951. Until that point, India's administrative control in Ladakh and Arunachal Pradesh (then NEFA) had been poor. In February 1951, India extended its administration to Tawang and began sending occasional patrols to Aksai Chin from Ladakh.[86]

When Panikkar departed China in June 1952, he remained confident that Beijing would respect India's trade and cultural interests in Tibet. But China's Premier Zhou Enlai directly

contradicted it just a month later.[87] During discussions in the
early 1950s between India and China, Beijing—led by Zhou—
initially did not seem keen to discuss the boundary issue. This
move was interpreted in some quarters in India as a sign of
China's acquiescence to India's position. At the advice of
Panikkar, Nehru did not raise the boundary issue with Zhou,
believing that it would lead to China pursuing a stronger
claim south of the McMahon Line. Instead, India opted for
ambiguity, believing that it was buying time to reinforce its own
positions on the ground. Indian maps in 1954 showed Aksai
Chin as Indian territory.

The same year, amid echoes of 'Hindi-Chini bhai-bhai
[India and China are brothers]', the two countries signed
a series of agreements. While covering trade and religious
pilgrimages, and designated routes for passage, the agreements
clearly mentioned the 'Tibet Region of the People's Republic of
China'. The two premiers also underscored non-aggression and
peaceful co-existence, among the five principles that became
known as Panchsheel. Additionally, India handed over postal,
telegraph, and telephone services in Tibet to China.[88] While
the agreements of 1954 were designed to mitigate suspicion
between the two countries, some in India remained sceptical,
and suggested that check posts be established at key locations
such as Demchok to prevent Chinese infiltration. A few Indian
officials believed that China had conceded nothing, while India
had given up significant leverage.[89] Sure enough, Indian political
or trade missions in Tibet—at Lhasa, Gyantse, Yadong, and
Gartok—became more restricted and isolated. Additionally,
differences soon emerged over Barahoti in the middle sector.
China began to publish maps that showed large tracts of Indian
territory to be parts of China.[90]

For its part, China retained suspicions that India was supporting Tibetan guerrillas. Rebellion had broken out among the Khampas of eastern Tibet in 1954 and began to spread. After 1956, the US Central Intelligence Agency provided training for Khampa rebels exfiltrated via India, East Pakistan, and Thailand, and also made arms and ammunition drops in Tibet.[91] The Dalai Lama visited India in 1956 and 1957 for Buddha Jayanti commemorations, and there were already calls by some of his supporters for him to remain there in the context of the spreading Tibetan revolt. Nehru urged the Dalai Lama to return and non-violently advocate for Tibetan autonomy.[92]

As the Tibetan situation worsened, so did discussions on the boundary and, coupled with concerns about the Dalai Lama, this prompted Zhou Enlai to fly twice to India in 1956 and 1957. In discussions with Nehru on these trips, Zhou referenced the McMahon Line, which Nehru interpreted as his acceptance of it.[93] But in September of 1957, India discovered that a road between Xinjiang and Tibet had been constructed through Aksai Chin. For China, this was strategically very significant as it could be used year-round to supply Tibet and was secure from the spreading Tibetan insurgency. The discovery should not have come as a complete shock to New Delhi: news and intelligence reports had pointed to its construction after 1952, but India only raised this in formal negotiations in October 1958.[94] While India was prepared to negotiate on Aksai Chin, where its claims were more tenuous, correspondence in 1958 and 1959 also indicated far more aggressive Chinese claims south of the McMahon Line in the eastern sector.[95] In the midst of all this, Nehru made a brief transit through Yadong—traversing some of the distance by pony and yak—on the way to Bhutan in September 1958. This made him the first national leader to visit Tibet since 1950 (his counterpart, Zhou, had not yet done so).[96]

After full-fledged rebellion broke out in Lhasa, the Dalai Lama sought asylum in India in the spring of 1959, followed by thousands of fleeing Tibetans. India also considered taking the Tibet issue to the United Nations but chose ultimately not to do so.[97] India's position remained that Tibet was a part of China, but it justified its provision of shelter for the Dalai Lama and his supporters on the grounds that Beijing had reneged on its 1951 agreement on respecting Tibet's cultural and religious autonomy. Yet Chinese government documents from a little later claimed that India still had designs to make Tibet a 'colony or protectorate'. Such paranoia was fuelled by a revival of Maoism.[98] Somewhat incongruently, despite the downward trajectory in India–China relations, India under V.K. Krishna Menon and Nehru continued to support China's entry into the United Nations.[99] They continued to be of the belief that bringing China into the international mainstream would make Beijing more likely to abide by rules and norms.

In August of 1959, clashes broke out between Chinese and Indian border security forces at Longju, a move that prompted the Indian Army to assume responsibility for security on the China border and to start preparing contingency war plans. India immediately put all Intelligence Bureau and Assam Rifles patrols under the direct command of the army.[100] In October, an Indian patrol was ambushed at Kongka-La in Ladakh, resulting in more hostile Indian public opinion. The next month, China proposed a demilitarized zone, but this was rejected by India because it favoured the PLA. Trust had been eroded and China had previously been vague about its claim lines. The delay in China's repatriation of Indians killed in action contributed to the souring mood, including in India's Parliament. Meanwhile, China rejected a counterproposal from India concerning patrols. All of this, including Nehru's release of correspondence with China to the Parliament and public, resulted in a hardening of India's position on Aksai Chin.[101]

In 1960, Zhou made a deliberately vague offer of 'reciprocal acceptance of present realities in both sectors' implying a swap: New Delhi would accept Aksai Chin as part of China and Beijing would accept NEFA as part of India. Mao may have authorized such an overture to India given his greater security concerns in Korea, Taiwan, and Indochina and domestic political turmoil. The offer was rejected by Nehru, who understood the hardening of the Indian political position on Aksai Chin and the requirements of parliamentary approval for territorial changes.[102] There were also suggestions from some Chinese officials that this deal was not entirely sincere.[103] Discussions nonetheless took place between Indian and Chinese officials in 1960 to review the historical record and showed a great disparity between their interpretations. In fact, in 1960, China advanced a new claim line in Aksai China farther to the west than what it had previously indicated in 1956.[104] The two sides therefore made no headway. As late as July and August 1962, negotiations and notes were being exchanged between Indian and Chinese officials. A last ditch offer by India to negotiate in July 1962 was rebuffed by China and was criticized by political leaders and the media in India.[105]

Although India had been preparing for conflict from 1959 onwards, several decisions were made which proved fatal in hindsight. Preparations were made only for a limited conflict with China and insufficient attention was paid to logistics. In fact, India's military budget *decreased* after 1960, as the country continued to prioritize development over defence. Even on the security front, not enough equipment was imported, although an agreement was signed for Soviet MiG-21 in the belief that it would help deter China. Indeed, Indian military leaders, including the former Army Chief Gen. K.S. Thimayya, who distrusted China from his experiences in Korea, understood that India was entirely unprepared for a major conflict.[106]

At the same time, the Intelligence Bureau assessed that China was only advancing in unoccupied territory, and therefore recommended more Indian posts. Nehru also had faith in international opprobrium deterring a major conflict with China. All of this contributed after 1959 to India's 'forward policy' of establishing posts and patrolling at advanced positions, in response to China's own forward positions. The forward policy seemed, at first, to work, deterring a Chinese patrol in Ladakh. But these posts were more observational than operational and were between old and new Chinese claim lines. China after all had been steadily building up its own forward presence for some time.[107]

But while negotiations and posturing had continued for years, the decision by Beijing to go to war was made quickly and decisively. In mid-1962, Beijing assessed that the United States would not intervene, and that India was not interested in negotiations. There was also a domestic political dimension, specifically Mao's keenness to overcome the disasters of his landmark economic programme, the Great Leap Forward. Two days after a major conference of the Chinese leadership in August 1962, military preparations began in earnest. In September, China occupied the Thagla ridge in NEFA, technically north of the McMahon Line according to treaty maps but south of the watershed, and thus Indian-claimed. The news of this caused a political furor in New Delhi, and evicting China became a question of Indian resolve. Sporadic firing broke out in late September, and after a final exchange of diplomatic notes, China decided on 6 October to inflict a punishing blow in the eastern sector. On 10 October, an advancing Indian patrol was decimated by Chinese forces at Namkachu. On 13 October, Nehru's remarks about the situation were misreported in the press as a promise to "throw out" the Chinese, leading to the *People's Daily* concluding the next day that a 'massive invasion of Chinese territory by Indian troops . . . seems imminent'.[108]

After approval by China's Central Military Commission on 18 October, the Chinese attack began in earnest on 20 October. The first line of Indian defences in the eastern sector crumbled, and a decision was made to fall back from Tawang. On 16 November, the PLA began its second phase of operations, which in three days broke Indian resistance in both western and eastern sectors. On 19 November, Nehru desperately wrote twice to US President John F. Kennedy requesting accelerated and urgent assistance, including air power.[109] But by the time the United States requested further details, China had indicated its intent of a ceasefire and a withdrawal in the eastern sector. Significantly, it appears that many of Nehru's key aides and other Indian foreign policy officials were kept in the dark about Nehru's desperate requests to Washington.[110] By 21 November China unilaterally announced a ceasefire and withdrew to its 1960 claim line in the west and to the McMahon Line in the east. The reasons for Beijing's ceasefire and withdrawal are unknown but were probably a combination of logistic unpreparedness for a sustained presence in the eastern sector (particularly with the onset of winter), satisfactory gains in the western sector, and the prospect of unwanted international involvement. But

Beijing's political objectives had been met: it had established its dominance over New Delhi and sent a signal to Moscow. In other words, China felt India had been put in its place.

Several lessons can be drawn from India's failures in managing differences with China between 1950 and 1962. The underlying causes of the conflict— the ambiguities of the boundary and the question of Tibet—were realities that India inherited from the British. But one of India's fundamental errors was its misreading of China's domestic politics, its ideological imperatives, and the international environment. Mao's position after the failure of the Great Leap Forward and the developments at the crucial August 1962 leadership meeting were completely missed. Zhou's silence and the contents of the 1954 agreements were mistakenly interpreted in New Delhi as China's acquiescence of India's positions. On balance, therefore, India's understanding of Communist China proved poor. On the international front, Nehru clearly underestimated the reputational costs that China was willing to bear. The Soviet Union, which had until 1962 been tilting towards India, ultimately opted to side more with China, in part for its support during the ongoing Cuban Missile Crisis.

There was also a dire lack of Indian preparation for a major conflict, whether in terms of military plans and equipment, logistics, or intelligence. This was understood by some military and intelligence officials, and belatedly by political leaders as well. Indian forces were not deployed at strength, with the Chinese enjoying an almost 3:1 advantage in the western and eastern sectors. Moreover, the Indian Air Force was not seriously utilized, with no offensive air support.[111] Particularly after China's 1964 nuclear test, the yawning security discrepancy led to greater calls for an Indian nuclear deterrent. The 1962 outcome, along with the 1965 war with Pakistan, also exposed deficiencies in intelligence which were partly remedied by the creation of the Research and Analysis Wing (R&AW) in 1968 for intelligence on foreign targets.[112] Finally, a lack of clarity about India's objectives with respect to the boundary also resulted in a mismanagement of public expectations and opinion.

Subcontinental Drift: India and Pakistan, 1947–1965

If deteriorating relations with China and the outbreak of war caused a sudden reversal in India's international ambitions, the rivalry with Pakistan proved more persistent. In part, its origins go back to Partition and the immediate competition over territory, resources, and reputation. But there were surprising strands of cooperation throughout. In December 1947, India and Pakistan signed an agreement to avoid double taxation. In January 1948, India released—at Mahatma Gandhi's insistence—two-thirds of the share of Reserve Bank cash balances it owed to Pakistan. After a month-long hiatus, the Government of Punjab agreed to release water to Pakistan in 1948, averting drought. Indian currency notes remained legal tender in Pakistan until September 1948, a full year after Partition. All of this occurred even as war was being waged in Jammu and Kashmir.[113] A subsequent crisis over refugees and minority rights was eased by the Nehru–Liaquat Pact of 1950, in which both countries committed to safeguard certain minority rights.[114]

In 1953, Nehru visited Pakistan, but the domestic situation in India limited his options for any real negotiations on resolving outstanding disputes between the two countries.

These circumstances included India's arrests of Jan Sangh leader Syama Prasad Mookerjee (who died in a Kashmiri prison) and of Kashmiri leader Sheikh Abdullah. Nehru found himself caught between Mookerjee's call for abrogation of autonomy and Abdullah's calls for independence. India also harboured concerns about US–Pakistan relations, which some in India such as V.K. Krishna Menon seemed to embellish. There were also doubts about the political viability of Pakistan's leaders. Between the assassination of Liaquat Ali Khan in 1951 and the coup that brought General Ayub Khan to power in 1958, Pakistan was led by a series of short-lived and weak governments.[115]

Despite the inability to achieve any significant outcome in 1953, the rest of the decade was in fact a rather propitious time for India–Pakistan relations. Protracted negotiations between Indian cabinet minister Swaran Singh and General Khalid Sheikh of the Pakistan President's cabinet resolved some of the ambiguities of the Radcliffe Line in Punjab. The Indus Waters Treaty was also settled by the two countries along with the World Bank in 1954. The Treaty gave India the exclusive right to the Beas, Sutlej, and Ravi rivers, while India agreed to allow the Indus, Jhelum, and Chenab to flow to Pakistan, but could use these rivers for run-of-the-river hydroelectric projects and for existing irrigation.[116] India and the World Bank paid Pakistan to compensate them for replacement canals, a move that faced resistance from many in India, including from within Nehru's government. In 1955, the Indian cricket team toured Pakistan. In 1959, Ayub even proposed a joint defence mechanism between Pakistan and India to counter China. This suggestion was rejected by Nehru because it would have required deviating from Non-Alignment.[117]

These developments—demarcating parts of the Radcliffe Line, the Nehru–Liaquat Pact of 1950, the Indus Waters Treaty, and a seemingly shared threat emanating from China—meant that Nehru's five-day visit to Pakistan in 1960 to formally sign the Indus Waters Treaty was perhaps the first real opportunity to completely normalize relations between the two countries. But India's high commissioner in Pakistan, Rajeshwar Dayal, who had established a strong personal rapport with Ayub, had instead been sent as UN special envoy to Congo. Ayub was stung by this move and other signs of what he perceived as Nehru's arrogance. '[T]he Congo was more important to India than Pakistan,' he later told Dayal, '*Woh* [Nehru] *mujhe hiqarat ki nazar se dekhte hain*. [He looks at me with contempt].'[118] No meaningful progress was made on Jammu and Kashmir at the 1960 summit.

The window for improved India–Pakistan relations began to close after the 1962 war with China. Pakistan began to see India as a 'defeated nation' (to use Zulfikar Ali Bhutto's phrase).[119] While the Indian economy began to slow, Pakistan's industrialization efforts picked up and its economy grew at rapid rates during much of the 1960s, primarily to the benefit of the elite. In March 1963, China and Pakistan demarcated their border, with Pakistan ceding parts of disputed Jammu and Kashmir—specifically, the Trans-Karakorum Tract—to China. India–Pakistan talks held in 1962 and 1963 went nowhere. A stopover visit by Nehru's successor Lal Bahadur Shastri would be the last visit by an Indian prime minister to Pakistan before the 1980s.

In April 1965, skirmishes began along the non-demarcated border between Sindh and the Rann of Kutch in present-day Gujarat. Two months later an agreement was signed with

British mediation. This gave rise to the belief in Pakistan that Kashmir could be settled through international arbitration. Due to a misunderstanding stemming from previous agreements, the Rann of Kutch agreement also left the status of Sir Creek on the Arabian Sea coast unresolved.[120]

It was in these circumstances that Pakistan launched Operation Gibraltar in August 1965. The plan had been approved by Ayub Khan earlier that summer, with the intention of using raiding parties and civil uprisings to bog India down in a guerrilla war in Jammu and Kashmir. Should India widen the conflict, Ayub felt, it would invite international mediation. Meanwhile, a second phase of the operation—called Operation Grand Slam—would involve an armoured thrust toward Akhnoor to cut off Indian supply lines to the Kashmir Valley. Pakistan's seemingly clever plan proved an abject failure. After the infiltration of about 5000 individuals by Pakistan, they found no indigenous uprising in Jammu and Kashmir. The infiltrators were neutralized, and the Indian Army responded with retaliatory attacks against infiltration points across the ceasefire line, capturing the key Haji Pir Pass.[121]

In September, Pakistan launched Operation Grand Slam, which caught India unawares despite advanced knowledge of Pakistan's armoured build-up. On 6 September, after cabinet approval, India launched a counter-offensive across the international boundary towards Lahore, widening the war. Pakistan countered with an armoured thrust that once again caught India off guard, and it survived only because of some luck and ingenuity. Knowing he was outnumbered, Major General Gurbaksh Singh flooded farmland at Asal Uttar near Khem Karan to bog down a Pakistani armoured division that threatened to break Indian lines. India was able to blunt the attack and destroy a large number of Pakistani tanks, and this prevented what might otherwise have been a catastrophic military disaster for India.[122] Meanwhile, on the diplomatic front, even as the U.S. suspended military assistance to both countries, Turkey, Iran, and Indonesia continued to provide material support to Pakistan in the form of arms, ammunition, and fuel. India also retained serious concerns about Chinese involvement, even if they did not materialize. The war ended with a UN-sponsored ceasefire on 23 September. In January 1966, the Soviet Union hosted an India–Pakistan summit at Tashkent. The resulting agreement returned captured territory by both sides but was overshadowed by the sudden death in Tashkent of Prime Minister Shastri.

While the 1965 war was brief and a stalemate, it had several important consequences. In many respects, it changed the future of the subcontinent. In the immediate aftermath, the Tashkent Agreement was criticized in both countries. Many in India, even at the time, lambasted the return of Haji Pir, which might have stemmed future infiltration from Pakistan. India also believed that while it did its part in returning relations to normal—swiftly repatriating prisoners of war and resuming overflights between West and East Pakistan—the sentiment was not reciprocated. In Pakistan, Ayub Khan's reputation and position deteriorated. While public propaganda had projected Pakistani efforts during the war as successful, the Tashkent Declaration came as a shock to many Pakistanis. Ayub Khan was soon replaced by his former protégé, General Yahya Khan.

The conflict also had longer term security implications for both India and Pakistan. In India, the war exposed India's intelligence failings, contributing to the creation of a separate external intelligence agency: the Research and Analysis Wing.

It also resurrected confidence in the Indian Army after 1962, while compelling it to rethink some of its acquisitions for armoured warfare. For Pakistan, its war experience led it to advance the use of sub-conventional forces against India and led to greater advocacy for nuclear weapons. With the US cutting off arms supplies to both sides, Pakistan began to turn more to China for defence supplies while India started relying more on imports from the Soviet Union. Meanwhile, East Pakistan, which had been left to its own devices, became resentful. Under Mujibur Rahman and the Awami League, it began to agitate for greater autonomy.[123]

Transitions, 1965–1971

The first two decades of Independence were therefore eventful for India on multiple international fronts. India secured territory in the wake of Partition, including through the use of military force. It managed for period to leverage competition between the US and the USSR to derive financial and technological benefits from both. In Asia and Africa, New Delhi assumed an important political leadership role, intervening diplomatically and in some cases militarily to resolve conflicts and shape international outcomes. But from the late 1950s onwards, the Indian economy slowed, the relationship with China deteriorated, differences with Pakistan grew more acute, and the balancing act between the United States and Soviet Union proved both difficult and, in some sense, inadequate.

The disaster of the 1962 Sino–Indian border war had a number of effects. It contributed to the deterioration of Nehru's health and his death in 1964. The India–China relationship saw the suspension of normal diplomatic relations and a military conflagration in Sikkim in 1967, in which India got the better of the People's Liberation Army. In September that year, Indian forces laid barbed wire to prevent clashes between patrols on the border at Nathu La. Chinese forces responded with machine gun fire, after which Indian forces used artillery, causing the PLA to suffer heavy casualties, possibly in the hundreds. Four days later, despite the threat of Chinese escalation, an uneasy ceasefire was brokered.[124]

Other transitions occurred during this period marked primarily by domestic preoccupations. India's cooperation with the United States increased after the 1962 war but military assistance and defence cooperation were suspended with the outbreak of the 1965 India–Pakistan War. As a consequence, India became gradually more dependent on military supplies from the Soviet Union, paving the way for a major agreement in 1971. The logic of the Cold War nonetheless continued to impose itself upon India in some curious ways. One incident during this period was the defection from the Soviet Union of Svetlana Alliluyeva, the daughter of its former leader Joseph Stalin (later known as Lana Peters). After becoming romantically involved with an Indian communist, Alliluyeva travelled to India. In early 1967, she approached the US Embassy in New Delhi, seeking asylum in the United States. Her defection put India in an awkward position, as it continued to balance its relationships with both the eastern and western blocs.[125]

Perhaps the greatest economic development of the 1960s for India was the Green Revolution. In 1965, high yield varieties of wheat, combined with fertilizer and irrigation techniques, were introduced into India after successful results in Mexico. The initiative was spearheaded by the American scientist Norman Borlaug and benefited from private American financial assistance and the political and technocratic leadership of C. Subramaniam in India. It had an almost immediate effect on Indian crop yields. While the United States had started to aggressively use food aid as a diplomatic lever, the Green Revolution helped to make India self-sufficient in grains.[126] It remains a potent example of how India's international partnerships, if leveraged correctly, can actually facilitate independence and autonomy.

But despite these developments, the vacuum created by Nehru's death in 1964 and that of his successor Shastri in early 1966, led to international affairs generally assuming a lower priority for New Delhi. By the early 1970s, this began to change with Indira Gandhi's consolidation of power. The split of the Congress Party, her concentration of executive power, and the nationalization of important sectors of the economy heralded the political shift.[127] Then, just nine years after its greatest military humiliation in 1962, independent India experienced perhaps its greatest military victory in Bangladesh.

3

1971–1991: Interventions and Alignment

Alignment: Tilting to the Soviet Union, 1971–1991

In many respects, India's approach to the last two decades of the Cold War—from 1971 to 1991—was different from the preceding quarter century. Geopolitically, the United States and China began to drift closer, driven by shared concerns about the Soviet Union. Their relationship, midwifed with the help of Pakistan, was consolidated by US Secretary of State Henry Kissinger's secret visit to China, followed by President Richard Nixon's historic trip in 1971. The People's Republic of China was welcomed into the United Nations as a permanent member of the UN Security Council and normal diplomatic ties were established between Washington and Beijing by the late 1970s. From India's standpoint, the US, China, and Pakistan were now perceived to constitute a dangerous coalition. Further developments took place domestically. While the first half of India's Cold War-era foreign policy had been dominated by

95

Jawaharlal Nehru's personality and worldview, the second half saw the strong imprint of Indira Gandhi. Economically, India remained relatively closed, even as other Asian economies became more globally integrated. Security challenges, including separatism and terrorism, intensified.

As a consequence, India's foreign relations during the 1970s and 1980s had two cardinal features. One was an open alignment with the Soviet Union following a Treaty of Peace and Friendship signed in 1971, in part to guard against the prospect of Chinese or American intervention in the Bangladesh Liberation War. While continuing with the rhetorical use of Non-Alignment, in practice India enjoyed much closer political, security, and economic ties with the Soviet Union than with the United States. Economically, the USSR offered low-interest loans on long-term timeframes that went directly to the Indian public sector. Just as notably, in the early 1970s, the newly strengthened relationship manifested in the use of Russian military equipment and technology by the Indian armed services. The USSR made licensed production easy and provided attractive financing terms and technical assistance. In time, Indian state-owned enterprises, particularly in the defence sector, grew accustomed to these arrangements. Moscow also provided other goods and services that India valued, such as critical components for its space programme.[1] A growing number of Indian students went to the Soviet Union and at times the USSR was India's largest bilateral trading partner. Politically, there was greater comfort against common foes in China and Pakistan. India often relied on Moscow's veto power at the United Nations to prevent foreign intervention in the Jammu and Kashmir dispute.

Nonetheless, there were evident limitations to this partnership. Defence relations were not always accompanied by technological transfers, and Moscow did little to help or encourage India's nuclear weapon programme. Privately, Indian military planners worried about the high costs of spares and uncertainties and lack of technical knowledge sharing. Indians often found attractive educational and work opportunities in the West—Europe and the United States—rather than in the Warsaw Pact countries, to some degree due to greater cultural and linguistic familiarity. In practice, differences also emerged over economic planning, with New Delhi—unlike Moscow— unable to manage all aspects of its domestic economy such as production and labour. The Soviet Union also occasionally put India in awkward positions, as after its decision to intervene in Afghanistan in late 1979.[2]

In the early 1980s, M.K. Rasgotra, India's foreign secretary at the time, recalled telling Indira Gandhi that India was in 'diplomacy stasis' concerning Pakistan, the United States, and China. 'The only major active relationship is with Moscow which is of course of central importance to our foreign policy,' he recalls assessing. But he also recognized the limitations of that relationship: 'we do not have any serious problems and a couple of visit to Moscow a year for consultations will suffice.'[3] These and other factors persuaded Indira Gandhi and later Rajiv Gandhi to explore cooperation with the United States, even if some of those early proposals never fully materialized. In 1981, Indira Gandhi met Ronald Reagan in Mexico, and their convivial personal rapport translated into a visit by the prime minister to the United States the next year.

At the same time, Indira Gandhi continued her leading role in the Non-Aligned Movement (NAM), hosting the group's summit in 1983 that featured seventy heads of state, vice-presidents, and prime ministers. India had to manage

the growing ideological fissures within NAM, which now
encompassed Communist countries such as Cuba and
conservative-leaning states in Asia, Africa, and Latin America.
The Summit also had to negotiate on contentious questions
such as the Soviet intervention in Afghanistan, the status of
Cambodia and the Iran–Iraq war.[4]

In 1985, less than a year after assuming the prime
ministership, Rajiv Gandhi visited Washington. In this
instance, more momentum in India–US relations meant that
cooperation with the United States went further, extending
to a deal for jet engines for India's indigenous fighter aircraft
programme. Both Washington and New Delhi began
discussions on more ambitious cooperation, extending to
economic and security issues. Despite these developments, this
attempt at balancing India's relations between the superpowers
in an era of Soviet *glasnost* and *perestroika* was limited by the
ongoing proxy conflict in Afghanistan and the United States'
continued military support to Pakistan, among other factors.[5]

Bangladesh to Brasstacks: India and Pakistan, 1971–1988

The second striking feature of India's foreign policy between
1971 and 1991 was its willingness to use force, albeit in a
more geopolitically constrained region limited to South Asia
and the Indian Ocean. This period witnessed a peaceful
nuclear explosion (PNE), the annexation of Sikkim, military
stand-offs with Pakistan and China, and interventions in Sri
Lanka, the Maldives, and the Indian Ocean region. But the
development that ushered in this era was the 1971 Bangladesh
Liberation War.

The Bangladesh crisis arose in part from structural realities: while the political and economic power in Pakistan lay in the West (especially the provinces of Punjab and Sindh), over half of the country's population was composed of ethnic Bengalis in the geographically detached East Pakistan. Student protests and growing resentment in East Pakistan following the 1965 India–Pakistan War led to calls for greater autonomy. In 1966, Sheikh Mujibur Rehman of the Awami League outlined specific demands for autonomy that included considerable independence on fiscal, administrative, and defence matters, including a separate currency for East Pakistan. He was accused of conspiring with India, tried, and jailed in 1968. The next year, Pakistan's military leader General Yahya Khan suspended the Constitution and declared martial law in Pakistan, to be followed by elections in 1970. To Yahya's surprise, Mujib's Awami League scored an overwhelming electoral victory in East Pakistan, winning 160 out of 162 seats, and thus giving it a majority. Zulfikar Ali Bhutto's Pakistan People's Party (PPP) finished a distant second with eighty-one seats. This undesirable outcome from Yahya's point of view resulted in an increasingly brutal military crackdown in February and March 1971. Pakistan banned the Awami League and branded Mujib and his supporters 'enemies of Pakistan'.[6]

India was initially wary about intervening in this situation, despite requests for asylum and other forms of support from Awami League members in March 1971. Violating Pakistani sovereignty could have had blowback effects, the Pakistani military was well-equipped, and there were concerns about Chinese intervention and a two-front war. In April, K. Subrahmanyam—a civil servant who was then heading the Institute for Defence Studies and Analyses think tank in New

Delhi—sent a memo to the defence minister and other senior officials. After laying out the options and counter-arguments, he made the case for a 'decisive intervention and withdrawal', and concluded that, 'It is obvious the benefits far outweigh the costs of intervention.'[7] But even as over six million refugees entered India from East Pakistan in less than 100 days after mid-April, and India's Border Security Force started providing some arms and training to Bangladeshi rebels (the Mukti Fauj, later Mukti Bahini), Indira Gandhi resisted military intervention. War plans were drafted by the Army only in the summer of 1971 and finalized in October.[8]

The international environment also played a role, most notably the US–China rapprochement engineered in July 1971 during Henry Kissinger's visit to China via Pakistan. Already, in mid-June 1971, Indian leaders had begun contemplating a Treaty of Peace and Friendship with the Soviet Union. Foreign Secretary T.N. Kaul, in fact, suggested that India offer similar treaties to the United States and Afghanistan, a notion rejected by Secretary to the Prime Minister P.N. Haksar. Indira Gandhi even suggested discussing such as agreement with China, with whom India's relationship was still frosty.[9] But these considerations were overtaken by news of Henry Kissinger's visit to Pakistan in July and the United States' tilt towards Pakistan and China.

Kissinger made it clear to Indian diplomats that the US would not help if China intervened in an India–Pakistan war. Haksar, Kaul, and D.P. Dhar accelerated outreach efforts to the Soviet Union, which after 1965 had begun to project itself as a neutral broker in South Asia and had even supplied arms to Pakistan in 1968. After lengthy negotiations, New Delhi and Moscow signed the Indo–Soviet Treaty of Peace, Friendship and Cooperation on 9 August. The treaty ensured that the

USSR would not supply arms to Pakistan in the event of war and opened the prospect of Moscow preoccupying Chinese troops along their border in the event of Beijing's intervention. Kaul argued that the treaty did 'not conflict with our conceptions of Non-alignment'.[10] Meanwhile, India's chargé d'affaires in Beijing, Brajesh Mishra, assessed that while China would continue to supply arms and support Pakistan at the UN, it would not intervene in a war between India and Pakistan. In addition to Chinese concerns about the Indo-Soviet Treaty, the People's Liberation Army was undergoing a significant political purge.[11]

While avoiding multilateral diplomacy at the United Nations, India also went on a diplomatic blitzkrieg between May and July, sending special envoys and informal representatives to capitals around the world. This effort enjoyed only mixed results. Despite the absence of diplomatic relations, Israel agreed to provide arms to India that were in turn supplied to the Mukti Bahini.[12] In October and November, Indira Gandhi went herself to Western capitals, and her tour included interactions with the media, during which she pressed India's—and Bangladesh's—case.

The year 1971 was also a case of India's soft power proving highly effective. Partially informed by positive sentiments for India and Indian culture, journalists, artists, and musicians in the West spoke out sympathetically for the Bangladesh cause. The best example was the Concert for Bangladesh organized at Madison Square Garden in New York by former Beatles guitarist George Harrison, which featured the likes of Bob Dylan and Eric Clapton. The event, which was initiated by Indian sitarist Ravi Shankar, raised funds for Bangladesh relief and increased public awareness by showcasing documentary footage of atrocities and refugee conditions. While many Western governments remained critical of India, the growing public perception in their countries was that a genocide was underway in East Pakistan.[13] The creation of Bangladesh as an independent country became an increasingly acceptable outcome.

By November 1971, conflict had essentially broken out on the East Pakistan border, one that involved armour, artillery, and aircraft. On 5 December, Pakistan opted for pre-emptive air strikes on India from the west, and this proved a fatal miscalculation. That evening, Indira Gandhi authorized Army Chief General Sam Manekshaw to go to war in the east. India benefited from larger forces in the theatre, control of airspace and the sea, and better intelligence and logistics. But believing that the capital Dhaka was too difficult to take, Indian war plans initially envisaged seizing large tracts of territory in the east, installing a Bangladeshi government, and using this leverage to force a political resolution with Pakistan. Plans changed between 9 and 11 December, when Indian forces from the east successfully reached the Meghna River. Without the means to cross the river, Lieutenant General Sagat Singh used helicopters to airlift troops and supplies to within 40–60 km of Dhaka. This opened the possibility of the fall of Dhaka and the complete surrender of Pakistani forces.[14]

Circumstances were already pushing for a decisive conclusion to the conflict. Indian intelligence learned that a US naval task force led by the aircraft carrier *U.S.S. Enterprise* was about to enter the Bay of Bengal, a development corroborated by a subsequent *New York Times* article. While the task force's objective was interpreted by India as either deterring an Indian attack on West Pakistan, evacuating Pakistani forces from the East, or bombing Indian communications, its arrival would clearly have impeded further Indian operations.[15] On 13 December, Moscow joined Washington in proposing a UN Security Council resolution that would call for a ceasefire between India and Pakistan. If agreed, it would have eliminated the possibility of a Pakistani surrender.

Instead, at that crucial moment, India stepped up the military pressure on Dhaka. On 15 December, Yahya told his commander in Dhaka Lieutenant General A.A.K. Niazi that 'resistance is no longer humanly possible' but also asked Zulfikar Ali Bhutto at the UN Security Council to accept a resolution.[16] Bhutto ignored these instructions, tore up the proposed resolution at the Security Council and walked out after a dramatic speech. By then, Niazi's proposal for a cessation of hostilities had reached New Delhi. India demanded unconditional surrender by the 93,000 Pakistani troops in the theatre and on 16 December, the head of the Indian Army's Eastern Command Lieutenant General Jagjit Singh Aurora and Niazi signed the Instrument of Surrender.

In June and July 1972, in the aftermath of India's victory in the Bangladesh War, Indian and Pakistani leaders met in the Indian hill station of Shimla. Pakistan sought and achieved the return of captured territory and of over 90,000 Pakistani prisoners of war. India got an agreement for a bilateral demarcation of a Line of Control (LoC), thus greatly reducing the possibility of third-party mediation on Jammu and Kashmir. The Shimla Agreement is widely seen in India as a missed opportunity. India had the upper hand but was unable to achieve a final settlement on Jammu and Kashmir. The blame is traditionally placed at the door of P.N. Haksar, who believed that more humiliating terms for Pakistan would have been akin to the 1914 Versailles Treaty for Germany and would therefore have perpetuated grievances and conflict.[17] Other considerations were also at play, including international sentiment. Many countries believed that India had already achieved an absolute victory in the dismemberment of Pakistan and creation of Bangladesh and were less sympathetic to further Indian demands. Moreover, rather than a bargaining chip, the Pakistani prisoners of war proved something of a liability and India (and Bangladesh) were keen to get rid of them.

Subsequent events made things even more difficult. On the one hand, India began to return prisoners in September 1973, Pakistan recognized Bangladesh in 1974, and India and Pakistan re-established full diplomatic ties in 1976. However, India's Peaceful Nuclear Explosion of 1974, Sheikh Abdullah's return to power as chief minister in Jammu and Kashmir, and the Indian annexation of Sikkim further decreased the appetite in Pakistan for normalization. Strangely, India–Pakistan relations initially improved following the coup that brought General Zia ul-Haq to power in Pakistan. Cricketing ties were re-established, consulates in Karachi and Bombay were opened, and an agreement was finalized for a hydroelectric dam in India over the Chenab River. India's External Affairs Minister Atal Bihari Vajpayee visited Pakistan in 1978, having already visited the other South Asian capitals, and India allowed Pakistan to enter the Non-Aligned Movement in 1979.[18]

The 1980s brought an end to this nascent bonhomie. The Soviet war in Afghanistan brought India and Pakistan on to opposite sides of a Cold War hotspot. India blocked Pakistan's re-entry to the Commonwealth. Meanwhile, as Zia faced popular protests in Sindh, Balochistan and the North-West Frontier Province (NWFP, now Khyber–Pakhtunkhwa), Indira Gandhi spoke up for democratic forces in Pakistan. India's concerns about Pakistan's nuclear programme also increased, as well as Pakistani concerns about a possible Indian strike on its Kahuta reactor. In 1984, India pre-emptively occupied the Siachen Glacier at an altitude extending to over 5000 metres as Pakistani maps had started to claim it, and Pakistani mountaineering expeditions had begun to venture into the vicinity. The glacier represented a gap in the demarcated Line of Control.[19] At around the same time, there were growing concerns about Pakistan's support for the Khalistan insurgency in Punjab— an insurgency that led eventually to the assassination of Indira Gandhi. For example, Indian intelligence found firm evidence, which was presented publicly, of Pakistani support for hijackers of an Indian airliner and for terrorists that sought refuge in the Golden Temple in Amritsar in 1984.[20] In 1986, India planned Operation Brasstacks, a massive armoured exercise and war game in western India, which alarmed Pakistan enough to lead to a large mobilization on its side, including of reserves.[21]

Atomic Purgatory: The Nuclear Programme, 1967–1991

India's nuclear development both fuelled and was informed by the rivalry with Pakistan, but it had wider implications for India's domestic development and relations with the superpowers. The process of weaponization—the actual design and manufacture of a nuclear device—began in 1967–68, under Homi Sethna, Raja Ramanna, and R. Chidambaram. But by 1970, it was clear that India lacked enough weapons grade plutonium for a full-fledged programme, and absent diverting some from Canadian-supplied reactors (which could be used for peaceful purposes), India would require a decade to produce enough for a suitable deterrent. In 1971, Sarabhai told fellow scientists at an international conference that India was prioritizing the development of nuclear explosives, hinting that they had successfully developed a basic design. The building and operation by 1972 of the Purnima research reactor helped ensure that that year, the go ahead for a PNE could been given. The decision was a culmination of the technological progress that India had made until that point, the death of Sarabhai and his succession by Sethna, the consolidation of Indira Gandhi's political position after the Bangladesh War of 1971, the continuing threats emanating from China and Pakistan, and recognition of the limitations of dependence on a superpower.[22]

On the morning of 18 May 1974, India detonated an underground nuclear explosive device. This made India the first country after the five recognized nuclear weapon powers to conduct a test. The yield was initially given as about 12 kilotons, similar to the American bomb dropped on Hiroshima in 1945. But it has been variously estimated between four and fifteen kilotons. The consequences were rather unexpected. First, while foreign aid to India did not stop (and in fact increased), external nuclear assistance evaporated. In April 1975, the Nuclear Suppliers Group met for the first time in London, creating a cartel to plug export control loopholes of the kind that had allowed India to produce its explosive device. Second, while the prestige of India's nuclear programme and the scientists involved was enhanced, the effort to achieve a nuclear deterrent actually withered and slowed down in the years that followed. Although the explosion was successful, not enough data was derived, and setbacks in the running of various reactors were only accelerated by the withdrawal of external support.[23] After the PNE, for international, technical and political reasons, India's nuclear weapons programme effectively slowed down.

For over a decade, a potential Indian test had been couched in peaceful terms, both for domestic and international audiences, even if it made little practical difference. In private budgetary discussions after the test in January 1975, the Defence Ministry said that nuclear weapons played 'no part in our defence preparedness which is based entirely on conventional weapons'.[24] Postponing a test might also have widened the gap with China, and there were already concerns about Pakistan's nuclear ambitions. Alternatively, could India have tested prior to the advent of the NPT in 1967, and thus become a formal nuclear weapon state? India may have had sufficient weapons-grade fissile material for a bomb by 1967, but it lacked other necessary elements and knowledge for an explosive device. Although India was no worse off than China economically or scientifically in the 1960s, China's nuclear programme benefited significantly from Soviet technological assistance and a focused, authoritarian regime.

Another effect of India's PNE of 1974 was the acceleration of Pakistan's nuclear programme. Pakistan's pursuit of a nuclear weapon capability actually dates back to the 1960s—when it began to receive civilian nuclear assistance from various foreign actors—and among its biggest advocates was Zulfikar Ali Bhutto. Bhutto's logic of pursuing nuclear weapons was driven by a few factors, among them the belief that India would imminently follow China's 1964 test, his scepticism of the US alliance, his concerns about a non-proliferation regime closing off the nuclear option, and India's growing military capabilities. In a 1965 interview, Bhutto famously declared that Pakistan would produce a nuclear bomb 'even if we have to feed on grass and leaves'.[25] Upon becoming prime minister after the 1971 war, Bhutto placed the Pakistan Atomic Energy Commission (PAEC) under his direct control. In

January 1972, he directed them to simultaneously produce plutonium through reprocessing, enrich uranium, and develop weapon designs. By March 1972, PAEC Chairman Munir Ahmad Khan presented plans that Bhutto quickly approved. From the outset, Pakistan's efforts benefited from Chinese assistance, including work on the Karachi Nuclear Power Plant (KANUPP) in the early 1970s.[26]

It was after India's PNE that A.Q. Khan—a Pakistani metallurgist working in the Netherlands—wrote to Bhutto, offering help with producing highly enriched uranium. In December 1975, Khan stole centrifuge designs from his employer and left the Netherlands. In 1976, he formally joined Pakistan's nuclear programme.[27] The same year, China and Pakistan signed an agreement for bilateral nuclear cooperation.[28] In 1981, Pakistan received 50 kilograms of highly enriched uranium and a 1966-vintage bomb design from China. In exchange, China was allowed to reverse engineer parts that Pakistan had acquired, including quite possibly A.Q. Khan's centrifuges. Khan also benefited from lax export controls, particularly in Europe, acquiring important parts from Switzerland, the Netherlands, and elsewhere. By the late 1970s and early 1980s, Pakistan's nuclear activities were well-known to others, including in the United States, with Zia and A.Q. Khan openly boasting of their capabilities.[29]

Throughout this time, the United States may have had reason to look the other way: some in Washington believed that Pakistan–China nuclear cooperation would help balance against the Soviet Union. Furthermore, the US legislation known as the Pressler Amendment, while widely heralded in India as a punitive measure against Pakistan, was in fact nothing of the sort. Rather, it enabled the United States to keep funnelling military and economic aid to Pakistan until 1990. By that time, Pakistan's nuclear development was advanced enough that the US president had no choice but to determine that Pakistan was in possession of a nuclear device and cut off military assistance. Not coincidentally, by then, Pakistan's support for the United States' assistance to the *mujahideen* in Afghanistan was no longer needed.[30]

Thus, the progress that Pakistan made in acquiring a nuclear weapon capability throughout the 1970s and 1980s became another impetus for India to pursue a nuclear deterrent. From 1974 onwards, Indian intelligence closely monitored Pakistan's nuclear programme. In April 1979, just as the United States cut off economic and military aid to Pakistan on non-proliferation grounds for the first time, India's Joint Intelligence Committee concluded that Pakistan's nuclear programme had made considerable headway. India's nuclear weapon initiative was therefore resumed, although not without further political, technical, and procedural delays. By 1983, Indira Gandhi authorized a further nuclear test, but swiftly reversed her decision. In 1985, Rajiv Gandhi authorized a task force—which included Army Vice Chief K. Sundarji and A.P.J. Abdul Kalam, among other military and scientific figures—to assess the costs of a nuclear deterrent. It concluded that a 'balanced minimum deterrent' with warheads in the 'low three digits' would cost less than 10 per cent of India's defence budget over ten years.[31] DRDO continued working steadily on weaponization and delivery systems throughout the mid- and late-1980s, despite Rajiv Gandhi internationally proposing an Action Plan for achieving nuclear disarmament in a timebound manner. India's first short-range Prithvi missile test took place in 1988, and a year later Pakistan tested its Hatf-I missile. But

India was still not in a position to conduct a nuclear test that would provide enough information for a proper deterrent.[32]

In the late 1970s and 1980s, financial, political, bureaucratic and technological factors played a role in impeding the nuclear programme, as did international circumstances and tighter export controls. All of this resulted in India's nuclear quest progressing only in fits and starts. By the end of the Cold War, India was in a difficult position. While its nuclear programme had made considerable progress and had successfully detonated a nuclear device, India effectively faced two nuclear-armed states in China and Pakistan. At the same time, it found itself outside the nuclear Non-Proliferation Treaty (NPT) and faced export controls and various international technology denials. The challenge that India consequently faced by the early 1990s was to achieve a sufficient nuclear deterrent against China and Pakistan while deriving access to civilian nuclear technology and reintegrating into the international nuclear architecture.

Uneasy Terms: India and China, 1974–1991

The 1962 Sino–Indian Border War had been a disaster for India, one that cast a long shadow on India's confidence, reputation, and overall outlook. But it is also possible that India may have overlearned some of those lessons. The 1967 skirmishes near Sikkim were one case in point. That sector was further transformed by India's annexation of Sikkim in 1975. Sikkim had been a British protectorate and that status had transferred to relations with the Republic of India in 1950. It had its own flag and currency under its hereditary leader, the Chogyal, but its defence and foreign policy were India's responsibility. In 1973, popular agitations for democratic rule began against the last Chogyal Palden Thondup Namgyal. In response to growing agitations, the Indian Army intervened. A vote in the Sikkim's Parliament and a referendum conducted in the presence of Indian forces in April 1975 showed overwhelming support for joining India, and within a month the Indian Constitution was amended to make Sikkim a state. Rather expectedly, the Chogyal, China, and Pakistan deemed the whole affair a sham.[33]

Relations between India and China remained frosty for fourteen years after the 1962 border war. Full diplomatic relations at the ambassadorial level were only resumed in 1976. But the same year as ambassadors returned to Beijing and New Delhi, China entered into an agreement to supply nuclear weapon assistance to Pakistan, a culmination of significantly closer relations between the two countries over the previous fifteen years. Between 1967 and 1979, China also provided training and arms to Naga, Mizo, and Manipuri rebels. Relations only began to improve with External Affairs Minister Atal Bihari Vajpayee's visit to China in February 1979, by which time China appears to have stemmed rebel support.[34]

After 1980, China's new leader Deng Xiaoping raised the possibility of a territorial swap or 'package deal' with India, during interviews and bilateral meetings with Indian officials. This was a loose offer to recognize the McMahon Line in exchange for India recognizing China's control of Aksai Chin, similar to Zhou Enlai's suggestion of 1960. In December 1981, Sino–Indian border talks resumed, and in 1983, China agreed to Indian demands for a sector-by-sector discussion. These revolved around resolving the boundary through minor territorial concessions by China in the western sector in exchange for a visit by Prime Minister Indira Gandhi in her capacity as chairwoman of the Non-Aligned Movement (a 'package deal-plus' option). While Beijing seemed open to the prospect of ceding some of the area between its 1956 and 1960 claim lines in Ladakh, the package deal-plus was rejected by New Delhi for domestic political reasons. Instead, the Indian government considered the possibility of exploring such a deal after the 1985 General Elections.[35] It is possible that Chinese proposals, like in years past, would not have been seen through to a full resolution.

In October 1984, Indira Gandhi was assassinated. The next year, with a new prime minister in power and changing international circumstances, China walked back its package deal-plus offer. In late 1985, Chinese negotiators pressed their claims south of the McMahon Line, to the surprise of the Indian side, a position that was reiterated a year later.[36] In 1986, Chinese forces occupied a vacant post, crossed the Thagla Ridge (which had been a flashpoint in 1962), and built barracks and a helipad in the Sumdorong River valley. Indian forces under General Sundarji retaliated with an airlift to the heights overlooking the Chinese outpost, on Longrola and Hathungla, with forward posts ten metres from China's. Beijing was apparently taken aback by the Indian response, and was even more incensed when that same year, India decided to make Arunachal Pradesh a state. These developments led to greater tensions with China in 1986 and 1987, which were only resolved seven years later after Rajiv Gandhi's visit to Beijing in late 1988 and the upgrading of border talks in the early 1990s.[37]

Interventions: India's Neighbourhood, 1975–1990

The unambiguous success of the 1971 Bangladesh War presaged a period of considerable Indian interventionism in its near abroad. But as the dynamics of the Cold War crept in closer, India's activities were mostly relegated to its neighbourhood and extended into the Indian Ocean. Although India—along with Sri Lanka—had led proposals to make the Indian Ocean a zone of peace after 1970s, in practice, India was active in ensuring that it was dominated by neither the United States nor the Soviet Union. Indian military support extended to countries throughout the region, such as a 1973 deal for the Indian Navy to train its counterparts in Oman and an arrangement between the Indian Air Force and Iraq from the late 1960s to the Gulf War.[38]

But India's military role often took more direct forms. In 1983, in Mauritius, differences between political allies-turned-rivals Anerood Jugnauth and Paul Bérenger raised the prospect of political strife and potential violence. The tensions had begun to assume a sectarian character—ethnic Indians versus Creoles—and Jugnauth asked Indira Gandhi for military assistance. While the prime minister agreed to help militarily, the operation was put on hold, largely because of differences between the Army and Navy. Instead, diplomatic and intelligence efforts were successfully used to shore up Jugnauth's coalition and prevent a coup.[39] Three years later, India under Rajiv Gandhi dispatched a frigate to the Seychelles, which helped to successfully avert a coup against left-leaning dictator France-Albert René.[40]

While the Mauritius and Seychelles cases involved only the threat of force, the Maldives intervention of 1988 was more than that. Operation Cactus involved India sending para commandos in two transport aircraft after the seizure of the capital Malé by about eighty Sri Lankan Tamil mercenaries. India's initial assault was complemented by additional forces from the Army, Air Force, and Navy. The operation, hastily planned and executed in sixteen hours with little intelligence support, was successful in its objective of restoring President Maumoon Abdul Gayoom to power.[41]

India's interventionist impulse was more muted, but not entirely absent, in Afghanistan and Nepal. In Afghanistan, India was a bit player for much of the 1980s as the country's civil war led to a Soviet invasion and a proxy conflict involving the United States, Saudi Arabia, and Pakistan. New Delhi had been caught in an awkward position by the Soviet invasion of 1979–80 and had to balance its own close relationship with the USSR with its genuine frustrations at Moscow's move. In the latter half of the decade, Rajiv Gandhi forged a stronger relationship with the Soviet-backed Afghan leader Mohammed Najibullah. There was also greater intelligence cooperation with Afghanistan facilitated by the Soviet intelligence agencies. In the late 1980s, India continued to assist Najibullah even as his support dwindled, the Soviets withdrew, and rival forces neared the capital. After his fall in 1992, Najibullah lived in a UN compound in Kabul. When the Taliban took the city in September 1996, they had him seized, castrated, mutilated, and shot, and his body hanged in public.[42] It was a macabre sign of things to come.

If Afghanistan saw a devastating and brutal civil war during the 1980s, Nepal experienced political upheaval, sporadic violence, and embargoes. Much of this had to do with the consolidation of power of King Birendra. In 1987, Birendra opted to tilt closer to China and the next year he concluded a secret agreement for intelligence sharing with Beijing and began to acquire military supplies from China. Birendra also endorsed Chinese infrastructure projects in the Terai region near India and enforced legislation that limited Indian labour. India saw these steps as cumulative violation of its prior agreements with Nepal, in particular the security and reciprocal elements of the 1950 India–Nepal Treaty of Peace and Friendship. In 1989, a prior trade and transit agreement between India and Nepal expired, and the result was an effective embargo on the country. Nepal's economy suffered as a result, and dissatisfaction with the King extended to the public. The year 1990 witnessed the popular Jan Andolan agitations by political parties, which included both the Nepal Congress and left. The King lifted the ban on political parties and elections were held in 1991. Nepal's new Constitution curbed the role of the King, and its democratically elected government pledged to remain sensitive to India's security concerns.[43]

More memorably, there was the 1987–90 Indian military intervention in Sri Lanka. The Sri Lankan civil war came about after many decades of simmering resentment by the Tamil minority, and after of a series of discriminatory laws and policies that had been advanced by majority Sinhalese-dominated governments. By the late 1970s, the movement had become militant and civil war broke out in the early 1980s. India was concerned about the rise of Tamil nationalism and its spread to India. It was also worried that Colombo might turn to other outside powers for support, including the United States, China, and Pakistan. This required India to play an active role in reconciling the situation, supporting Tamils, but also ensuring that their demands for a Tamil nation (*eelam*) were not realized. Initially, the main Tamil militant group— the Liberation Tigers of Tamil Eelam (LTTE) and its leader Velupillai Prabhakaran—benefited from Indian intelligence support and enjoyed considerable popularity among Indian Tamils. India also made relief efforts to besieged Tamil

civilians by air in 1987. In July of that year, India brokered an
accord to ensure peace, in which the Sri Lankan government
in Colombo made certain concessions to the Tamils. As part
of the agreement, an Indian Peace Keeping Force (IPKF) was
dispatched to Sri Lanka, initially to oversee disarmament and
maintain law and order.[44]

Agreements between the Sri Lankan government and
the LTTE broke down over questions of amnesty and the
ceasefire and spiralled into conflict involving the IPKF. An
operation launched by India in October 1987 to take control
of the town of Jaffna proved disastrous, with Indian forces
suffering seventy fatalities.[45] The Indian military presence
on the island grew larger over the following years, but the
effort suffered from several shortcomings. One, as India
learned early on, it consistently underestimated the LTTE
as a fighting force. Two, India suffered from the ambivalence
and later hostility of the Sri Lankan government, on whose
behalf it was supposedly fighting the counterinsurgency. Sri
Lankan President J.R. Jayewardene initially used the Indian
presence to deal more forcefully with a separate insurgency in
the south, but his successor Ranasinghe Premadasa reached a
clandestine understanding with the LTTE and even provided
them arms in a bid to rid his country of the Indian military
presence. Three, the Sri Lanka war was unpopular in India,
and became an issue in the 1989 General Elections. By 1990,
the IPKF had lost over 1000 soldiers. With its intervention
opposed by all parties, an inability to realize a political
outcome, and a new government in New Delhi, Indian forces
withdrew.[46] But the war followed them home. In 1991, Rajiv
Gandhi was assassinated by an LTTE suicide bomber while
on the campaign trail for the General Elections.[47] Despite

the disaster of the IPKF intervention, Sri Lanka did not splinter, the LTTE was eventually defeated two decades later, New Delhi patched up relations with Colombo, and India managed to minimize external involvement. Nevertheless, the IPKF saga ended two decades of Indian interventionism in its region.

India's interventionism did have some positive outcomes form India's standpoint. India's relations held relatively steady with Bhutan (with whom a 1949 Friendship Treaty endured), Bangladesh became independent under Mujibur Rehman, and Sikkim became a part of India. By the early 1990s, Nepal democratized and acknowledged Indian security concerns. Even in Sri Lanka, the possibility of a Tamil *eelam* was forestalled, despite the operational disasters of the IPKF intervention. Indian intervention also dampened the influence of outside powers in its immediate periphery. This included serious attempts by Nepal to draw closer militarily to China in the 1980s, by the United States to prevent a decisive Indian victory in Bangladesh in the early 1970s, and by various actors—including the United States, the Soviet Union, China, Pakistan, United Kingdom and even South Africa—to increase their influence in the Indian Ocean basin.

Nonetheless, India's approach was hardly an unmitigated success. In fact, many of India's smaller neighbours were sometimes successful in using relations with extra-regional powers to gain leverage with India. In Nepal, Chinese aid came close to matching Indian aid in 1976–77. In the late 1980s, King Birendra made attempts at deepening military and intelligence cooperation with China. Bangladesh also established military relations with Beijing after Mujib's death in 1975. In 1977, under Ziaur Rehman's leadership,

Bangladesh began to receive arms from China. In 1979, senior military exchanges between Bangladesh and China began and two-way chief of staff visits became annual affairs. Over the following years, Bangladesh became the second largest recipient of Chinese arms, after Pakistan. In 1986–87, during the Sumdorongchu stand-off between India and China, President Hussein Muhammad Ershad reportedly assured Beijing that he would not permit India to move its forces through Bangladeshi territory. The relationship between China and Sri Lanka also grew. From the 1950s onwards, China provided subsidized rice and railway equipment to Sri Lanka and from 1980 military support, including naval vessels, small arms, and transport aircraft.[48]

But India's response to developments in the 1970s— particularly in Bangladesh and Sri Lanka—had other consequences. Efforts at regionalism were half-hearted and poorly designed. The year 1985 saw the establishment of the South Asian Association for Regional Cooperation (SAARC). The effort to create SAARC was led by Bangladesh, with support from Sri Lanka, but there were reasons for hesitation on the part of India. One fear was that the coalition might hem India in, much as the Association of Southeast Asian Nations (ASEAN) had narrowed power imbalances in Southeast Asia between Indonesia and other countries. For this reason, India insisted on unanimity in decision-making within SAARC. At the same time, Pakistan perceived SAARC as a potential vehicle for India to exert its regional dominance. As such, the agenda was watered down and relegated to less controversial issues. In the years that followed, differences between India and Pakistan ensured that regional institutionalism could not proceed very far or very quickly.[49]

Belated Liberalization: The Economy, 1971–91

During the latter years of the Cold War, India may have navigated the superpower rivalry through a closer relationship with Moscow and the fitful pursuit of a nuclear deterrent, managed rivalries with Pakistan and China, and intervened more in its near neighbourhood. But another legacy of this period was the degree to which its economy remained closed, even after many Asian economies had begun to open, integrate, and liberalize. In fact, just as Asian economies such as South Korea, Taiwan, and parts of Southeast Asia began to experience miracle growth, India took a turn to the left. During this period, India witnessed Indira Gandhi's populism, the Emergency (1975–77) when elections and civil liberties were suspended, and a fragile Janata Party-led government from 1977 to 1980. It was the 42nd Amendment to the Indian Constitution, introduced in 1976, which added the word 'socialist' to the preamble.[50]

The economic direction of the country during this period was the subject a good deal of domestic criticism, although not enough to shape the balance of opinion among Indian leaders. In the 1970s, the prominent economist Jagdish Bhagwati argued that India's mixed economy had failed both as socialism and as capitalism, growing too slowly and failing to reduce inequality.[51] Similarly, the legendary industrialist J.R.D. Tata believed that India had benefited from the mixed economy until the mid-1960s but that after that India had missed an opportunity to liberalize. He estimated that 'employment would have grown more quickly in all sectors; production would have increased considerably and shortages removed; and Government revenues too would have materially increased, which in turn could have been utilized for developmental programmes'.[52] Some of the criticism of the mixed economy even came from within the corridors of power. In a highly publicized 1975 interview, Indira Gandhi's son Sanjay Gandhi described free enterprise as 'the quickest way to grow' and said he believed in removing government controls on industry.[53]

But there was also a great deal of resistance to change. Vested interests—politicians, bureaucrats, even business leaders— dampened the prospects of an overhaul of the license-permit-quota Raj. As a result, the 1980s saw several pro-business, but not exactly pro-market reforms.[54] Rajiv Gandhi's first budget of March 1985 simplified licenses, reduced duties, lifted curbs on company assets, and cut tax rates. This was roundly criticized by the left, and any benefits that industry derived at the top were offset by the droughts of the late 1980s.[55] GDP per capita growth between 1982 and 1992 averaged 3 per cent, more than double the previous decade. But in the words of the economist Arvind Panagariya, the developments of the 1980s were less 'systematic and systemic' than what followed.[56] Fiscal and current account deficits remained high, and the fundamentals of the licence-permit-quota Raj remained intact. Thus, while India may have enjoyed an opportunity between the mid-1960s and late-1980s to embark upon a process of liberalization and integration with the world economy, a combination of politics, ideology, and vested interests prevented that from occurring.

The 1970s and 1980s were, in hindsight, difficult decades for India and its place in the world. International and domestic circumstances meant that India was often on the defensive and constrained. These years saw India having to deal with—but rarely resolve—some contentious problems which would have lasting challenges for a post-Cold War and post-liberalization India.

The five major challenges remained the rivalry with Pakistan, difficulties with China, the unresolved question of India's nuclear deterrent and status, a restive neighbourhood, and unrealized economic potential. These would be compounded by terrorism, separatism, and the dissolution of India's closest partner—the Soviet Union. These circumstances presaged several crises in the early 1990s that compelled India to take on—and in some cases finally address—its most pressing challenges.

4

1991–2008: Liberalization and US Unipolarity

The Year of Change, 1991

India experienced several fundamental changes in and around 1991 that sharply altered its international environment, its economy, its domestic politics, and its national security. These developments could perhaps be traced to three military interventions. The first was India's intervention in Sri Lanka after 1987 against Velupillai Prabhakaran and his Liberation Tigers of Tamil Eelam (LTTE). Despite the withdrawal of Indian Peace Keeping Forces (IPKF) in 1990, the assassination of former Prime Minister Rajiv Gandhi by the LTTE during the campaign for the 1991 general elections created a political vacuum at the Centre in New Delhi. After elections that year, P.V. Narasimha Rao, an improbable candidate, became India's prime minister for the next five years.[1]

A second military intervention that left a lasting impact was the Soviet invasion of Afghanistan somewhat earlier in December 1979. What followed was a ruinous war waged by the Soviet Army against Afghan *mujahideen* backed by the United States, Pakistan, and Saudi Arabia.[2] The Soviet misadventure in Afghanistan contributed indirectly to political developments in Moscow with unforeseen results. In August 1991, a failed coup in the Soviet Union against Mikhail Gorbachev resulted in the dissolution of the Communist Party of the Soviet Union. The collapse of the USSR was quite sudden and relatively peaceful, a result of factionalism, failed reform, economic malaise, and the attractiveness of the Western economic, social, and political model. In the previous two years, from 1989 to 1991, the USSR had lost much of its influence in Central and Eastern Europe. By the end of 1991, fourteen new post-Soviet countries emerged in Eastern Europe and Central Asia, leaving an economically broken Russia. India's closest international partner for the previous two decades had dissolved.[3]

But the employment of insurgent Islamist forces against the Soviet Army in Afghanistan also had direct security consequences for Pakistan and India. It was this conflict that contributed to an infrastructure in Pakistan that financed, recruited, trained, and equipped terrorists. Starting in 1988–90, these terrorist forces began to be deployed with considerable effect against India. An insurgency in Jammu and Kashmir flared up. Shortly after, India began to feel the brunt of international terrorism against urban civilian targets, especially after the Mumbai blasts of 1993.[4] Pakistan provided support and shelter to the planners and executors of these operations.

The third military intervention was the occupation of Kuwait by Saddam Hussein's Iraq in August 1990. Operation

Desert Storm, in which US-led forces ousted Iraqi troops the next year with relative ease, resulted in a spike in global oil prices. India, heavily dependent on oil imports, had been running years of current account and fiscal deficits, and increased oil prices exhausted its foreign exchange reserves. This resulted in a balance of payments crisis, during which India had to ship gold to foreign lenders to secure emergency financing. These developments prompted Rao, Finance Minister Manmohan Singh, and others to push through a package of policy changes in 1991 and 1992 that included abolishing industrial licensing for most industries, ceding government authority on the location of industries, eradicating public-sector monopolies in ten sectors, dropping investment controls for large corporations, raising foreign direct investment (FDI) caps to 51 per cent in many sectors, allowing private enterprises to enter into technology transfer agreements, and removing import controls for capital goods, intermediate goods, components, and raw materials.[5] Tariff reforms were accompanied by the devaluation of the rupee, from Rs 18 per US dollar in 1991 to Rs 31 two years later.

The early 1990s were therefore a very precarious time for India on multiple fronts. For a few years, India's domestic politics featured embattled prime ministerships. P.V. Narasimha Rao (1991–1996), Atal Bihari Vajpayee (for sixteen days in 1996), H.D. Deve Gowda (1996–97) and I.K. Gujral (1997–98) all had to contend with coalitions and factionalism. Economically, the results of the 1991 liberalization reforms took some years to reveal themselves. High rates of economic growth were not immediately obvious. The country confronted continuing insurgencies or separatist sentiments in its north, south, east, and west. Amid this difficult backdrop, India managed to break many long-standing taboos in its external relations.

This period saw the rise of economic diplomacy as an essential element of India's external engagement after decades of relative isolationism. A realization that India's economic future would be intertwined with Asia's led to the initiation of the 'Look East' policy. In the process, India initiated official relations with the Association of South East Asian Nations (ASEAN) in 1992. That same year, India normalized diplomatic relations with Israel. There was also some tentative outreach to the United States, including on defence ties. And in the early 1990s, a series of border management agreements were signed between India and China added new dimensions to that relationship. Finally, in 1995, the Rao government decided to approve a nuclear test, although this was not carried out as a result of economic conditions, US warnings, and forthcoming elections.

Despite these considerable changes, India's scholars, analysts and commentators of international affairs were often slow to appreciate new developments. For example, there was significant ideological resistance against exploring opportunities for closer relations with other power centres, most notably the United States. Similarly, many Indians initially had deep moral and practical reservations about the necessity and wisdom of pursuing a nuclear deterrent, even as Pakistan's programme advanced and international non-proliferation efforts narrowed India's options. A political obsession with Pakistan often came at the expense of relations with other smaller neighbours and an appreciation of the growing challenge posed by China. And the language of India's international relations remained constrained by outdated notions of Non-Alignment and developing world solidarity. As the future National Security Adviser Shivshankar Menon later noted, '[I]n the early 1990s it was hard to be nonaligned when there was no one to be aligned with or nonaligned against.'[6]

The conceptual confusion at the time about the state of international affairs was not restricted to India. Most thinkers and writers of international relations were also unsure how to navigate the post-Cold War world. For some, it was merely a unipolar moment, an opportunity for the enlargement and consolidation of a US-led international order. Inspired by the German philosopher G.W.F. Hegel, Francis Fukuyama argued that liberal democracy could mark the endpoint of man's ideological evolution: the 'End of History'. A belief even took hold in business and academic circles that the state would become increasingly irrelevant in international politics, giving way both to powerful supranational entities (such as the European Union) or non-state actors (such as multinational corporations). Others were more pessimistic. Samuel Huntington argued that the world would be characterized by a 'Clash of Civilizations,' and that the main global challenge could possibly be Islamist terrorism. Still others warned of American arrogance and overreach. Certain sceptics took this further and believed that the answer to many international problems lay in global disengagement by the United States. It was only a very small minority that argued consistently that the rise of new powers, particularly China, would result in a return of great power politics. In time, some of these predictions would prove partly vindicated—but only partly.[7]

Tentative Openings, 1991–1998

Amid the conceptual haze, a new post-Cold War world created ample new opportunities for policymakers. For India, a significant series of steps between 1991 and 1994 helped establish what became known as the Look East Policy. Initially, it served a primarily economic value. Rao sought investment and trade opportunities as he travelled to South Korea, Singapore and elsewhere in Southeast and Northeast Asia, but he also sought alternative economic models. New Delhi's efforts were initially limited. India did receive some official development assistance (ODA) from Japan, while South Korean companies successfully entered the Indian market. Southeast Asia also saw more of a strategic vacuum after the end of the Cold War: Russia had closed bases at Da Nang and Cam Ranh Bay in Vietnam and the United States departed from the Philippines. In this context, the desire of Southeast Asian economies to engage with India increased. 'Looking East' was also a less contentious way in India of introducing market forces and cooperating with US allies and partners, which meant that it also helped India 'Look West'. In 1992, India established official contacts with the Association of Southeast Asian Nations (ASEAN), an institution that had once been associated with anti-communism and viewed by New Delhi with a great deal of scepticism.[8] The military aspect of this engagement also slowly took off. In 1995, the Indian Navy began the Milan multilateral exercises, initially involving Indonesia, Singapore, and Thailand.

The other significant diplomatic breakthrough immediately after 1991 was with Israel. India had recognized Israel in September 1950; at the time, the two countries were already working together at the United Nations and India was following a precedent set six months earlier by Iran. Although Israel had a consul in Bombay from 1953, India opted not to establish diplomatic ties because it felt it was necessary to compete with Pakistan for support from Muslim-majority countries on issues such as Jammu and Kashmir. A series of crises in both West and South Asia in the late 1960s and early 1970s opened prospects for a diversification of India's West Asia policy, but New Delhi was also constrained by a greater dependence on oil imports from the Gulf states. That did not stop Indira Gandhi from accepting military assistance from Israel in the run up to the 1971 Bangladesh War. However, in 1975, India recognized and initiated diplomatic ties with the Palestinian Liberation Organization (PLO) and after the Israeli attack on Iraq's Osirak nuclear reactor, India expelled Israel's consul in Bombay in 1982, marking a low point in relations.[9]

By the late 1980s, it became clear that the absence of India–Israel diplomatic ties was hindering other efforts, including Rajiv Gandhi's attempted outreach to the United States. In the early 1990s, several factors converged: the initiation of a renewed Israel–Palestine peace process, India's defence requirements after the collapse of the Soviet Union, China's decision to start diplomatic ties with Israel, and the Organisation of Islamic Cooperation's vocal support for Pakistan in the Jammu and Kashmir dispute. During Palestinian leader Yasser Arafat's visit to India in 1991, he made it clear that they did not object to India's normalization of ties with Israel, an argument used by proponents such as Rao to counter sceptics in the Indian government, such as the minister Arjun Singh. India's decision to establish diplomatic ties with Israel was made on 29 January 1992.[10]

Not coincidentally, the Indian opening of relations with Southeast Asia and Israel also facilitated an improvement of ties with the United States at this time. In the early 1990s, the US Army's Pacific commander, Lt Gen. Claude M. Kicklighter, proposed to explore tentative military-to-military cooperation.

In 1994, Rao visited the United States, with the tone and context now considerably different from past prime ministerial visits. In 1995, the Indian Air Force chief visited Washington, and two years later, the vice chairman of the US joint chiefs of staff reciprocated, marking the senior-most US military staff visit to India since 1953. US First Lady Hillary Clinton's 1995 trip to India was meant to pave the way for a presidential visit later. But the India-US relationship was hindered by two factors during this period: one was India's nuclear weapon programme and New Delhi's refusal to sign the nuclear Non-Proliferation Treaty (NPT); the second was the Clinton administration's propensity to regard India and Pakistan as a problem to be solved like the Balkans, Israel–Palestine dispute, or Northern Ireland. Furthermore, urgent issues often took priority for Washington. As US Deputy Secretary of State Strobe Talbott later lamented, 'the Clinton administration paid less attention to [India] during its first six years in office than the president wanted'.[11]

The post-Cold War situation was also more auspicious for an altered Indian relationship with China. In 1992, Rao authorized a Border Peace and Tranquillity Agreement with China, which was signed in September 1993. China appeared keener to stabilize the border with India following the Tiananmen Square protests and domestic and international political turmoil it was confronting. The initial agreement effectively recognized a Line of Actual Control (LAC), created a mechanism to resolve continuing differences as to where the LAC lay, limited troop levels, required the prior notification of military exercises, partly insulated the bilateral relationship from the boundary dispute, and committed both sides to not use force to settle the issue. In 1996, an Agreement on Military

Confidence-Building Measures was signed as a follow-up, which reduced military forces, forbade military exercises larger than one division near the LAC, and requested prior notification for exercises larger than one brigade.[12] These were subsequently followed up by agreements in 2003 that established Special Representatives for the border, and a series of agreements in 2005, 2012, and 2013 to manage border frictions.

After Look East, Israel, the United States, and China, perhaps the most significant legacy of Rao's tenure was in the nuclear sphere. This was prompted primarily by international conditions. In May 1995, the United States and most of the international community proposed to extend the Nuclear Non-Proliferation Treaty (NPT) indefinitely. From India's standpoint, this created a permanent system of nuclear 'haves' and 'have nots'. Just as worrying for New Delhi was that the NPT conference of 1995 also pledged to conclude a Comprehensive Test Ban Treaty (CTBT) no later than 1996 and initiate negotiations towards a ban on fissile material production for explosive devices. These steps would have permanently closed off the nuclear option for India, while legitimizing the nuclear arsenals of China and the other four nuclear weapon states in perpetuity. That same year, the United States considered watering down sanctions on Pakistan for its proliferation activities, adding to concerns in India about the need for a nuclear deterrent. Nuclear tests were now urgently required to perfect and demonstrate its technology and confirm India's nuclear deterrent.

By August 1995, preparations for a nuclear test site at Pokhran were underway. Under scientists A.P.J. Abdul Kalam (India's future president) and R. Chidambaram, India finalized weapon designs. In December, the *New York Times* reported that US intelligence had detected preparations for an Indian nuclear test.[13] In a phone call with US President Bill Clinton, Rao said that India would not act irresponsibly, and tests were delayed. Elections were around the corner, the US had made its displeasure known, and India's economy was still too vulnerable to withstand international sanctions.[14] Although Vajpayee wished to authorize tests in 1996 upon becoming prime minister after the General Elections, he agreed to postpone the decision to after a vote of no confidence in Parliament, which his government did not survive.[15] Nuclear tests were therefore delayed, but the option remained on the table.

If the early- and mid-1990s heralded some new openings, other developments were far more worrying. One was the rise of a new kind of international terrorist threat with close links to Pakistan. In 1988, amid growing public dissatisfaction and an adverse political climate, the Kashmir Valley saw terrorist explosions followed by an increase in rioting and disturbances the next year. Pakistani assets—funds, arms and trained terrorists—filtered into the Kashmir Valley. Pakistan's involvement in these efforts was not new: various forms of covert activity had been employed since 1947. But the beginnings of a sub-conventional war under the cover of Pakistan's nuclear weapons marked a distinctly new phase.[16] In August, India reinforced its military presence in Jammu and Kashmir and in Punjab. In December 1989, within days of the swearing in of the new government of V.P. Singh, the daughter of India's home minister, Mufti Mohammed Sayeed, was kidnapped. Five militants were released in exchange, and this 'opened the floodgates of insurgency' in the words of one senior Indian intelligence official.[17] In December 1989, Pakistan conducted a major military exercise near the border with India. After

January 1990, assassinations, threats, and overall violence in Kashmir resulted in the fleeing of some 3,00,000 Hindus—Kashmiri Pandits—from the Valley. That month, Pakistan's foreign minister, Lieutenant General Yaqub Khan, delivered an intimidating message to his Indian counterpart, implying the possibility of war. In March, Pakistan's prime minister, Benazir Bhutto, promised a '1000-year war' for Kashmir.[18]

An attempt by both New Delhi and Islamabad to arrest the slide in relations in late 1991 and 1992 proved unsuccessful. In December 1992, the demolition of the Babri Masjid mosque in Ayodhya saw reprisals in Pakistan, including the destruction of over 120 temples, as well as churches and gurdwaras.[19] After a series of bomb blasts in Mumbai in March 1993, its planners—including Dawood Ibrahim, the leader of organized crime syndicate D-Company—were found to have sought sanctuary in Karachi, and Pakistan's Inter-Services Intelligence (ISI) was assessed to have had a role in planning and executing the attacks. In October, terrorists stormed the sacred Hazratbal Mosque in Srinagar resulting in a siege by Indian forces, one that was eventually resolved peacefully.[20] But from this point onwards, the Kashmir dispute and Pakistan-supported infiltration and terrorism began to dominate the India–Pakistan agenda.

The BJP emerged as the largest party in the 1996 elections. But after its leader Atal Bihari Vajpayee lost a vote of no confidence in Parliament, the coalition governments of prime ministers H.D. Deve Gowda and I.K. Gujral between 1996 and 1998 proved short-lived. This period was notable for one development: the so-called Gujral Doctrine. Gujral—like Rao and Vajpayee—had previously served as external affairs minister and had occasionally clashed with his colleagues for what were seen as 'dovish' views, particularly on Pakistan. As part of Deve Gowda's cabinet, he outlined a series of five principles for his government's neighbourhood policy that he would continue to espouse as prime minister. These included non-reciprocity, a shared commitment in South Asia not to allow territory to be used against others' interests, non-interference, mutual respect for territorial integrity and sovereignty, and the peaceful bilateral settlement of disputes. These principles did resonate positively with Bangladesh, with which India had had more difficult relations since 1977 and enabled some repair in ties. Certain elements of the Gujral Doctrine also found favour with subsequent governments. However, the Gujral Doctrine was also widely criticized in India for being unrealistic and ignoring security concerns and differences between India and its neighbours, particularly Pakistan.[21]

Shakti and Shanti: The Nuclear Tests and Their Aftermath, 1998–2005

Immediately after returning to power at the head of a coalition government following the 1998 General Elections, Vajpayee gave the order to test nuclear weapons. The tests conducted between 11 May and 13 May 1998 became known as Pokhran-II after the test site (Pokhran-I being the peaceful nuclear explosion of 1974). The immediate political implications were sharp and negative. On 4 June, the foreign ministers of the five permanent members of the UN Security Council— the United States, China, Russia, France and the United Kingdom, all nuclear weapon states under the NPT—issued a strong statement calling for the prevention of an arms race in South Asia, strengthening non-proliferation, and dispute resolution between India and Pakistan. This was supplemented by the 6 June UN Security Council Resolution 1172 that was even harsher. US sanctions included suspending defence sales, denying government credit and loans, prohibiting loans from international financial institutions, a hold on loan guarantees, a denial or delay of visas for Indian scientists, and the suspension of aid, with the exception of food and humanitarian assistance. As spelled out by the United States, the criteria for lifting sanctions were five-fold: India should sign the Comprehensive Test Ban Treaty (CTBT), freeze fissile material production and work towards a permanent ban, limit its ballistic missile development, align export controls with international standards, and resume dialogue with Pakistan on the causes of tension, including Kashmir.[22] From New Delhi's point of view, these were completely unacceptable demands.

But India managed a careful counter-offensive. Led by Vajpayee and Jaswant Singh (who transitioned from Deputy Chairman of the Planning Commission to External Affairs Minister), India banked on the fact that access to its large market would get the US Congress and European governments to advocate for a swift relaxation of sanctions. While engaging in a dialogue with the United States and other countries, India played for time, and its gamble paid off. Within six months, the US Congress approved a legislative amendment to allow the president to waive some sanctions, and by early 1999, the Europeans—led by France and Italy—were suggesting to Washington that the threshold for lifting sanctions should be reduced. The rejection of the CTBT by the US Senate forced Clinton to drop his hard-line position, and in October 1999, he spoke to Vajpayee about the possibility of visiting India. By the end of the month, Clinton waived most of the remaining sanctions on India, setting the stage for his ground-breaking visit to India in March 2000.[23]

India's relations with the European powers and Russia, who were already more sympathetic to New Delhi's position on nuclear matters, rebounded quickly. Japan—which had taken a much tougher line on India's nuclear tests as the only victim of nuclear bombings—also began to normalize relations with the visit to India of Prime Minister Yoshiro Mori in August 2000 and the announcement of an India–Japan 'Global Partnership'.[24] Another visitor to India in July that year was Australian Prime Minister John Howard. In hindsight, the year 2000 marked the beginning of efforts to resurrect relations between India and its future Quad partners: the United States, Japan and Australia.

The nuclear diplomacy that followed the 1998 tests was intertwined with the growing profile of the Indian economy. By the late 1990s, the initial liberalization efforts after 1991 were starting to have an effect. India's private sector was beginning to thrive, foreign investment began to pick up, and certain sectors saw more gradual reform over the course of the 1990s and early 2000s. For example, in civil aviation, initially only private Indian-owned 'air-taxis' were allowed, and then foreign investment by non-aviation businesses in domestic airlines, before international routes were opened to private airlines. Competition eventually proliferated, prices came down, and quality improved without the shock privatization of state-owned enterprises and large-scale job losses. Such incrementalism often proved more politically palatable than 'big bang' reforms.[25]

Perhaps the most far-reaching set of economic developments in the 1990s resulted from a combination of deliberate policy changes, prior conditions and plain luck. In 1985, the US-based advanced electronics company Texas Instruments (TI) established a research and development facility in Bangalore but struggled with government clearances and regulation. In 1991, partly as a response to TI's experience, the Ministry of Communications and Information Technology established Software Technology Parks of India (STPI), which was meant to facilitate single window application clearances from only one government entity, allow for 100 per cent foreign equity investment in software, provide tax incentives, and ensure dedicated high-speed data connectivity infrastructure. India already had a large number of skilled English-speaking engineers, many trained at the Indian Institutes of Technology (IIT) and other such institutions. In the late 1990s, concerns over calendar dates in computer software—known as the Y2K problem or Millennium bug—created a massive global demand for low-cost computer engineers. Together, these conditions created the perfect cocktail for India's software boom.[26] 'Y2K has been a godsend,' the vice president of the tech firm Satyam declared to a foreign journalist in 1998.[27]

India's economic potential, which came to the fore after 1998, also had a positive effect on India's relations with China. Defence Minister George Fernandes had justified India's nuclear tests by declaring nuclear-armed China as India's 'potential threat No. 1'.[28] But in time, India and China attempted to cooperate both on economic and trade issues and on matters of global governance. Chinese Premier Zhu Rongji's 2002 visit to India attempted to highlight the economic complementarities of the two economies. 'You [Indians] are number one in terms of software, we [Chinese] are number one in terms of hardware,' Zhu said in Bangalore, 'Together we make the world's number one.'[29] For their part, Indian leaders recognized that China was a positive pace-setter and that its ascent gave other rising powers such as India the space to follow in its slipstream.

Repeated Betrayals: India and Pakistan, 1999–2003

Although the late 1990s and early 2000s—the period immediately following the nuclear tests—saw improved Indian relations with both Washington and Beijing, this time was marked by crises involving Pakistan. The first was the Kargil War of 1999. Vajpayee had made efforts to normalize relations with Pakistan after the tests, including a bus journey to Pakistan in 1999 and the Lahore Declaration. This historic agreement enabled a series of confidence building measures between the two countries for the new nuclear context and set a new baseline for relations after the Shimla Conference of 1972. But even as Vajpayee and Pakistani Prime Minister Nawaz Sharif were working to improve ties, Pakistan's Chief of Army Staff General Pervez Musharraf implemented a plan to infiltrate soldiers across the Line of Control (LoC) in the Kargil sector. This position gave Pakistani forces access to the heights over a major highway connecting the Kashmir Valley with Ladakh.[30]

India detected the Kargil intrusion in May 1999 and launched army and air force operations to evict the occupying forces. New Delhi opted to keep the conflict limited, particularly given the presence of nuclear weapons on both sides, and Indian pilots were instructed to attack Pakistani targets while remaining in Indian air space. Although Pakistan initially denied that its troops were involved, insisting that the infiltrators were irregulars, India publicly released a wiretapped conversation proving Musharraf and the Pakistan Army's complicity in the incursion.[31] In early July, Nawaz Sharif hurried to Washington where, to his surprise, he was harshly criticized by US President Bill Clinton. Pakistan realized that it did not have the support of the United States and international community, and by mid-July, India successfully managed to clear the infiltrators and return the LoC to the status quo ante.[32] For India, the Kargil War marked the first time that the United States had supported its position in a conflict with Pakistan, but it also exposed deep flaws in India's intelligence collection, analysis, and dissemination.

Another incident at the end of that year added further to India's woes. In December 1999, five Pakistan-based hijackers boarded an Indian Airlines flight in Kathmandu, IC-814, and diverted it first to Amritsar, then Lahore, then Dubai and finally Kandahar in Afghanistan, which was then under the control of the Taliban. One passenger was killed. Jaswant Singh and other Indian officials found themselves negotiating with the Taliban leadership: Mullah Omar, Mullah Akhtar Mansour and others. After eight days of negotiations, India managed to secure the release of the hostages in exchange for three terrorists in Indian custody: Masood Azhar, who later founded Jaish-e-Mohammed, Omar Saeed Sheikh, who would go on to murder *Wall Street Journal* reporter Daniel Pearl and Mushtaq Ahmad Zargar, who ran training camps in Pakistan. India assessed a close Pakistani role in supporting the hijackers and the Taliban during the hostage crisis, and subsequent developments appeared to corroborate this. In the 1990s, India had supported the Northern Alliance—a loose anti-Taliban coalition—and especially ethnic Tajik leader Ahmad Shah Massoud by extending arms and some aid. As India could not play a security role in Afghanistan on its own, it required cooperating with Iran and Russia, who harboured similar concerns about the Taliban in that period.[33]

In the summer of 2001, Indian and Pakistani leaders met in Agra for a historic two-day summit. The two sides had planned to discuss managing nuclear escalation, the Kashmir dispute, and terrorism. But talks broke down and no agreement was signed, in part due to a lack of trust in Pakistan's leader General Pervez Musharraf, weak commitments on cross-border infiltrations, and the political climate. The failure of the Agra Summit was overshadowed a few months later by the 11 September 2001 attacks in New York and Washington, DC—masterminded by Osama bin Laden and his organization al-Qaeda from a safe haven in Afghanistan—which suddenly made transnational terrorism centred in Afghanistan and Pakistan an international issue. India was supportive of the US invasion of Afghanistan to topple the Taliban government and eliminate al-Qaeda.

But as bin Laden was trapped in the border region of Tora Bora in late 2001, Pakistan-based militants attacked India once again. This time, their target was the Parliament in New Delhi. This incident, in which a high-profile hostage situation was narrowly averted, gave a pretext for Pakistan to withdraw its forces from the Afghan border and redeploy against India. Bin Laden managed to slip into Pakistan, where he would remain in hiding for the next decade. India, meanwhile, authorized a large-scale mobilization of forces against Pakistan, known as Operation Parakram. Tensions were further raised in May 2002, when the families of Indian soldiers—including ten children—were massacred by Pakistan-based militants at Kaluchak in Jammu and Kashmir. Although cross-border infiltrations from Pakistan continued, Musharraf informed US diplomats in June 2002 that they would decrease. India's military began to stand down from its mobilization in late 2002, due to the high costs, unwelcome international attention, and the presence of nuclear weapons on both sides, but having secured a notional commitment from Pakistan to stem cross-border terrorism. In November 2003, India and Pakistan agreed to a formal ceasefire along the International Border and Line of Control.[34]

Atomic Closure: Nuclear Diplomacy, 2004–2008

The post-Pokhran-II era witnessed a resolution of sorts: a civil nuclear agreement with the United States. Starting in the early 2000s, a small minority in the US government—concerned about the prospect of China's rise as a peer competitor to the United States—began to consider how best to facilitate India's rise as a balancer in Asia. India reciprocated: Vajpayee had called India and the United States 'natural allies' and after the 9/11 attacks discussions progressed on a variety of previously taboo topics such as ballistic missile defence cooperation and even the possibility of India sending peacekeepers to Iraq following the 2003 US invasion (a proposal that came remarkably close to fruition).[35] Even with a surprise change in government in India in 2004 from the BJP to a Congress-led United Progress Alliance (UPA) coalition, cooperation with the United States continued and accelerated with close coordination in relief efforts after the December 2004 Indian Ocean tsunami.[36] This early manifestation of cooperation among what became the Quad—India, Australia, Japan, and the United States— occurred despite strident opposition from India's communist parties, who were then supporting the Indian government.

The central hindrance in the burgeoning relationship between New Delhi and Washington was India's nuclear status, which ensured that it could not have access to a range of nuclear, defence, and dual-use technologies (which could serve both military and civilian purposes). The solution would be to create an exception for India in US law and at international export control entities such as the Nuclear Suppliers Group, while getting India to harmonize its export controls with international standards. In the aftermath of India's nuclear test, a proposal for a similar exception had been floated by the Indian government. Several other countries, notably France, had openly talked about such a possibility. But many in the US establishment were sceptical, believing that a civilian nuclear agreement with India would compromise Washington's relations with China and Pakistan, provoke an arms race, and set a negative precedent for international non-proliferation efforts by appearing to 'reward' India.[37]

The US efforts to increase India's access to sensitive technology were incremental between 2001 and 2004, embodied in a set of initiatives known as the Next Steps in Strategic Partnership (NSSP), whose objective was to gradually reduce export controls to India in critical areas, including defence, space, and nuclear technology.[38] During his second term beginning in 2004, President George W. Bush and his advisors opted for a more ambitious proposal that the Manmohan Singh government had also been advocating. This was the landmark India–US civilian nuclear agreement, announced on 18 July 2005 by the two leaders in Washington, DC. Essentially, this was an agreement to let India preserve its nuclear weapon arsenal while receiving access to US and international commerce, as well as technology for energy and other peaceful purposes. In exchange, India would have to separate its military and civilian nuclear programmes and place the latter under safeguards in line with standard international practice.[39] While the Clinton administration had demanded five criteria for the lifting of sanctions after 1998, Bush was asking for only one (harmonization of export controls) in exchange for international acceptance of India as a de facto nuclear weapon power. The next three years saw considerable attention and resources devoted to finalizing and implementing this agreement, which faced significant opposition in both countries. In India, the political opposition, some nuclear scientists, and the government's Communist supporters in Parliament resisted the deal. They argued that it would erode India's nuclear and strategic autonomy and bring India too close to the United States.

In March 2006, during Bush's visit to India, a separation plan that split India's civilian and weapons programmes was announced. Legislation to enable the agreement by the US Congress (what became known as the Hyde Act) was passed, after considerable lobbying by the Indian government, Indian–American community, and US big business. In July 2007, a so-called 123 Agreement that enabled nuclear trade between India and the United States was signed, but efforts then stalled for a year due to political wrangling between the Indian government and its Communist supporters in Parliament. The next year, after the Congress's loss in Uttar Pradesh state elections, alliances shifted, and the Congress-led government managed to secure the support of the Samajwadi Party (SP). In 2008, a vote of no confidence was held in the Indian Parliament and Manmohan Singh survived. Rather unusually, an Indian government had staked its very existence on a major foreign policy decision.[40] As George W. Bush's tenure was coming to an end in late 2008, events proceeded quickly. Within months, India signed a safeguards agreement with the International Atomic Energy Agency for its civilian programme. The culmination of this complex process was a meeting of the Nuclear Suppliers Group (NSG) in Vienna in September 2008. Bush and US Secretary of State Condoleezza Rice called up world leaders, while Indian diplomats went on a round-the-world blitz to secure support for an exception by the NSG for India. China remained the last country to hold out, but once isolated it reluctantly agreed to a waiver for India.[41] After thirty-four years, India had broken free from restraints on civilian nuclear and dual-use technology denials by the international community.

The direct material benefits of this hard-fought agreement were not immediately delivered. This was due to several factors, including the Fukushima nuclear accident in Japan (when an earthquake and tsunami caused a shutdown and radiation leak), the passage of nuclear liability legislation in India that placed a significant burden of risk on foreign investors and thus deterred investment, and financial woes among international leaders in the civilian nuclear industry. However, the indirect benefits were much more evident. India's nuclear status ceased to become an irritant in its relations with the United States and its European and Japanese allies. This allowed India's relations with these powers to assume a truly strategic dimension. Already, from 2005 onwards, India's defence cooperation with the United States had steadily improved. India acquired its first major American defence platforms in several generations, including heavy lift transport aircraft, maritime surveillance planes, helicopters, and artillery. Military exercises also increased in regularity and sophistication, particularly in the maritime realm. In 2007, India, the United States, Japan, Australia, and Singapore took part in a massive naval exercise (called Malabar) in the Bay of Bengal. This corresponded with a working level meeting that year between the foreign ministries of India, the United States, Japan, and Australia, which came to be known as the Quad.[42]

Closing Chapters: India's Neighbourhood, 2005–2008

One other outcome of the major developments between 1998 and 2008—the Kargil War, normalized economic relations with China, the civilian nuclear agreement with the United States, and the strong performance of the Indian economy—was the 'de-hyphenation' of India and Pakistan.[43] For much of independent India's history, the two countries were closely associated with each other in the minds of the international community. India's foreign relations—as with West Asia—were often guided by calculations of competing for influence with Pakistan. Policymakers in Washington, London, Moscow, Beijing, and other capitals had traditionally been sensitive of needs to 'balance' relations between New Delhi and Islamabad. But it was over the course of this period from the late-1990s to early-2000s that India managed to a large extent to dilute that association and be treated on its own merits. The rising profile of the Indian economy was the primary factor, but India's behaviour during crises with Pakistan, and Pakistan's continued support for international terrorism, contributed to these evolving perceptions.

Perhaps the last gasp of India–Pakistan hyphenation was the 26/11 terrorist attacks in Mumbai in November 2008. For the previous few years, as cross-border infiltration declined following the 2003 ceasefire, Pakistan-based terrorist groups had begun a new strategy of targeting urban centres in India, such as

Mumbai, Delhi, Bengaluru, and other cities across India. High-level talks between India and Pakistan continued despite these regular incidents of terrorism. The two countries continued to be engaged in a formal Composite Dialogue on a range of issues, while a backchannel between special representatives of the two leaders made progress towards a deal on Jammu and Kashmir. The process began unravelling as Pakistani President Musharraf faced popular protests in 2006 and 2007. Elections following the assassination of Benazir Bhutto in late 2007 resulted in a weak civilian government in Pakistan. But the November 2008 attacks in Mumbai—televised in real time around the world and targeting foreigners—brought an end to this phase of difficult India–Pakistan talks. The Composite Dialogue was suspended. While in previous years, major attacks had resulted in fears of external intervention by New Delhi, India in fact received greater international sympathy and New Delhi benefited from intelligence and investigative cooperation with Western agencies after 2008. India also initiated a major rehaul of its intelligence and counter-terrorism apparatus. US relations with Pakistan deteriorated after this time, culminating in the May 2011 raid on Abbottabad in which Osama bin Laden was killed. This incident also contributed to the popular international perception of Pakistan as a centre of international terrorism.[44]

Two additional regional developments of considerable significance occurred during this period. One concerned Nepal, which had become embroiled in a civil war between the government and Maoist forces. In February 2005, King Gyanendra—who had succeeded his brother in 2001 following the massacre of most of his family—seized absolute power and declared a state of emergency. Indian diplomats and intelligence

agencies brokered a deal between the seven major political
parties and the Maoists, with India serving as a guarantor of
a proposed accord between them. In 2006, a comprehensive
peace accord was signed between the political parties and the
Maoists, that ended the civil war. But the constitutional crisis
involving the king continued. Popular protests began, and
the next year, after receiving assurances, Gyanendra agreed
to withdraw from an executive role. India helped ensure the
army's backing for this transition. But while the king continued
to advocate for a constitutional monarchy, the Nepali public
had become more hostile to any form of monarchy. In 2008,
Nepal's monarchy came to an end after over two centuries and
the country became a republic.[45] But the consequences included
a left-wing turn in Nepal's national politics, with implications
for its foreign relations, including with India.

The other momentous regional development was the end
of the long-running Sri Lankan civil war. In December 2006,
the Sri Lankan army began a major offensive, sweeping into
the Eastern Province with the help of the defection of a former
LTTE commander. The next year, it began its campaign in
the Northern Province, resulting in the fall of Kilinochchi and
Jaffna. By April and May 2009, the last remnants of LTTE
support were holed up in a small coastal area along with
large numbers of displaced civilians. While the international
community pushed for a ceasefire, India coordinated closely
with the Sri Lankan government, advocating safe zones for
civilians and providing medical, infrastructural, and de-mining
assistance, while politically protecting President Mahinda
Rajapaksa and other Sri Lankan leaders from international
mediation and allegations of war crimes. The final assault in
mid-May resulted in a bloodbath that also saw the death of

the LTTE leadership, including Prabhakaran. The result was that after almost three decades, the Sri Lankan civil war came to a decisive end.[46] For India, this eliminated what was once a major national security threat. But, in time, it opened a new set of issues with its southern island neighbour.

The decade after India's 1998 nuclear tests was therefore eventful. This period featured multiple crises with Pakistan that contributed over time to a 'de-hyphenating' of relations, the resetting of India's ties with the United States and its allies coupled with the mainstreaming of India's nuclear programme, the fast growth in India's economy, and important developments in the Indian subcontinent. But this trajectory was not inevitable and a series of developments in and around 2008 presented bumps in the road.

5

2008–2024: Opportunities and China's Rise

Pauses and Drifts, 2008–2014

As in 1991, the year 2008 marked a set of major developments that altered India's strategic environment in some significant ways. But rather than serve as a catalyst for major geopolitical, economic and security developments, it initally led to a period of some stasis. In September 2008, India received a unanimous waiver from the Nuclear Suppliers Group, enabling civilian nuclear and dual use commerce with India. The meeting in Vienna was dramatic, with China proving the major hold-out, and significant Indian and American lobbying required to ensure consensus.[1]

But just two months later, a group of terrorists carried out a major attack in Mumbai, killing numerous civilians at luxury hotels, public places, and a Jewish centre. The perpetrators were Pakistanis who had arrived by boat across the Arabian

Sea. Although the United States immediately attempted to mediate and prevent an escalation of tensions, the nature of the attacks and clear Pakistani complicity had a number of effects, improving law enforcement and counter-terrorism cooperation with the United States and Israel, driving changes to India's intelligence and coastal security institutions, and adversely affecting Pakistan's international image.[2]

These events were, in time, overshadowed by another major development. In August and September of 2008, a bubbling mortgage debt crisis in the United States resulted in the failure of major financial institutions, including Bear Stearns and Lehman Brothers. The financial contagion spread to Europe, where many vulnerable economies in the Eurozone found themselves mired in debt. Political constraints within the Eurozone, which was a monetary union but not a fiscal union, resulted in fissures within the European Union. The financial crisis was compounded by a sharp rise in global energy prices, contributing to economic distress in the developed and developing worlds.[3] But the fact that China and India (at least until 2011) recovered well in the following years, while the United States and Europe saw an economic downturn, contributed to the pervasive notion that the West was in decline and Asia was ascendant.

The major geo-economic crisis of 2008 coincided with geopolitical moves. In August 2008, Beijing hosted the Summer Olympics, symbolically announcing its arrival as a world power. Shortly after, China surpassed Japan to become the world's second largest economy. In late 2008, Beijing launched its first naval flotilla to the Indian Ocean on the premise of counter-piracy operations. This marked the first major actions by the People's Liberation Army outside its claimed territory.

Developments were no less significant in Europe. Following a NATO Summit in which leaders opened the possibility of Georgia and Ukraine joining the alliance, Russia under Vladimir Putin intervened militarily in Georgia, after differences erupted over Russian-backed breakaway regions. The move also sent a signal to the West and further perpetuated frozen conflicts in the Russian periphery.[4]

That year also saw political developments of significance. In November 2008, Barack Obama was elected president in the United States. His historical victory was, in part, a repudiation of the foreign and economic policies of George W. Bush and (to a lesser degree) Bill Clinton. Early in his presidential tenure in 2009, Obama and his advisors expressed interest in reaching an accommodation with China (a so-called 'G2') and mediating between India and Pakistan on Jammu and Kashmir.[5] These naturally raised hackles in New Delhi.

After elections in early 2009, the new Congress-led United Progressive Alliance government (known as UPA-II) responded to these developments. The following few years were marked by less enthusiasm in building ties with the United States and Europe. Instead, New Delhi's focus on Asia increased and it made attempts to improve relations with China, including further agreements on border management in 2012 and 2013. Beginning in the early 2000s, trade relations between India and China grew from a negligible amount to $73 billion in 2012. People-to-people contacts also increased, and India and China identified aspects of a shared agenda.

During this period, New Delhi and Beijing held similar positions on climate agreements proposed by Europe and the United States, and they cooperated as part of the BASIC coalition (Brazil, South Africa, India and China). In negotiations with the United States, this group brokered a tentative outcome at the 2009 Copenhagen Climate Summit, one they believed protected the interests of developing economies. Similarly, both India and China lobbied for greater voting shares at international financial institutions, and eventually collaborated on the Asian Infrastructure Investment Bank (AIIB) and the BRICS New Development Bank (comprising Brazil, Russia, India, China and South Africa), where they could exert greater influence on institutional lending.[6] At the United Nations Security Council, the two countries shared similar concerns about humanitarian intervention, sovereignty, and the Responsibility to Protect (R2P) commitment.[7] These efforts, and particularly the involvement of India in BRICS, allowed India to exchange the rhetoric of developing world solidarity for that of an emerging major power.

During this period, India also increased formal trade and economic ties with Asian economies. After having entered into trade agreements with the likes of Sri Lanka, Thailand, and Singapore in the late 1990s, India finalized more ambitious trade deals with larger economic entities—the Association of Southeast Asian Nations (ASEAN), South Korea, and Japan—between 2009 and 2014. A trade agreement was also contemplated with China. But in time, India's trade deficits widened with these Asian economies and in some cases, as with Japan, the volumes of direct trade flattened. In India, this led to growing concerns that it had not benefited sufficiently from these trade agreements.[8]

The years between 2009 and 2014—marked by scepticism of closer relations with the United States and its European allies, closer coordination with China and BRICS, and a spirit of what some called 'Nonalignment 2.0'—slowed the pace of the major trends in India's foreign relations between 1991 and 2008.[9] Relations with the United States and Europe grew increasingly frustrated. The civil nuclear agreement was offset by India's nuclear liability law of 2010, as well as anti-nuclear sentiments following the Fukushima nuclear accident in Japan in 2011. A low point in India–US relations in late 2013 was a highly visible and public disagreement over the arrest of an Indian diplomat by US authorities in New York, although this incident may have been more a symptom than a cause of poor relations. With Europe, trade talks ground to a halt and political relations were infected by India's arrest of two Italian marines, who in 2012 killed Kerala fishermen in international waters mistaking them for pirates. India's ties with Denmark too were held back by a somewhat unusual extradition case, further contaminating India's relations with the European Union.[10]

New Delhi's relations with Beijing, despite some convergence on economic and global governance issues, also faced a number of frustrations. In some sense, Beijing brought its newfound confidence after the Olympics and global financial crisis to the border negotiations with India. China issued visas to individuals from Arunachal Pradesh that were stapled rather than affixed to their Indian passports to undermine India's claims to that state. It also began to issue more maps claiming Indian territory and suspended some military contacts with India's Northern Command. Despite boundary talks and agreements in 2012 and 2013, Chinese attempts at changing the facts on the ground at Depsang in 2013 led to their most high-profile border stand-off since Sumdorong Chu in the late 1980s and early 1990s. Furthermore, despite India's attempts at developing a broader consensus with China, it was hampered by economic factors. While India's initial economic recovery after the global financial crisis in 2009–2010 was strong, the years after 2011 saw a deceleration, compounded by budgets that deterred foreign investors. One bright spot remained India's relations with Japan, which saw steady progress on military and economic matters, including a visit by Prime Minister Shinzo Abe for Republic Day in 2014.

India's relations with Pakistan fared little better during this period. Efforts at reviving talks, including at a meeting of the Indian and Pakistani prime ministers at Sharm el-Sheikh in Egypt in 2009, were heavily criticized in India.[11] Although Prime Minister Manmohan Singh desired a visit to Pakistan, resistance within his own party prevented one from taking place. Despite attempts at insulating dialogue from terrorism, continuing terrorist attacks against civilian targets in India, domestic political tumult in Pakistan, and growing frustrations in New Delhi ensured that India–Pakistan relations remained in turmoil without resolution.[12]

Reengagement: India's Neighbourhood, 2014–2019

An opening was created once again with the election of Narendra Modi as India's prime minister on the back of a large parliamentary majority in 2014. Modi's first act was one of foreign policy—inviting the leaders of Pakistan, Afghanistan, Nepal, Bhutan, Bangladesh, Sri Lanka, the Maldives, and Mauritius to his oath-taking ceremony. This proved a way to start a dialogue with his counterpart in Pakistan, while also emphasizing the importance of the neighbourhood to his foreign relations. Modi's first bilateral overseas visits as prime minister were to Bhutan and Nepal. In Nepal's case, no Indian prime minister had visited in twelve years. The symbolism of these developments was meant to signal the renewed attention that India would give to its near abroad.[13]

In practice, despite the strong signal of intent, India's neighbourhood relations sometimes proved bumpy. Bhutan—a major recipient of Indian grant and military assistance—remained steadier, even as its polity and public space became increasingly democratized and its outlook more international. With Bangladesh, Modi had the political capital to implement what his predecessors could not: a major Land Boundary Agreement. With a historic visit in 2015, India and Bangladesh swapped islands of territory that had prevented their boundary from being settled. A year earlier, India and Bangladesh had resolved their maritime dispute, with India opting to abide by international arbitration in Bangladesh's favour.[14] These agreements paved the way for greater integration between India and Bangladesh, including road, rail, and electric grids. Issues of migration and border deaths, which had long dominated bilateral relations, also became easier to address. In the years that followed, Bangladesh became the largest recipient of Indian state-backed lending, often for infrastructure projects such as railways and power plants.

New Delhi's ties with Afghanistan also saw an upswing during this period. President Ashraf Ghani had begun his tenure by trying to broker an agreement with Pakistan and distancing himself from India. The breakdown of that arrangement led to a warmer relationship with New Delhi, including a Trilateral Transport Agreement involving India, Iran, and Afghanistan; an India–Afghanistan air freight corridor; and the conclusion of a number of major infrastructure projects, such as the Salma Dam which was renamed the Afghan–India Friendship Dam.[15]

Relations proved more challenging with Nepal, Sri Lanka, and the Maldives. With Nepal, Modi's successful visit and India's speedy delivery of relief assistance following a devastating 2015 earthquake were offset by political developments in Kathmandu. The promulgation of a new Constitution in Nepal was perceived by ethnic Madhesis to be discriminatory. The subsequent agitations along the India–Nepal border led to closures of commercial traffic, for which Nepal's leaders blamed India. Eventually, despite only marginal constitutional changes, the blockade ended, but the episode left some lasting bad blood between Kathmandu and New Delhi. Concerns about China's growing political and economic influence in Nepal contributed to differences, as did the resurrection by Nepal of smaller territorial disputes. It would take some years before India could restore positive relations with most major political stakeholders in Kathmandu and offer greater economic opportunities—particularly in purchases of hydroelectric energy—to Nepal.[16]

Sri Lanka also saw swings in relations with India tied to domestic politics and Colombo's relations with China. Under Mahinda Rajapaksa, Sri Lanka took on major loans for infrastructure development in and around Hambantota, including a port and an airport. The non-commercial nature of these loans and the control and management of these assets by Chinese entities sparked concerns in New Delhi. A tipping point was the appearance of a Chinese submarine in Colombo Port in 2014. Relations with India stabilized somewhat following a change in government the next year, although the levels of accumulated external debt proved hard for Colombo to manage.[17] The leasing of Hambantota Port to a Chinese entity for commercial use did little to ameliorate Indian worries. Although India continued to provide economic aid to Sri Lanka—including for housing and railways—concerns about

Chinese lending, infrastructure projects, and political influence translating into a security presence persisted.

India's relations with the Maldives proved equally volatile, with the consolidation of power by Abdulla Yameen and financial backing from China resulting in the imposition of an emergency in 2018. Eventually, elections and a peaceful transition of power led to in the reestablishment of cooperative relations between New Delhi and Male. But lingering anti-India sentiment was to translate into a growing 'India Out' movement in the years ahead.

Until only a few years earlier, New Delhi had believed that China's growing profile in the smaller South Asian countries was not necessarily detrimental to Indian interests. In practice, Beijing's relations with each country were different. With Sri Lanka and the Maldives, China's approach had been primarily economic, involving infrastructure lending, investment, and tourism, although it was no coincidence that these countries occupied important strategic locations in the Indian Ocean. With Bangladesh, China's PLA had an older relationship with the military dating to the 1970s and 1980s, when Dhaka had turned to Beijing for military equipment. With Nepal, economic and military relations were initially weaker, but China had stronger party-to-party relations with political stakeholders in Nepal's new republic. Yet India began to find that these ties were being leveraged by Beijing to promote anti-Indian propaganda, political influence, and security advantages.

Addressing these developments required a new approach. This included improving the diplomatic priority afforded India's neighbours, including regular visits and bilateral coordination mechanisms. Additionally, New Delhi began to place a much greater emphasis on connectivity, facilitating the exchange of trade, capital, people, and energy. The smaller South Asian countries began to receive more lines of credit from India's Export–Import Bank, including for major infrastructure and connectivity projects. Border checkpoints and customs were upgraded. Agreements for energy purchases and cross-border electric grids were established. And India became quicker at providing humanitarian assistance following tropical storms, rains, earthquakes, and other natural and manmade disasters.[18]

As part of its Neighbourhood First approach, India also made attempts at recasting regionalism, which had long been held hostage to India–Pakistan differences in the South Asian Association for Regional Cooperation (SAARC). At the 2014 SAARC Summit in Kathmandu, India went ahead with plans for a South Asian satellite involving all other countries after Pakistan blocked consensus. This 'SAARC-minus' approach reflected growing frustrations with Pakistan's intransigence. India also upgraded its profile, funding, and presence in the Bay of Bengal Initiative for Multi-Sectoral Technical and Economic Cooperation (BIMSTEC), a long moribund grouping involving South Asian countries minus Pakistan and Afghanistan, but also involving Myanmar and Thailand.[19] In some cases, India opted for smaller mini-lateral solutions, such as a motor vehicle agreement among the BBIN countries (Bhutan, Bangladesh, India and Nepal). After Bhutan expressed objections over the possibility of greater tourist and commercial traffic to their country, this proposal focused on improving overland connectivity between Nepal, India, and Bangladesh.

The Indian government also attempted to extend its neighbourhood—conceptually and practically—to the Indian Ocean. This broader conception incorporated Mauritius and, to a lesser extent, the Seychelles. As with other regional relationships, India increased the frequency of high-level visits and state-backed grants and loans, including for defence articles and infrastructure. It was in a speech in Mauritius that Modi outlined his vision for Security and Growth for All in the Region (SAGAR).[20] India also contributed to patrolling these countries' Exclusive Economic Zones and adding capacity, providing technical assistance, and building out infrastructure on strategic islands. In addition, New Delhi expanded national security adviser consultations with Indian Ocean island countries, and entered into agreements to improve their maritime domain awareness.

The one exception to the flurry of diplomacy, economic engagement, connectivity, and regional integration remained Pakistan. For the first two years of his government, Modi made repeated attempts at engagement with Islamabad, despite continuing Pakistani transgressions. His invitation to Nawaz Sharif to New Delhi in 2014 was met with intensified firing on the Line of Control and Pakistan's insistence on meeting with the Hurriyat, a coalition of Kashmiri separatists. Progress at a July 2015 summit in Ufa in Russia was eroded by Pakistan's cancellation of national security advisor talks. In December 2015, Modi's stopover visit in Lahore on a return to New Delhi from Kabul was followed immediately by a terrorist attack in Pathankot. India's controversial invitation to a Pakistani' Joint Investigative Team (JIT), in the hopes that it would enable reciprocal access to Pakistan, was followed by the detention, trial, and sentencing to death by Pakistan of a former Indian naval officer Kulbhushan Jadhav as an alleged spy.[21]

Relations, already testy, went into deep freeze following the killing in Jammu and Kashmir of Hizbul Mujahideen commander Burhan Wani in July 2016, which triggered wider violence in the Kashmir Valley. Pakistan used these events to once again attempt to internationalize the dispute. Furthermore, a terrorist attack in Uri in September 2016 was followed a ground assault by India on terrorist targets across the Line of Control ('surgical strikes'). Economic relations also remained fraught, with the Pakistan Army preventing Nawaz Sharif from recognizing most favoured nation (MFN) status for India, and Pakistan undermining Afghan and Indian proposals for a collective transit trade agreement. Furthermore, Pakistan's army chief, General Qamar Javed Bajwa, urged that Sikh pilgrims be offered a special corridor to access Kartarpur in Pakistan, an attempt that India believed was intended to fan pro-Khalistan separatist sentiments.[22] Just before the 2019 General Elections, a major terrorist attack on Indian forces in Pulwama led to Indian Air Force strikes at a terrorist training facility in Balakot. The following day, a skirmish between the Indian and Pakistani air forces following retaliatory attempts by Pakistan led to the downing of an Indian aircraft and capture of its pilot, Abhinandan Varthaman. With tensions high, his swift release by Pakistan helped defuse the situation.[23] Despite India's strong focus on improving neighbourly relations between 2014 and 2019, Pakistan remained the outlier.

Rebalance: China, the US, and the Indo–Pacific, 2014–2019

As prime minister, Modi also found himself immediately embroiled in relations with great powers. In September 2014, just months after his inauguration, Modi invited China's paramount leader Xi Jinping to his home state of Gujarat. While the optics were positive, China's People's Liberation Army

(PLA) attempted an incursion around Chumar in Ladakh. While eventually defused, the timing of the PLA's actions was seen as a message to New Delhi and cast a pall upon the visit. Relations remained frosty over China's opposition to India's entry into the Nuclear Suppliers Group, its refusal to subject Pakistan-based terrorists to UN sanctions, and its advancement of the China-Pakistan Economic Corridor (CPEC) through Pakistan-occupied Kashmir. Furthermore, India boycotted the Belt and Road Forum in 2017, which was attended by many international delegates, including from Japan and the United States. Instead, India issued a statement arguing that infrastructure and connectivity financing should be transparent, financially and environmentally sustainable, beneficial to local communities, and respectful of recipient countries' sovereignty and territorial integrity.[24]

In June that year, Chinese and Indian forces entered into a standoff at Doklam, around the de facto border trijunction with Bhutan. China's road construction in territory disputed with Bhutan resulted in an intervention by Indian Army units. While China's media engaged in sabre-rattling and painted India as the aggressor, India argued that China had violated written agreements with Bhutan in 1988 and 1998 to maintain the status quo and a 2012 understanding with India to not unilaterally define tri-junctions with third countries. India had security commitments to Bhutan dating from the 1949 Bhutan India Treaty of Friendship, which had been updated in 2007. These included training and support for the Royal Bhutan Army.[25] India was also conscious that Chinese encroachment into Bhutanese territory would have potentially severe consequences for Indian security in the Siliguri Corridor in the south. Although the Doklam stand-off was resolved after a tense two months—just prior to a Party Congress in China and a BRICS Summit—it led to both China and India reinforcing their military positions in the vicinity. In contrast to prior border stand-offs in 2013 and 2014—in which India had angrily criticized Chinese provocations—the Doklam stand-off also gave a preview of China's rhetorical belligerence and war-mongering. Another effect was greater public debate in Bhutan about relations with India and China.[26]

After 2018, efforts were made at improving high-level engagement between New Delhi and Beijing. Modi and Xi took part in an 'informal summit' at Wuhan, and Modi reciprocated in 2019 by inviting Xi to Mamallapuram near Chennai. Yet, despite a rhetorical cooling of temperatures, neither side made significant progress or concessions to the other. The most significant material benefits were minor adjustments to trade in specific goods. Developments in 2019 and 2020 were to reveal the hollowness of some of these high-level diplomatic engagements.

Modi's early diplomatic frustrations with China contrasted with a warm visit to the United States almost immediately after Xi's 2014 visit to India, despite having previously had his visa denied by Washington as chief minister of Gujarat. In addition to being feted by the White House and State Department during his 2014 visit, Modi headlined a massive event for the diaspora at Madison Square Garden in New York City. Such diaspora engagements would become a hallmark of Modi's political and foreign policy outreach, with similar events later organized in London, Sydney, and Houston, among other places. Modi's visit also soon translated into a reciprocal one to India by US President Barack Obama. Not only did Obama become the first US president to visit India twice in his tenure, but he became the first American leader to be hosted for Republic Day. One of the outcomes was a Joint Strategic Vision for the Asia-Pacific and Indian Ocean Region, which presaged future cooperation between India and the United States in the Indo–Pacific.[27] Another significant development involved India becoming a Major Defense Partner of the United States, a status that granted it many of the benefits of US treaty allies, such as access to advanced defence technologies, but without any obligations such as a mutual defence treaty, combined commands, or basing arrangements.

The notion of the Indo–Pacific had been in circulation for some time in academic circles. But it took off with its adoption by the Japanese, Australian, Indian, and—eventually—US governments.[28] Modi's first visit to the United States after Donald Trump's election as US president made some progress in bilateral cooperation in 2017. This contrasted with other world leaders' challenging meetings with Trump, who had campaigned on an anti-establishment platform. Nevertheless, under Trump, the United States began to officially articulate its Indo–Pacific strategy following Secretary of State Rex Tillerson's visit to India in September 2017 and the release of a National Security Strategy in December of that year.[29] Notionally, the Indo–Pacific recognized the Pacific and Indian Oceans as a strategic continuum, the importance of the maritime domain for security and commerce, and the role of India in the regional balance of power. It contrasted with the narrower vision for the Asia–Pacific that had been in vogue in the early 1990s, and which led to the exclusion of India and the Indian Ocean in forums such as the Asia Pacific Economic Cooperation (APEC) summit. India did not issue an official and public Indo–Pacific strategy, but Modi articulated India's approach to the region in a speech at the Shangri-la Dialogue in Singapore in 2018.[30]

Relations with the United States, Japan, and Australia all began to take off in this period. Bilateral and trilateral military exercises involving all three military services proliferated. India concluded a series of foundational agreements with the United States that enabled mutual logistics support, secure communications, and geospatial data sharing—agreements that the United States had long insisted were necessary for strong functional military-to-military interoperability. Political consultations also increased in frequency and seniority, with India eventually establishing '2+2' dialogues—involving the external affairs and defence ministers—with all three partner countries. Civilian nuclear agreements and defence logistics agreements were concluded. (India also concluded maritime logistics agreements with other Indo–Pacific countries such as France, Oman, and Singapore.) Eventually, relations between India, Japan, Australia, and the United States were elevated to the Quad among the foreign ministers and Australia was reincorporated into the Malabar naval exercises for the first time since 2007.[31]

In the Indian Ocean, India stepped up its resources and capabilities after 2017. These included policy changes in the Indian Navy to ensure year-round patrolling by surface vessels, submarines, or aircraft in seven identified zones around the Indian Ocean, from the Gulf of Aden to the Strait of Malacca. These mission-based deployments also ensured greater operational readiness, with vessels travelling armed and equipped. Greater resources were also placed in bilateral white shipping agreements, information fusion centres for maritime domain awareness, and bilateral liaison arrangements to share maritime security information with partner countries. Logistic agreements—

including those involving refuelling and replenishment—also proliferated between India and Indo–Pacific partners. These helped to increase the number of turnaround points used by the Indian Navy, improving its operational reach and effectiveness.

Although Indian Ocean and relations with Quad countries improved steadily, another aspect of India's Act East policy proved somewhat more frustrating: engagement with Southeast Asia. India had rhetorically elevated its 'Look East' Policy to 'Act East' in a bid to widen the agenda beyond economic relations, increase the scope to the broader Indo–Pacific, and add urgency to its agenda. As part of this effort, India hosted all ten leaders of the Association of Southeast Asian Nations (ASEAN) for Republic Day celebrations. India began to increase security cooperation with several southeast Asian states over the next decade, including training arrangements with Singapore, joint naval exercises with Vietnam and Thailand, and military exports to Myanmar and the Philippines. But while trade relations with Vietnam and Indonesia increased and financial and security cooperation with Singapore deepened, India's outreach to Southeast Asia proved difficult. In part, connectivity projects in Myanmar proved slow while trade negotiations marginalized Indian concerns. Ambivalence in some Southeast Asian countries about security cooperation, including in the South China Sea, impeded efforts. In time, efforts at engaging ASEAN as an institutional bloc gave way to more fruitful bilateral engagements with certain partners.

Experiments: The Economy and Institutions, 2014–2019

The Indian government under Modi attempted to reach out to some new constituencies between 2014 and 2019. Some of this represented an attempt to source investment and technology. For example, an agreement was brokered with Japan to finance and help establish India's first high speed rail line. On a visit to California, Modi also reached out to Silicon Valley, inviting major corporations to contribute to Indian digital infrastructure in various ways. New kinds of financial arrangements—whether tax agreements with Mauritius or a currency swap with Japan—were also finalized. However, perhaps the most transformative technological development in this period was indigenous: the continued adoption and development of India's biometric identification system, its links to mobile phones and bank accounts, and its employment for digital payments.[32] At the same time, the government expressed reluctance to enter into new trade agreements and none were concluded during Modi's first five-year term.

Internationally, India began reaching more to international blocs in various regions in an organized manner. In 2014 and 2016, India held summits with the leaders of Pacific Island countries. These fourteen countries had not previously received much attention in New Delhi, except for Fiji, which boasted a large Indian community. In 2015, India also hosted an Africa Summit, with over forty African leaders visiting India to bolster outreach to that continent. (The first such summit had been held in 2008, featuring fourteen African heads of state and government. A second followed in Addis Ababa in 2011.) In practice, while India's engagement with Africa increased, it was more focused on eastern and southern Africa, which benefited from historical ties, Indian communities, geographical proximity, and economic dynamism. In addition to the ASEAN Summit, India also engaged the five Central Asian Republics and later the Nordic countries at the leadership level. India–EU

Summits, which had been held with leaders of Brussels-based institutions since 2000, were complemented by a hybrid Leaders' Meeting in 2021. In each of these cases, discussions focused on what India could offer including in terms of investment, technology, or market access, and in turn how it could benefit from regional partnerships to source commodities, financing, and political goodwill.

Perhaps the most radical new relationships in this period were forged in West Asia (the Middle East). Hosting Abu Dhabi's crown prince (and later president of the United Arab Emirates) Sheikh Mohammed bin Zayed Al Nahyan (popularly referred to as MbZ), for Republic Day in 2017 contributed to major breakthroughs in India's relations with the United Arab Emirates and Gulf States. On regional issues, there was a meeting of the minds and shared concerns about radical Islamism. Outreach to the UAE also facilitated better relations with Saudi Arabia, which for many years had been a close partner of Pakistan. Regional developments following the 'Arab Spring' and the economic imperatives had gradually elevated India's importance for the Gulf Arab states. The relationship between India and the Gulf was no longer about just the diaspora and fossil fuel energy exports, but increasingly also about trade, investment, technology, security, and education.[33] The sizeable Indian diaspora also helped ensure strong cultural links, including the building and inauguration by Modi of a temple—BAPS Hindu Mandir—in Abu Dhabi in early 2024. In other regional developments, Modi also used his political capital to further elevate relations with Israel. In 2017, Modi became the first Indian prime minister to visit Israel, following reciprocal visits by the two countries' presidents.

A final major development of Modi's first term involved shifts on nuclear and climate diplomacy. As part of capitalizing on the India–US civilian nuclear agreement, India became a member of the Missile Technology Control Regime, the Wassenaar Arrangement (which governs the export conventional and dual-use weapons) and the Australia Group (which controls the spread of chemical and biological weapons). Membership at the Nuclear Suppliers Group continued to be blocked by China. In terms of climate negotiations, while India had earlier worked with the 'BASIC' coalition—including China, Brazil and South Africa—to negotiate with the West at the Copenhagen Climate Summit in 2009, a different outcome was managed at the Paris Climate Summit in late 2015. This time, India worked with hosts France not only to commit to a nationally determined contribution (NDC)—helping to ensure that the Summit was a success— but announced the co-development of an International Solar Alliance (ISA).[34] The ISA was somewhat new territory for Indian diplomacy, in that it involved the establishment of a treaty-based international organization. India's experience in this respect brought a new angle to its multilateral diplomacy and was replicated with the founding of a Coalition for Disaster Resilient Infrastructure (CDRI) and other issue-specific international institutions.

New Mandate: Domestic and Foreign Policy, 2019–2020

Modi and the BJP won re-election in 2019 with an even larger political mandate. For the first ten months, his government focused on major domestic objectives, some of which had been longstanding BJP positions. The first—in August 2019—involved nullifying Article 370 of the Constitution, a temporary provision that had granted Jammu and Kashmir special status. Furthermore, Jammu and Kashmir was made into a Union Territory and divided, with the region of Ladakh becoming autonomous. The move elicited criticism from Pakistan and, to a lesser degree, China, and India expended diplomatic capital to explain to the international community that this was a strictly domestic matter. (For its part, Pakistan had more than once changed the status of Pakistan-occupied Kashmir.) Some of the international criticism related less to India's actual action as the means it employed, such as the detention of Kashmiri political leaders, localized Internet cut offs, and the use of president's rule to bypass the assembly. Over the subsequent years, improvements in the Kashmir Valley such as local elections, higher tourism, and improved law and order were seen in New Delhi as a vindication of its move.

No sooner had the controversy over Article 370 died down than India passed a Citizenship Amendment Act. CAA did not affect existing citizens' status, but created a fast-track for religious minorities from Afghanistan, Pakistan, and Bangladesh. These minorities were specified, with Muslims noticeably excluded. Defenders saw this as rectifying some of the wrongs of Partition and the Nehru–Liaquat Pact. Critics argued that it would set a bad precedent and be used alongside a proposed National Register of Citizens to discriminate against Muslims.[35] CAA resulted in sizeable protests in India, which also invited international attention, but India took the view that other countries—including the United States and Europe—had regularly created selective pathways for citizenship.

Finally, the government passed Farm Laws intended to reduce corruption in agriculture by giving farmers more access to markets, and marginalizing middlemen. Ironically, such measures had long been requested by developed economies who believed India's agricultural policies were distortionary. Nonetheless, the Farm Laws generated protests led by some farmers, especially some communities in North India in and around Punjab and Haryana. It became an issue in already divisive local politics and also led to the mobilization of diaspora groups, including some Sikh communities in the United States, Canada, and the United Kingdom. Much of the international coverage mischaracterized both the laws and the nature of protests. But eventually, concerned about the national security implications, the government retracted the Farm Laws. Thus, between May 2019 and March 2020, India's focus was on domestic priorities that assumed an international dimension.

Three Crises: The Pandemic, China and Russia

The Covid-19 pandemic which began in Wuhan, China, in late 2019 but spread rapidly around the world over the next year, was a watershed moment in many respects. India was deemed particularly vulnerable, given its economy and public health infrastructure. India responded by quickly issuing a nation-wide lockdown, one which initially mitigated the spread of the disease, but which had major implications for the economy. Emergency efforts at manufacturing basic supplies at scale—including pharmaceuticals, medical devices, and personal protective equipment—underscored the vulnerability of supply chains and the need for domestic manufacturing capability. India also undertook a massive repatriation mission, bringing stranded Indians back home, an exercise that would prove useful in other humanitarian and disaster relief contingencies. Initially, India was deemed to have fared relatively well as many countries in Europe, West Asia, and the Americas fared poorly, with large numbers of infections and deaths. But this optimism proved premature. The rapid spread of the Delta variant of the pandemic in India in 2021 had devastating consequences. From previously providing pandemic supplies to the rest of the world, India focused on the emergency sourcing of oxygen concentrators and other supplies. Over the following years, the race to vaccinate and document vaccinations took precedence, as multiple waves of the pandemic continued to spread around the world.

The pandemic contributed, at least in part, to another shock in the spring of 2020. Forces of China's People's Liberation Army (PLA), initially in the process of conducting scheduled military exercises in Tibet, deployed rapidly at a number of forward points along the disputed Western Sector of the Line of Actual Control (LAC) in Ladakh. The four main friction points were (north to south) the Galwan Valley, Hot Springs, Gogra, and the north bank of Pangong Tso, with further disagreements in the far north at Depsang and in south-east Ladakh at Demchok.[36] In contrast to border stand-offs in 2013, 2014, and 2017, Chinese forces deployed in far larger numbers with full armaments (including armour and artillery) and logistical capabilities. Areas that were once effectively 'both men's land'—in that they had featured patrols by both Indian and Chinese forces—had now seen patrolling patterns disrupted. Instead, Chinese and Indian moves and countermoves led to close-up and sometimes overlapping deployments.

The reasons for China's actions along the LAC in Ladakh can only be speculated upon and may perhaps come to light in future years. The scale of deployment required the approval of China's Central Military Commission (CMC), chaired by paramount leader Xi Jinping. It is known that the PLA had conducted war games and exercises involving Ladakh since at least 2006.[37] In 2019, the PLA inducted new equipment designed for mountain warfare among units in its Western Command. Forestalling Indian infrastructure in the Shyok River Valley that would improve supply lines to India's northern-most military facility at Daulat Beg Oldi may have been another motive. There may also have been political reasons, with Xi believing that he would not get major concessions from India after the Wuhan and Mamallapuram summits. Finally, China's decision may have been opportunistic: it had already recovered from a first wave of the Covid-19 pandemic, while India—including the Indian Army—remained constrained by lockdowns and pandemic protocols.

Regardless of China's reasoning, its mobilization along the LAC had immediate effects on relations. India initiated a counter-deployment and engaged in negotiations. In June, the Indian belief that China was not following through on its commitment of disengagement in the Galwan Valley resulted in violence in which twenty Indian soldiers and several Chinese soldiers died. (China does not release information about combat deaths, but posthumously honoured four soldiers.)[38] The first violent deaths on the LAC in almost a half century proved a shocking development. India immediately retaliated with economic steps, banning certain Chinese technology, imposing greater scrutiny upon public procurement and Chinese investment, and eventually excluding Chinese companies from 5G telecommunication contracts.[39]

In late August 2020, the Indian Army conducted a military operation to seize heights on the southern bank of Pangong Tso. Conducted in stealth, the moves came as a surprise to

Chinese forces and led to perhaps the most tense moment in India–China relations since the 1960s. India leveraged its gains to broker a mutual disengagement at Pangong Tso in early 2021.[40] Over the next few years, similar agreements were negotiated by military commanders at the other major friction points.[41] But the large-scale armed deployment of Chinese and Indian forces in close proximity to one another and improved infrastructure fundamentally altered the LAC, making it much more volatile. Major conflict, which might previously have required days or weeks of preparation, could now break out instantly.

India was not alone in facing the brunt of Chinese assertiveness following the outbreak of the coronavirus pandemic, suggesting that the causes were not necessarily India-specific. In May 2020, China's National People's Congress advanced a national security law for Hong Kong with wide extra-territorial implications in a manner that undermined prior commitments to the region's autonomy and the notion of 'one country, two systems'. Australia's government and businesses suffered a major cyberattack attributed to China, as well as trade restrictions. Chinese territorial claims in Bhutan were advanced in areas that had not featured previously in negotiations. Chinese vessels intimidated Malaysian and Vietnamese shipping in the South China Sea, and Chinese military activity in Japan's exclusive economic zone and Taiwan's airspace saw an increase. Diplomatically, China's 'wolf warriors' openly criticized US, European, British, and Brazilian leaders. China also detained and charged two Canadians with espionage.[42]

The deterioration of China's relations with India— along with other Indo–Pacific countries—contributed to the elevation and restructuring of the Quad immediately following Joe Biden's assumption of the US presidency in January 2021.

The group comprising India, the United States, Japan, and Australia agreed to meet annually at the leadership level and established working groups on health, climate change, and critical and emerging technologies.[43] The logic was to deliver public goods to the Indo–Pacific in a coordinated manner without heightening security tensions. In time, the number of working groups and deliverables proliferated to include infrastructure, investment, scientific education, and maritime governance.[44] Meanwhile, the Malabar naval exercises among the Quad countries became more regular and sophisticated and various other mini-lateral and Quad-plus groupings proliferated on an issue-by-issue basis.

Bilateral relations between India and other Quad countries also expanded, especially with Australia after the re-election of Scott Morrison in 2019 and with Japan under Shinzo Abe and his successors. With the United States, India's cooperation extended to a special initiative on Critical and Emerging Technologies (iCET) led by the National Security Advisers, which advanced practical cooperation on defence, space, semiconductors, 5G telecommunications, and biotechnologies, among other areas.[45] During Modi's state visit to the United States in 2023, a number of major defence agreements were unveiled, along with India's joining US-led groupings on critical minerals and space cooperation.[46] Deteriorating ties with China also had important domestic defence implications in India: it helped accelerate procurement of critical kit, helped consolidate the position of the Chief of Defence Staff, and further strengthened the National Security Council Secretariat.

The third major geopolitical shock came over a year and a half after Galwan. Russia—after a major military build-up east of Ukraine and in Belarus in late 2021—initiated a 'special military operation' in late February 2022. Although it had intervened through proxies in the Donbass in eastern Ukraine to control large portions of Luhansk and Donetsk *oblasts*, and annexed Crimea in 2014, the 2022 invasion was on a massive scale. Russian forces entered from Belarus and attempted to seize Hostomel airport outside the Ukrainian capital Kyiv. It also made ingresses in eastern Ukraine and in the south from Crimea. While the northern axis to Kyiv failed to take the capital and the eastern axis made limited progress, Russia made surprising gains in the south to take over much of two additional oblasts. Moscow's objectives to decapitate the leadership in Kyiv and incorporate Ukraine into a larger Russian-led union failed. But after setbacks in the Kharkiv sector in late 2022, the front stabilized and Russia's military industrial superiority shifted leverage in its favour.

For India, its enduring friendly relations with Russia had gradually been becoming more complicated. Strategic Russian technologies such as defence, nuclear, and space remained very important for India, but had not always been accompanied by technology transfers. Still, Russia remained open to, for example, leasing nuclear-powered attack submarines to India, something that the United States and its allies were still unwilling to countenance. Although India was not a major importer of Russian oil and gas, it had investments in oil and coal infrastructures, especially in Russia's far east. But beyond these considerations, trade and people-to-people contacts between India and Russia had withered and active Indian efforts at broadening the commercial relationship proved frustrating. By contrast, New Delhi's ties with Europe had begun to take on greater priority, encompassing trade, technology, counterterrorism, labour mobility, and defence.

But the war in Ukraine had several immediate consequences. India had been one of only three foreign destinations for Putin since the outbreak of the pandemic (the other being to Geneva to meet US President Joe Biden and to Beijing just weeks before initiating the Ukraine War). Even in late 2021, he gave little hint of his intentions to New Delhi.[47] Once war broke out, India's immediate priority was the evacuation of over 20,000 Indian citizens from Ukraine, including numerous university students. The evacuations from Kharkhiv and Sumy proved particularly complicated, requiring delicate Indian negotiations with both Moscow and Kyiv.

India had four other immediate concerns. One, it had to secure a continuing supply of Russian defence equipment, maintenance, and spares, particularly given urgent requirements on the LAC with China. Two, India required energy as Europe and the United States placed sanctions on Russian oil and gas, and Europe began to source more from the Middle East, which had been India's biggest traditional supplier. Although Russian oil had traditionally been too expensive for India, it was now price competitive, and large-scale imports were required to stabilize domestic and international prices. A third concern was food security, particularly grain shipments from Ukraine and Russia, as well as fertilizers. Finally, India became increasingly worried about Russian overdependence on China having deleterious effects on its own security. On 4 February 2022, Putin had travelled to Beijing where he agreed to a 'no limits' friendship with 'no "forbidden" areas of cooperation'.[48] Given these various considerations, India initially abstained on UN resolutions condemning Russia and refused to openly criticize its actions. Over time, New Delhi offered mediation on certain specific matters, called for investigations of alleged war crimes in

Bucha, and provided some humanitarian assistance to Ukraine. At a meeting in Samarkand, Modi told Putin in person that: 'Now is not the time for war', perhaps the most public criticism a foreign leader had given in person to the Russian president.[49]

Taken together, the pandemic, the border clashes with China, and the Russian invasion of Ukraine had tremendous consequences for India's economic and commercial policies. National and economic security considerations meant that critical supply chain vulnerabilities could no longer be justified. These events proved an impetus for an Indian industrial policy focused on critical manufacturing and technologies. To this end, India unveiled subsidies in the form of production linked incentives (PLI) with early gains in electronics manufacturing. Special efforts were made in areas such as semiconductors and solar panel production.[50] In addition to subsidies, India fast tracked regulations and policies concerning artificial intelligence, space, and drones. It made further investments in research and development and coordinated supply chain approaches with friendly partner countries.

Trade policy also adjusted. India had previously decided not to join the Regional Comprehensive Economic Partnership (RCEP) with fifteen other countries led by ASEAN. A major concern was that the trade deficit with China would widen given lax rules of origin stipulations in the agreement. But India's trade policy then pivoted toward more complementary advanced economies and away from competing Asian manufacturing centres. After a decade without concluding trade agreements, India swiftly finalized deals with Mauritius, the United Arab Emirates, Australia, and an economic grouping of Norway, Switzerland, Iceland and Liechtenstein. Trade negotiations with the United Kingdom, Canada, and European Union were resuscitated, and deals began to be considered with countries such as Oman, Israel, and Bangladesh.

This new flurry of economic diplomacy was not restricted to trade agreements. India joined three out of four pillars of the US-led Indo–Pacific Economic Framework (IPEF) and concluded a supply chain agreement in that format.[51] Strategic and technological cooperation with the European Union was elevated with the creation of an India–EU Trade and Technology Council (TTC). India also began entering into a series of mobility agreements, including with some European countries, that would structure migration from India. Bilateral trade, defence, diplomatic, and technology relationships between India and European countries—including the Nordic, Baltic, Mediterranean, and Central and Eastern European countries—also saw an upswing. A new global rebalance was underway, encapsulated in initiatives such as the Quad, I2U2, IMEC, iCET with the United States, the TTC with the European Union, new security partnerships with countries like the Philippines and Armenia, infrastructure investments in the Indian Ocean and beyond, and technology tie-ups with South Korea and Taiwan. The post-pandemic world was beginning to have some major effects on India's domestic economy and international partnerships.

Regional Turmoil: South and West Asia, 2020–2023

If global developments were transformative after the outbreak of the Covid-19 pandemic, events in South and West Asia proved equally dramatic. In August 2021, the United States decided to withdraw its military from Afghanistan after two decades and began negotiations with the Taliban that included a release of prisoners. While the Afghan government under Ashraf Ghani had been expected to survive a US withdrawal, particularly given investments and years of US-sponsored training for the Afghan National Security Forces (ANSF), the Taliban swiftly swept into all major urban centres in the country. In the chaos that followed, foreigners and Afghans were evacuated out of Hamid Karzai International Airport in Kabul. India managed to extricate its diplomats and other citizens, but after decades of backing anti-Taliban forces, New Delhi found that its long-time adversary was now in complete control of the country.

India had been excluded from negotiations in the lead up to the US withdrawal. The United States needed Pakistan to bring the Taliban to the negotiating table and sidelined New Delhi. Russia also excluded or downplayed India's role in a parallel Moscow process. Yet while India initially appeared to be among countries most adversely affected by the Taliban's return, New Delhi soon engineered direct negotiations with the new leaders in Kabul. The return of tensions between Afghanistan and Pakistan may have helped. Without initially offering recognition to the Taliban government, India re-established a diplomatic mission in Kabul, provided grains and humanitarian relief, and continued its technical assistance as part of prior aid projects. At the same time, security concerns prevented India from reissuing visas to Afghans, including many students who had been attending institutions of higher education.

As with India's west, turmoil erupted to India's east in Myanmar following a coup by military leader Min Aung Hlaing against the elected government of Aung San Suu Kyi in 2021. For India, this revived memories of the late 1980s and early 1990s, when India initially backed the civilian leadership in that country. Instead, India initially attempted to not engage politically with the Myanmar junta, so as to avoid lending credence to the coup d'état, while continuing bureaucratic and military-to-military engagement. This was motivated by a few factors including continuing Indian assistance projects and vaccine aid, managing the long land border, and stemming infiltration and the spread of the Covid-19 pandemic. Another implicit consideration was not ceding space to China, which had long benefited from Myanmar's international isolation. India's provision of a second-hand Russian submarine to Myanmar represented a new form of engagement with the country.

A crisis—in this case an economic one—also broke out in Sri Lanka, where debt levels proved unsustainable following a decline in tourism as a result of the pandemic. Although Sri Lanka had earlier turned to China for loans, the severity of the crisis resulted in a suspension of imports, fuel shortages ,and an inability to pay government salaries. India stepped in with a sizeable financial package, worth over $4 billion.[52] For India, a bilateral financial assistance package of this scale was unprecedented. As part of ensuring a positive outcome, India voluntarily committed to standards established by the Paris Club, a grouping of creditors of which India is not a member.

Developments proved no less stable in West Asia. India had been steadily improving ties with the Gulf Arab states—led by the UAE and Saudi Arabia—as well as Israel. Relations with Qatar and Turkey remained more difficult and while ties with Iran often lacked substance in terms of trade, energy, or diaspora, it retained utility for connectivity, counterterrorism, and Afghanistan-related contingencies. The Abraham Accords—brokered by the Trump Administration in the United States—fully normalized Israel's relations with several Arab countries, including the UAE,

Bahrain, and Morocco. More quietly, Saudi Arabia and Israel began to cooperate. For India, this represented an opportunity of working with some of its closest regional partners on a shared agenda. It was in this backdrop that India, Israel, the UAE, and the United States established a grouping called I2U2 to deepen economic cooperation.[53]

A more dramatic consolidation of these trends revealed itself at the G20 Summit in New Delhi in September 2023. The United States, India, UAE, Saudi Arabia, and European participants agreed to an India–Middle East–Europe Corridor (IMEC). IMEC would connect India to the Gulf, Israel, and Europe through port, railways, and other infrastructure, but was subject to Saudi Arabia's normalization of ties with Israel.[54] But this heady development was overtaken by the attack on 7 October 2023 by Hamas forces in Gaza against Israeli civilian targets. The attacks, and subsequent Gaza war, put India in a predicament. New Delhi initially stood firm with Israel against terrorism and on the question of the release of Israeli hostages in Hamas custody. At the same time, it called for humanitarian corridors, provided some medical provisions to Gaza via Egypt, and reinforced the necessity of a 'two state solution'. While not derailing India's long-term plans for regional integration with the Gulf and Israel, the Gaza War proved a complicating factor.

Vasudhaiva Kutumbakam: G20 and the Global South, 2022–2023

Another major development of the post-Covid period involved a reengagement with the Global South. The idea of the Global South had been popular in historical and developmental circles but not in international relations. But a number of common agenda points began to make themselves felt. The countries of the Global South—despite their many differences—shared colonial histories and belated development trajectories, which together contributed to their marginalization at institutions of global governance. Their economic distress, as a consequence of the coronavirus pandemic, resulted in greater calls for debt sustainability and better representation at international financial institutions. Inadequate climate financing for vulnerable developing countries also led to greater advocacy for climate justice and action. The Russian invasion of Ukraine—coupled with Western sanctions—resulted in more vociferous demands for energy, food, and health security. India shared many similar concerns and saw an opportunity to better position itself as a leader in the Global South.[55]

In part, India sought to elevate its engagement with the Global South through regional summits (as with Africa, the Pacific Island states, ASEAN, or Central Asian Republics). It also opened up new diplomatic missions, including in Africa and Latin America. But concrete contributions often involved India's burgeoning foreign assistance program. Although modest relative to Western donors, India's support for projects in over seventy countries was used to strategically increase goodwill, improve market access, and provide public goods. India's assistance also extended to humanitarian assistance and disaster relief and expanded training programmes, often focused on developing economies.[56] A particular effort that helped to extend Indian goodwill in the Global South involved the Vaccine Maitri initiative, through which India supplied over 300 million vaccines to over 100 countries during the Covid-19 pandemic, a combination of grants, commercial sales and contributions to the global COVAX initiative.

A major opportunity for India to elevate the Global South's agenda occurred during its presidency of the G20 in 2022–2023. In January 2023, India hosted a 'Voice of Global South' virtual summit, featuring leaders from 125 non-G20 countries, to solicit their inputs on global affairs. For India, the G20 process proved a grand affair, with India hosting preparatory and official working group meetings in some 60 cities across the country.

The Summit itself in September 2023 was the most high-profile international conference in independent India's history, with most major world leaders—barring Xi Jinping of China and Vladimir Putin of Russia—in attendance. In addressing the G20, Modi evoked the Sanskrit phrase 'Vasudhaiva Kutumbakam (the world is a family)' as a fundamental principle of India's global conduct.[57] Substantively, India managed to broker a consensus document despite severe differences over Ukraine.[58] But of longer-term consequence, India's presidency included the addition of the African Union to the G20 group and commitments to focus international financial institutions on climate action. Another development of some consequence involved efforts at popularizing India's experience with digital public infrastructure (DPI). Over sixty countries had expressed some interest in India's model of digital identification and payments and the G20 Summit proved an opportunity to highlight these developments. The G20 Summit of 2023 served an important symbolic and political purpose. But perhaps more importantly, it had some consequences for the representation of the Global South, the revitalizing of multilateral climate finance, the internationalization of digital public infrastructure, the restructuring of West Asia, and India's ability to negotiate consensus on matters of war and peace.

Conclusion: Major Transformations after 1991

It is tempting to find continuity in any historical overview of India's relations with the world. Indeed, there are some consistent themes, whether the role of trade and technology, the quest for a balance of power in Asia, and regional rivalries. But equally, India's global interactions have seen some major transformations, and these are important to recognize. A number of important trends after 1991—with periods of acceleration in 1998–2008 and 2014–2024—are worth highlighting.

One, over the past three decades, India has emerged from relative economic isolationism and is now increasingly integrated with the global economy. The Indian economy is significantly larger than it ever was and, in addition, more robust and diversified. Its gross exports, foreign exchange reserves, and overall macroeconomic health, are in far stronger shape than in the past and absolute poverty has declined. The trappings and behaviour of the fifth- (and probably soon, third-) largest economy are radically different from a country that was once dependent upon food aid or concerned about a balance of payments crisis.[59] Rather than protectionism, India now strives for economic competitiveness in a globalized world, requiring the integration of its foreign policy with its defence, trade, industrial, financial, education, technology, energy, health and agricultural policies. Barring China and Pakistan, India's relations with most other countries are primarily collaborative, rather than competitive. This creates unprecedented opportunities for India.

Two, in contrast to a period where it was preoccupied with a narrower South Asian neighbourhood, India has begun to play an active role in a wider Indo–Pacific region, with implications for the Asian balance of power. In part, this is a natural consequence of the de-hyphenation with Pakistan, which until at least 2008 remained a limiting factor. There are antecedents in the pre-Independence and immediate post-Independence period. Whether in terms of trade, security, or institutions, India can now play a larger role in a broader region.

Three, India has established better relations with the United States and its allies (including in Europe, Japan, Australia, and Israel) than at any point in its history. These relations are broader than some of its old partnerships, as with the Soviet Union during the height of the Cold War, and now extend to military cooperation, business, education and technology. With the Anglophone world, in particular, India enjoys stronger relations by virtue of its large and growing diaspora. These improved relationships are also closely linked to another transformative change: India having achieved both nuclear security and legitimacy. The nuclear deterrent was an important objective in an era when India was much more insecure. Demonstrating a nuclear capability, followed by negotiations to not be commercially or technologically disadvantaged for its nuclear arsenal, removes major shackles on India's economic and technological development.

Four, India has exchanged the rhetoric of third-worldism for that of a rising power. Again, this has antecedents in the immediate post-Independence period but carries more credibility with the stronger performance of the Indian economy. In that sense, India's recent emphasis on the Global South is very different from that of Non-Alignment, in that it is much more an aspect of great power competition than a recusal from it. An India that had less hesitation in associating first with the BRICS (until that group's limitations became apparent), followed by the Quad, is indicative of this repositioning.

Finally, for all its progress, India faces a major strategic challenge in China. The People's Republic of China is a single-party state that continues to claim large tracts of Indian territory and whose economy has risen faster than India's since the 1980s. China's rise initially presented economic and institutional opportunities for India. But recent developments— on the disputed border, in the Indian Ocean region, on trade and economic issues, and at international institutions—have made clear the degree to which Beijing's policies offer major impediments to India's rise, its near abroad, its maritime security, its regional aspirations, and its global objectives.

While the major transformations in India's foreign policy between 1991 and the present have often been structural and cumulative, the historical record also shows that leadership and decision-making mattered. Taken together, the changes in India's position and international circumstances have been significant. Sufficient time has elapsed since 1991 to ensure that a realignment in India's approach to global affairs is readily apparent.

Part II

Strategy | राष्ट्रीय नीति

6

Atmanirbhar Bharat: Security and Prosperity

Understanding the Present

India is entering a decisive period as it defines its role in the world. Its developmental trajectory is positive. Its economy has more than tripled as a share of the world since 1992. Its demographics are entering a period of peak workforce, even as total fertility has begun to fall below replacement levels. The geopolitical environment, while fluid, is far more favourable than in the past, when India had to deal with decolonization and Partition, aid dependence, separatist movements, and major wars without the benefits of food security, a global market and a nuclear deterrent. Diplomatically, India now has a wide variety of partners—including among major powers such as the United States, Europe, Russia, and Japan and countries in the Global South—with which it enjoys largely cooperative and constructive partnerships.

189

But the world is also changing. The United States remains a major superpower, but there is a growing domestic political consensus in that country around resetting its international obligations and revisiting the terms of globalization. China has risen as a major power in its own right. Although it confronts its fair share of economic and political difficulties, it is focused on displacing the United States as a regional and global power. A long-term great power competition—akin to the Cold War but in a more globalized context—is already underway. Other major economies—including the European Union, United Kingdom, and Japan—are struggling with the challenges of demographics, immigration, slower growth, unsustainable welfare, and military dependence on the United States. Russia is preoccupied with war and has deepened its dependence on China. The rise of developing economies in Asia has created new opportunities but also direct economic competitors for India. India's neighbours are in many respects democratizing and engaging new partners. West Asia (the Middle East) is reshaping itself, with greater normalization between the Gulf Arab states and Israel coexisting with continuing tensions involving Iran and the Palestinian question. Africa and Latin America are also transforming in a variety of ways, with individual countries and sub-regions moving in different directions and at varying speeds.

Under these conditions, India faces several strategic challenges. One, it must continue to prosper, secure itself, and modernize at a time when the international system, globalization, and global governance are undergoing significant changes. The idea that unfettered globalization renders benefits without risks can no longer be assumed. This will require a different approach to accelerating India's development. Two, India has a continuing need to ensure a peaceful and well-integrated neighbourhood in the face of its smaller neighbours' polarized domestic politics and the presence of more international partners. Three, India faces a formidable challenge from an assertive People's Republic of China, one that extends from their disputed boundary to regional competition, from economic and technological difficulties to institutional differences. Managing China's rise and assertiveness will require a judicious use and application of resources on India's part to maintain a balance of power in Asia, in the Indo–Pacific, and in world affairs. Four, India has long faced a persistent challenge from a revisionist Pakistan, which has used its military, intelligence, and terrorist resources to undermine Indian interests under a nuclear umbrella. While the Pakistan challenge has in some ways become easier to manage for India, as the power disparity has shifted in India's favour, it has not disappeared entirely. Fifth, although there are many non-traditional and transnational challenges to India's welfare— including climate change, food and energy security, pandemics, terrorism, inflation, trade disputes and the proliferation of weapons of mass destruction—India's ability to respond to them is often inhibited by strong vested interests at multilateral organizations that manage the international order. This extends to both competitors and, on some issues, even partners.

India will therefore need to accelerate its development trajectory and strengthen its security, compete more effectively in its immediate and broader region, and shape international institutions and norms in its favour on matters concerning war and peace, economic exchange, and governance the global commons. Addressing these challenges will require taking diverse steps over the coming years and decades. But, to start, foreign policy will have to begin at home.

Background: The Limits of Globalization

The objective of accelerating India's domestic development to increase the fundamentals of its power can be premised on four propositions. One, India's political and economic circumstances are unique. Two, India derives considerable advantages from international partnerships. Three, liberalization alone will not address all of India's development challenges. Four, India must invest in the foundations of national power: security and prosperity. Each of these deserves a more detailed explanation.

India's political and economic circumstances are unique. At Independence, and for decades that followed, India was incredibly large, poor, diverse, and democratic. Taken together, these qualities presented it with conditions that almost no other country had to confront as it sought to modernize and accelerate its domestic development. For all its gains in the decades since, India is still a developing country. Absolute poverty may have sharply declined, but Indian policymakers still place priority on development needs and objectives, including affordable health and housing solutions, food and energy security, basic education, the efficient delivery of public goods, and employment for a large workforce transitioning out of agriculture. Meeting these objectives remains crucially important and still heavily informs India's policies concerning international trade, its desire to attract foreign investment, its net outward migration, and its approaches to climate change and the energy transition.

At the same time, in the aggregate and by virtue of its large population, India has potential and capabilities that few other countries can match. It enjoys the technical and scientific capabilities that enable a nuclear deterrent and a world-class space programme. It can offer massive scale, whether the size of its military, the growth of its civil aviation sector, its digital ecosystem, or its energy and agricultural production. India is home to more billionaires than any other economy after the United States and China. While on average Indian incomes, health metrics, or educational standards may not yet be at global standards, it has long offered pockets of world class excellence in terms of business, medicine, scientific research, manufacturing, innovation, and scholarship. It will soon be the world's third-largest economy, although well behind the United States and China for the foreseeable future. Narrowing that gap will present a medium-term challenge. But the paradox of Indian power is that it is simultaneously both a developing economy and enjoys many of the advantages of a major power. These features are not contradictory—and may even be used to complement one another.

India derives considerable benefits from international partnerships. The world presents India with many opportunities. One, India can attract foreign financing, including state-backed, multilateral, and private investment and loans. Investment can be both direct (e.g. foreign direct investment or FDI) or indirect (e.g. portfolio) investment. Two, India can gain knowledge and technology through research and development collaboration, educational exchanges, training programmes, and joint ventures. Three, it can learn best practices from other countries and systems. Four, India can source critical commodities—such as energy, agricultural products, or other raw materials—that it cannot produce domestically. Having privileged diplomatic relations with source countries is especially helpful when those commodities are highly sought after. Five, it can gain access to export markets, which would both create jobs at home and help lower costs for domestic consumers. Beyond exports, the competitiveness of Indian businesses in foreign environments strengthens the corporate sector at home. Six, India derives earnings and other advantages from foreign labour markets, including in terms of remittances and skill development. For all these reasons and more, foreign relations are intrinsically tied with India's domestic development.

Indeed, India already benefits from a bewildering array of international partners. The United States, European Union, Japan, United Kingdom, Gulf, and Singapore are important foreign investors in India. India sources energy from, among others, Iraq, Saudi Arabia, Russia, Qatar, Nigeria, the United States and UAE. It imports critical defence equipment from Russia, France, Israel, and the United States. A large number of Indian students receive their education at institutions in the United States, Canada, European Union, the Gulf, Australia ,and elsewhere. India's top export destinations include the United States, Gulf, European Union, China, Bangladesh, Singapore, and the United Kingdom. Strengthening and diversifying these partnerships will remain a crucial element of India's foreign relations, with direct implications for citizens at home.[1] Continued, sustained and productive diplomatic partnerships with advanced complementary economies—including, but not limited to, the United States, the European Union (and its member states), Japan, United Kingdom, Canada, Australia, the Gulf Cooperation Council, Russia, South Korea, Taiwan, Israel and Singapore—will remain a high priority for Indian diplomacy.

The world also presents India with risks and threats that must be mitigated, which is another reason for proactive international engagement. For example, other countries can offer sources of radicalization and safe havens for terrorists, hackers, and pirates. Competing economies often manufacture and export goods using unfair trade practices that undermine Indian industry and employment. As the Covid-19 pandemic showed, infectious diseases originating in other countries can easily spread to India. There is a temptation on the part of some Indian commentators to suggest that India should not distract itself with international affairs and focus only on its domestic economic and military transformation. But this view is not just simplistic, it is short-sighted, even dangerous. India—like almost every successful country in history—will have to proactively engage and manage its international environment if it is to accelerate its domestic transformation.

Liberalization alone will not address India's development challenges. From the outset, India experimented with various ways to increase its power and capabilities, with mixed success. Initially, this included sourcing economic and technical assistance, often in the form of aid, from the United States, Europe, and British Commonwealth, and subsequently from the Soviet Union, Warsaw Pact, and Japan. Although India grew faster after Independence than it had under colonial rule, state planning and nationalization efforts contributed to a relatively closed economy persisting until the 1990s. By then, it lagged many other Asian economies in its development. Beginning with liberalization measures in 1991, India leveraged a more open international economic system. Its trade volumes grew, its services sector prospered, its financial markets became more sophisticated, and Indian human capital strengthened from unprecedented education, health, and employment opportunities. Although India's economy has fared much better since the late 1990s, and it has grown on average much faster than the rest of the world, it has fallen behind China, a large neighbouring country that enjoyed similar per capita incomes as recently as the late 1980s.

Conventional thinking presumed that if only India liberalized more—further reducing tariffs, opening up its economy, and increasing the ease of doing business—it would grow faster. But this presumption began to run into some problems. The biggest was that not all markets were truly open in all sectors during the era of what some have called 'hyper-globalization', creating an uneven playing field. Many major economies guarded their agricultural sectors, which were politically sensitive and benefited from large state subsidies. Some advanced economies, such as the European Union, raised regulatory barriers and maintained hurdles for foreign businesses. But perhaps the most egregious was China, which as a non-market economy heavily subsidized industry, utilized systematic campaigns of corporate espionage, and blurred the lines between the state and private enterprise.[2] In time, China became the hub of a disproportionate amount of the world's manufacturing. Those economies that integrated with China's value chains prospered from this arrangement, as did major resource exporters. But despite ever increasing wages, China's market distortions, increased efficiencies enabled by technology, and the sunk costs of businesses helped ensure that manufacturing did not move to lower-wage economies such as India. While India could have certainly done more to liberalize and compete in an earlier era, at some point indiscriminately reducing trade and economic barriers would have rewarded non-market practices in China and further exacerbated structural imbalances in the global economy.[3]

India's persistent trade deficits in the 2000s were compounded by other factors. The global financial crisis of

2008–09, challenges in the Eurozone, Brexit, and Donald Trump's election in the United States further dented the neo-liberal consensus in the West. The coronavirus pandemic after 2019–20 exposed India's vulnerability to supply chain disruptions, including for basic medical supplies. Geopolitical tensions, particularly the India–China border clashes and the Russia–Ukraine war, exacerbated concerns about economic interdependence. India was affected—directly or indirectly—in terms of its defence imports, energy sources, and food security. The idea that further liberalization is the only way forward to accelerate India's development trajectory is now in doubt. India will continue to benefit from sourcing investment, technology, knowledge, and raw materials from the rest of the world, as well as continued access to overseas export and labour markets. But it will have to balance these considerations with other factors such as national security, economic security, international competitiveness, and domestic employment.

India must invest in security and prosperity. Any country, particularly in an era of intensifying global competition, must invest in the basic foundations and instruments of power. A major objective of foreign relations is to make yourself more secure and prosperous. From these bases, other kinds of power accrue including technological advancement, diplomatic weight, and strong cultural appeal or attraction ('soft power'). Of course, not all countries with considerable national power use that power wisely or effectively. Translating power into influence is ultimately a product of leadership, systems, institutions, and culture.

While the agenda of leveraging foreign relations for domestic development is broad, touching upon almost every aspect of public policy, two priorities stand out. The first involves national security. Defence and security remain the sole preserves of the government and in a difficult regional environment such as India's will always be afforded a priority in national budgetary allocations. India has a large standing army with expeditionary potential and battle experience, a potent air force, a blue water navy capable of operating in deep waters and the open seas, and a nuclear weapons capability. Few countries beyond the five permanent members of the UN Security Council (the United States, Russia, China, France, and the United Kingdom) can boast all these attributes. At the same time, India's military and national security apparatus needs to constantly upgrade its capabilities—whether planning and management, defence industrial production and technology, recruitment and training, posture and operations, or intelligence—to meet its emerging challenges. While India's ability to deal with non-state actors (such as terrorists, separatists, and pirates) and with Pakistan (a country that, despite its nuclear arsenal, suffers from resource disadvantages vis-à-vis India) may be difficult, they are more manageable. The challenge of China, which enjoys a significant resource and technological edge over India, presents a much more difficult proposition.

The second priority relates to India's economy. While the management of a large and diverse economy such as India's is a complex exercise, India's shortcomings are particularly acute on the industrial and technological sides, with implications for employment, education, infrastructure, health, agriculture, environmental, energy, and trade policy. India's developing economy is unusual in having been led by consumption and services rather than savings and manufacturing (as characterized the development of several other Asian economies). As agriculture becomes more productive, an insufficient industrial base has implications for employment and economic security. For the foreseeable future, Indian policymakers will be focused on boosting domestic manufacturing, including in critical and emerging technologies, while ensuring economic security and sustainable development. This will essentially require an industrial policy as a basis to address India's development challenges rather than simple liberalization. Instead of a rejection of globalization, a new Indian approach to the international economy should be seen as a part of globalization's great rebalance.

Priority 1. Improve Military Preparedness

India has the largest active-duty military in the world. In addition, it has sizeable reserves, large and numerous paramilitary forces under the home ministry, police forces, multiple intelligence agencies, and entities responsible for border management, coastal security, and cyber security. Together, these comprise its national security apparatus.[4] This large and varied defence and security infrastructure is necessary given India's numerous and diverse security challenges, which have ranged from terrorism and insurgencies to international peacekeeping and conventional conflict against other states. India's spending on defence has not been unusually high in recent years, remaining between 2.4 and 3 per cent of its gross domestic product since 1990.[5]

India has dealt with these diverse challenges, with some success but not without its fair share of difficulties. Domestic conflicts, including insurgencies, have seen a steady decline in recent years, including in Jammu and Kashmir, in North-East India, and against Naxalites in central India. Terrorist incidents have also fallen, at least against civilian populations in urban areas by cross-border terrorists. Most recent cross-border terrorist attacks—such as at Gurdaspur, Udhampur, Uri and Pulwama—have been against military, paramilitary, or police targets. A few high-profile incidents in recent years have served as periodic reminders of the resilience of domestic security threats. But the broader trends concerning domestic security remain mostly positive.[6]

The prospect of major conflict with either China or Pakistan has declined with the introduction of nuclear weapons. Although India and Pakistan fought three large-scale conventional wars between 1947 and 1971, the only major conflict since their 1998 nuclear tests was an important but limited war in Kargil in 1999. Nuclear deterrence improves with a 'triad', the ability to deploy nuclear weapons by land (missiles), air (aircraft), and sea (submarines), something India has been developing since demonstrating its nuclear capability.[7] Nonetheless, conventional deterrence remains a necessity in localized or limited contingencies. As the 'surgical strikes' across the Line of Control have indicated, limited Pakistan-related contingencies might still be required to deter terrorism and counter military adventurism. India may enjoy a resource and technological advantage against Pakistan, but that should not lead to complacency.

With China, India faces a much more daunting challenge, as the border stand-offs of 2013, 2014, 2017, and 2020 made clear. China has recently undergone significant military reforms within the People's Liberation Army (PLA), that have resulted in a smaller standing military force, upgraded equipment, and joint commands.[8] Its economic and technological edge, coupled with improved military infrastructure in Tibet and Xinjiang—

including new or improved airfields, helicopter landing pads, missile silos, and road and rail infrastructure—means that the PLA poses a serious challenge to India on the border. Moreover, China's aggressive intentions in the East China Sea, Taiwan Strait, and South China Sea, along with its growing presence in the Indian Ocean region, raise the prospect of a Chinese military challenge to India's south, north, east, and west.[9]

Addressing the China challenge—in addition to a variety of other continencies on land, at sea, in the air, and in space—necessitates several significant changes in India's defence structures, some of which are already underway. These include improvements to national security management and coordination; command, plans, and operational readiness; personnel (including recruitment and training); and procurement (including acquisitions and research and development). In all these areas, India faces a need to coordinate between the three military services, between the military and civilian bureaucrats in the Ministry of Defence, between the defence ministry and finance ministry (on budgetary matters), and between the defence ministry and external affairs ministry (on foreign procurement, military diplomacy, and overseas operations).[10] Over time—and considering also its growing security responsibilities in a broader region amid China's rise and the United States' resource constraints—India will have to increase its expeditionary capabilities, including its ability to conduct amphibious operations, air-to-air refueling, and special forces operations.

National security management has evolved since the creation of a Defence Committee of the Cabinet in 1947. After 1962, India had an Emergency Cabinet Committee which was bureaucratized into a Committee of Secretaries. In

1990, the government of V.P. Singh created the first National Security Council assisted by a Strategic Core Group of military, intelligence chiefs, and secretaries from relevant ministries. A permanent National Security Council was established only in April 1999 after India's nuclear tests, along with an office of the National Security Advisor to coordinate policy. In recent years, the National Security Council Secretariat has expanded to include designated coordinators for cyber security and maritime security. The Cabinet Committee on Security (CCS) remains the primary sanctioning body for defence procurement, law and order, and foreign policy while the national security advisor is the key official advising the prime minister on matters of national security and foreign policy. [11]

Strategic plans and operational readiness are the primary responsibility of the military services themselves. Until recently, the three services have operated relatively autonomously with service chiefs enjoying both staff and command functions. This sufficed in 1971 but was beginning to prove inadequate by the 1990s. For example, the Kargil War of 1999 revealed glaring gaps in communication and operational execution between the Army and Air Force. A series of government advisory committees have recommended a move to joint commands and the separation of staff and command functions. Although India did create a chief of defence staff (CDS) position and made it a secretary in a new Department of Military Affairs within the defence ministry, the move towards joint commands remains a work in progress.

Recruitment is another important matter and has implications for the defence budget. Although India has had a large standing army, pensions for former soldiers are beginning to consume greater portions of the defence budget.

To address this, the government proposed the Agnipath scheme involving shorter-term recruitment. The intention was in part to gradually reduce pensions, bring down the average age of enlisted soldiers, and free up budgetary space for military upgrades and modernization. The proposal proved controversial, including with serving and former service members. Nonetheless, changes to defence budgeting and allocations are necessary to meet India's objectives, including facilitating the shift from a manpower-intensive force to a well-trained, -equipped, and -prepared military. As resources are freed up for capital expenditure, important decisions will also need to be made about allocations between services and issues related to infrastructure and procurement within each service.

While questions of defence management and recruitment are primarily internal, the question of defence industrial production has critical external implications. Most major countries have indigenous defence industries, both for national security reasons and for their domestic political value. India has long intended to develop an indigenous defence industry and in fact has both a lengthy history of defence production and a sizeable defence industrial complex. Nevertheless, the country remains reliant on defence imports for a number of reasons that include a historic inability to take advantage of economies of scale, difficulties in absorbing technology, unpredictable defence spending, uncertain requirements on the part of the services, opacity in public sector undertakings and indigenous R&D facilities, political apathy, and a preference for low costs over high quality. As a result, despite having one of the largest defence budgets after the United States and China, about a quarter of which is allocated to capital expenditure, India has historically remained dependent on defence imports, including for critical components. Its defence exports were also, until recently, meagre.[12]

India's approach to defence industrial production is changing rapidly. For almost two decades after about 2000, India inched towards greater diversification of defence procurement, more sustainable and realistic indigenous content requirements, and greater domestic competition involving the private sector. India also made attempts at convincing partners to reduce export controls, sign bilateral security agreements, and increase defence ministry engagements with key constituencies. In time, its defence exports grew from a low base of $145 million in 2014 to $2.6 billion in 2023.[13] But the Russia–Ukraine war after 2020 proved something of an inflection point. Russian attrition in the conflict, supply chain constraints, and difficulties in making payments prompted a further Indian push toward defence indigenization and technology transfers in new contracts.

In addition to meeting the needs of the Indian armed services, the scope for exports in armaments and ammunition is considerable. Potential areas include aircraft engines and marine turbines; anti-tank and anti-air missile systems; armoured vehicles, artillery, small arms, and munitions; drones and counter-unmanned aerial systems; maritime surveillance; and maintenance, repair, and overhaul. Another critical area in which greater efforts will need to be expended by India involves shipbuilding, particularly larger hulls for both commercial and military purposes.

Although the direction is clear, certain steps would accelerate the process of defence indigenization. This would include greater predictability in procurement specifications (including timelines and budgets) to ensure long-term private sector investment, better alignment between threat perception and qualitative requirements, more consistency between requests for information (RFIs) and requests for proposals (RFPs), and closer public-private coordination. These steps could help accelerate India's attainment of an indigenous defence industry that would meet its national security needs and compete in export markets. Procurement processes should encourage competition, including between domestic public sector undertakings (PSUs), the private sector, and foreign vendors, in order to derive maximum benefits and build redundancies. Overall, India must prioritize its operational requirements (including in terms of quality), taking into account budgets and timelines, in a manner that develops a robust domestic industrial base.

Priority 2. Implement an Industrial Policy

As with the quest for security, India has been on the quest for prosperity since Independence. Initially, attempts were made to stimulate growth and development through state planning and foreign assistance. Although India became more agriculturally self-sufficient, its economy reified in the 1970s and 1980s. The early 1990s opened the door to the prospect of liberalization, encouraging market forces at home and investment from abroad. The blueprint for economic growth became one of liberalization, free trade, and market economics, even if in actuality there remained political resistance in many quarters. The 2008–09 financial crisis and the triple crises of Covid-19, China, and Ukraine in 2020–22 have now led to a rethink. The objective of liberalization to stimulate growth and development now had to be balanced with national security, supply chain concerns, and competing industrial policies. The world is no longer flat, if ever it was.

For India, there is an added consideration. India's growth after 1991 was driven by services (rather than manufacturing and agriculture) and consumption (rather than investments and exports). Not only did this result in supply chain vulnerabilities, but it also contributed less to employment, particularly as India's agricultural sector began to become more efficient. Stimulating manufacturing at home could partly solve several challenges for India, including narrowing its persistent current account deficits, strengthening its corporate sector, improving resilience, and increasing employment.

An industrial policy has therefore become critical. This necessity has been reflected in the slogan of 'Make in India'. But translating 'Make in India' into a real industrial policy has required a series of steps, and a focus on key sectors. After the pandemic, the contours of an actual industrial policy in India began to be reflected in large-scale government subsidies (including production linked incentives, or PLI); massive infrastructure spending on roads, railways, ports, airports, electric grids, and broadband; regulatory and customs changes; and bilateral and multilateral trade, investment, training and supply chain agreements with foreign partner countries. Although an Indian industrial policy could potentially apply to several sectors, critical and emerging technologies have been given priority due to their strategic importance, growth potential, and economic security vulnerabilities. Taken together, these new and strategic technologies have the potential to transform virtually every aspect of the Indian economy.

The priorities identified by India include computational hardware, physical and digital infrastructures, clean and green energy, transportation, health and biotechnologies, and defence and aerospace. Particular effort has gone into attracting foreign manufacturing exemplars in these areas, with the calculation that their successes in India could create a replicating effect. To this end, India's central and state governments have provided hundreds of crores in subsidies, both PLIs and upfront funding for semiconductors, green hydrogen, and artificial intelligence. In addition, the government has attempted to provide new or improved regulatory guidelines for defence, AI, space, drones, and geospatial policies and created dedicated nodal agencies in government for semiconductors, quantum technologies, and green hydrogen. Efforts are also underway to improve the R&D ecosystem through research funds and incentives for private sector R&D. Furthermore, India has attempted to coordinate with partners on standards, investment, technology transfers, and supply chains, including through such mechanisms and the initiative for Critical and Emerging Technologies (iCET) with the United States, the Trade and Technology Council (TTC) with the European Union, the Global Partnership on AI, the Minerals Security Partnerships, and the Indo–Pacific Economic Framework (IPEF).[14]

India's trade policy has also shifted considerably. After entering into a series of trade agreements with Japan, South Korea, and the Association of Southeast Asian Nations (ASEAN) in the early 2010s, India's trade negotiations slowed. This was in part due to a belief that India had not benefited sufficiently from these agreements; indeed, its exports to these countries and regions did not meaningfully appreciate in the years that followed these trade agreements.[15] Much hinged on the outcome of the Regional Comprehensive Economic Policy (RCEP) negotiations that would have included not just ASEAN, Japan, South Korea and India, but also China, Australia and New Zealand. As negotiations progressed, India believed that its own concerns—such as mobility and rules of origin—were systematically sidelined, and that ultimately Indian interests would have suffered from joining. Concerns about the widening trade deficit with China played a particularly strong role.

But after refusing to join RCEP, India reoriented its trade negotiations, concluding a succession of deals with Mauritius, the United Arab Emirates, and an interim trade agreement with Australia. It also signed an agreement with a group of four non-EU European economies: Norway, Iceland, Switzerland and Liechtenstein. That agreement included investment provisions that made such an agreement more attractive to India. Overall, India's trade strategy has attempted to improve market access to complementary advanced economies from which India's exports can benefit. Negotiations were consequently revived with, among others, the United Kingdom, Canada and European Union.

Still, India will need to continue to take steps to improve conditions for its industrial policy. These include creating regulatory and customs predictability, improving logistics, expediting legal arbitration and increasing workforce skills. Sustained outreach to the large and successful Indian diaspora—which can often act as bridges between foreign economies and India's ecosystem—is also necessary. In recent years, foreign investors have been appreciative of India's macro stability; its fiscal health; its infrastructure spending; favourable demographics; increased digital payments; large science, technology and engineering workforce; greater financial inclusion; and growing start-up ecosystem. There have also been some efforts at improving policy predictability and exit paths for investors. While currency depreciation is a concern, foreign investors are learning to factor that in. Their major concerns remain the long duration of legal disputes, inadequate skill development, lack of Centre–State government coordination, and insufficient private capital expenditure.

A stronger Indian economy—particularly one that is able to improve labour productivity, human capital, and manufacturing—would benefit India in many ways from a foreign policy standpoint. It would increase its tax revenue and therefore provide more resources for military and security spending, intelligence collection and management, and Indian diplomatic capacity. Additionally, it would mean more resources for foreign grants and lending, thus increasing India's international profile as a creditor. It could strengthen India's hand as a monetary power and potentially improve the performance and profile of state-owned enterprises and private corporate entities. The Indian market will also become more highly sought after, a source of potential leverage. A stronger and more competitive economy will, in time, mean a greater international role and profile for Indian businesses, its media, its academic institutions, and its cultural and religious groups. It is by no means a foregone conclusion, but a more secure and prosperous India will naturally contribute to a more powerful and influential India on the world stage.

Lessons Learned: The Perils of Isolationism

India has long been on a quest for self-reliance. This remains justifiable, insofar as it is unwise to create unnecessary dependencies that other powers might exploit in a competitive international environment. This sentiment has a tradition in the Independence movement, with Mahatma Gandhi's call for domestic textile production (khadi) as part of the Swadeshi movement. In recent years, the government of Narendra Modi has advertised 'Make in India' and called for Atmanirbhar Bharat ('self-dependent India'). But that objective, however necessary, should not be conflated with isolationism. Indeed, the success of Atmanirbhar Bharat requires investment, technology, talent, know-how, and market access from the rest of the world. An overview of India's own history reveals how periods of isolationism led to its missing out on opportunities, resulting in a more hostile international environment. By contrast, most major powers of the past 200 years—including the United States, Russia, China, or Japan— took considerable advantage of their international circumstances. It is worth recalling examples, both from India's own experience and that of others, of countries leveraging international relations to improve their own domestic trajectories.

Education and agriculture offer some early examples from newly independent India. For example, the Indian Institutes of Technology (IITs)—now the pride of many Indians—were developed with considerable international support, including from the United States, United Kingdom, Germany, Soviet Union, and United Nations. Similarly, the Green Revolution was helped considerably by American technology on wheat strains and their application in Mexico, as well as funding from private US entities. Despite these early successes, higher education and agriculture have been two areas where India has been more wary about leveraging international resources in recent decades.

There are further examples in Indian public health. Even as India's per capita incomes in the early 2000s were a century behind the West's, its public health indicators were only a half century behind. In fact, rising living standards accounted for only about a quarter of the increase in life expectancy between the 1930s and 1960s.[16] Instead, India—along with other developing countries—benefited from the spread of medical research, public health expenditure and awareness, vaccinations, improved water supply, better sanitation, pest eradication, and other steps to stop the spread of communicable and non-communicable diseases. Although much of the credit for these improvements goes to domestic health professionals and policymakers, India would not have made such swift strides without, for example, assistance from multilateral bodies such as the World Health Organization (WHO) in eradicating polio or private foundations' efforts to improve immunization and counter elephantiasis. Similarly, India's telecommunications revolution—now spearheaded by Indian companies such as Airtel and Reliance Jio—was initially made possible due to the use of equipment from the likes of Ericsson and Nokia, and the outsourcing of information technology services to companies like IBM. Entering the Indian market successfully required these corporations to depart from some of their traditional revenue models, which they were only willing to do this because of the scale afforded by the Indian market.[17]

One of the clearest examples of average Indians gaining from external partnerships is the advent of rapid transit systems in urban India. While Kolkata has had a metro rail system since the early 1980s, the recent boost to Indian public transportation began with the demonstrated success of the Delhi Metro. The Delhi Metro Rail Corporation (DMRC) was established in 1995, and construction of the rail network began in 1998. The first section of a metro line opened in 2002 and the first phase of the Delhi Metro consisting of three lines was completed in 2006. Today, the Metro network is in the world's top 10 by length and ridership. The Delhi Metro has also become a model for other cities, with dozens more transit systems in operation or under construction, and even more are being planned.

But the construction of the Delhi Metro, particularly in such a short amount of time, would have been impossible without external contributions. The Japan International Cooperation Agency (JICA) supported 60 per cent of the costs of Phase I, 54 per cent of the costs of Phase II, and 49 per cent of the costs of Phase III through soft loans. The trains were initially built in South Korea by Hyundai Rotem along with Mitsubishi, with subsequent manufacturing of rail compartments in India enabled by technology transfers. A newer generation of vehicles was manufactured by Canadian-based firm Bombardier in Germany, with manufacturing once again moving to India. The entire Delhi Metro enterprise benefited from partnerships with, among others, British construction firms, US software companies, German electronic automation, and even personnel training from Hong Kong's Mass Transit Railway. Thus, a very Indian project—one that has led to replication and services millions of people daily—was in fact a very international initiative.[18] Ultimately, what the examples from India's education, agriculture, health, telecommunications, and transportation sectors show is that in an increasingly globalized world India's national interests are inescapably international in nature.

India is not the only rising power that benefited from such external partnerships; indeed most have. The United States took advantage not just from waves of migration, from Europe, but also material economic and military resources from France and other European powers. Before and after World War II, an influx of Jewish and German scientists contributed decisively to an American technological edge in its global competition with the USSR.[19] Meanwhile, Russia advanced tremendously thanks to external assistance in its rapid domestic transformation into a European and global power after the seventeenth century. This included Peter the Great's import of shipbuilding and other technologies from western Europe and extended to the Soviet Union's use of German scientific capabilities after World War II.[20]

But for India, more illustrative examples of domestic transformation come from Asia. Japan, for example, had remained an isolated, feudal society until its leaders suddenly discovered the modern advancements made by the United States and Europe in the 1850s and 1860s. Soon after the Meiji Restoration, between 1871 and 1873, a group of almost 100 Japanese led by the nobleman Iwakura Tomomi went on a round-the-world mission. The Iwakura Mission's primary purpose was diplomatic, to revise what Japan saw as unequal treaties with other countries. But it was also a tour of study: it was meant to discover what had made the West so successful. It resulted in a discovery of education systems, industrial centres, and dockyards in the United States, Europe and elsewhere. Students accompanying the mission were left to study overseas, with the objective of returning to accelerate the process of Japan's modernization.[21]

The modernization effort that followed in Japan was swift, but more difficult and painful than many often appreciate. It was financed initially by silk and tea exports overseas, particularly to a rising United States. The government faced fiscal constraints, having had to compensate feudal landowners. Efforts to modernize the Japanese military, using conscription, led to riots in what had to date been a hierarchical, casteist, warrior society. Private universities arose to rival Japan's state-supported institutions but were often criticized as hotbeds of radicalism. Industrialization did come about eventually, but only in the late 1880s and early 1890s. It was a full three decades after the Iwakura Mission that Japan announced itself on the world stage with a decisive military victory over Russia, then a major European colonial power.[22]

China embarked upon a similar transformation over a century later. In 1978, China's leader Deng Xiaoping made a path-breaking visit to Japan: the first ever by a Chinese leader to that country. During this visit, he accompanied Nissan's chairman for a tour of one of his car company's plants, which had just installed robots in its auto manufacturing lines. Deng was impressed to learn that the plant produced ninety-four cars per worker per year.[23] The next year, four special districts were established in China that could use a 'special policy, with flexible measures' to attract foreign investment. 'Modern management systems' were adopted not only by Chinese enterprises but also government and party units. In these regions, experimentation was encouraged in industry, construction, labour, finance, foreign currency, and even local voting, while efforts were made to preserve the primacy of the Chinese Communist Party, constrain markets to serve public welfare, and ensure ultimate state control over key enterprises, land, and planning.[24]

A big part of China's push involved courting investment. Two-thirds of FDI into China between 1979 and 1995 came via Hong Kong and efforts were made to appeal to the Chinese diaspora in Taiwan, the United States, and Southeast Asia. But more importantly, policies began to change in practice and not just in theory. Single-stop decision centres were established to arrange for electricity, transportation, construction, labour, and permits for investors. The most successful regions and townships were those that centralized official decision-making from one government office. There were other things that Communist China had to learn: the practice of setting prices for foreign investors that were neither exorbitant, nor so low as to not raise revenue; an acceptance that investors would be deterred without high returns on investment, which meant that concerns about the exploitation of Chinese labour had to be relaxed; and that assurances were required on contracts, timeliness, dispute resolution, legal procedures, sanitation, efficiency, and customer service. The results of these and other transformative lessons, given what has happened in the intervening decades, are plain enough to see.

India can learn something from Japan and China's past modernization experiences, as large non-Western powers that transformed rapidly. Obviously, India's circumstances are different, so other countries' histories offer imperfect blueprints. But what they do indicate is that national transformation, even when successful, is neither painless nor easy. And yet what is also clear is that both Japan and China benefited considerably from various forms of external support. Japan's opening would have been impossible without importing industrial techniques from Europe and accessing the US market. China gained from its diaspora outreach efforts in Southeast Asia, its import of technical skills and knowledge from Hong Kong, its exposure to countries like Japan, and unprecedented global market access, including to the United States and Europe. If India could take one lesson from these experiences, it would be that modernization efforts cannot be accomplished entirely on one's own. Just as its foreign policy begins at home, India's domestic policy will have to have an inherently international character.

7

Neighbourhood First: A Stable Periphery

Background: The Problem of Neighbours

In addition to the challenge of accelerating domestic development and thereby enhancing Indian power, one of the outstanding issues that India has had to confront is a challenging and sometimes volatile neighbourhood. India has five privileged relationships in its immediate periphery. For India, each of these countries is important it in own right. But each also has its own unique features and complexities. India's ties with all five of these neighbours have sometimes been fraught but, unlike relations with Pakistan or China, have been more cooperative than adversarial.

The first, Bhutan, initially opted for economic and political isolation in the 1940s and 1950s, a decision which India respected and indeed facilitated. The 1949 India–Bhutan Friendship Treaty, amended and renewed in 2007, involved India's support for Bhutan's security.[1] India has a standing mission in Bhutan

216

to train and equip the Royal Bhutan Army (RBA), known as the Indian Military Training Team (IMTRAT). The RBA also sends trainees to the Indian Military Academy and National Defence Academy and Bhutan's diplomats have trained alongside Indian Foreign Service (IFS) officers. Bhutan's military forces also coordinate closely with the Indian Air Force for support and logistics. Additionally, Bhutan is also by far the largest recipient of Indian government grant assistance.

Although India signed a Treaty of Peace and Friendship with Nepal, and initially had similar defence arrangements to those with Bhutan, the security dimension of relations became diluted much earlier. Beginning in the 1950s, Nepal adopted a more independent foreign policy. In 1960, Nepal reached a border agreement with China and in 1969, Indian military forces left the country at Kathmandu's request. But the country still enjoys certain special relations with India, including reciprocal working rights and an open border, which facilitates economic and social interactions between the two countries. Millions of Nepal's citizens find work in India. Nepalese soldiers still serve in the Indian armed services, specifically the Gorkha regiments. The Indian government still pays pensions to tens of thousands of Nepali citizens as veterans of the Indian Army.[2]

Bangladesh, a large country of over 170 million people, has an unusual relationship with India for several reasons. India was involved in the creation of the country in 1971 and 1972, and many of Bangladesh's laws and political practices were modelled on India. While India worked to help Bangladesh set up the structures of an independent state in the 1970s, the assassination of Sheikh Mujibur Rahman and a series of military dictatorships saw a cooling of relations after 1977. At its core, Bangladesh saw a political conflict between two ideologies and

identities, which had origins in the violence surrounding the
1971 Bangladesh War. One was a vision of the Awami League
that played up Bengali identity and contested the more radical
strains of Islamism. For example, under Sheikh Hasina, Mujib's
daughter, Awami governments sought justice against those
deemed guilty of war crimes in 1971. An alternative ideology
found expression in the Bangladesh National Party (BNP),
which was eventually led by Khaleda Zia, the widow of former
President Ziaur Rahman, as well as other religiously-inspired
movements.[3] India looms large in this political and ideological
competition in Bangladesh, and New Delhi has sometimes
found willing partners in Bangladesh's leadership in pursuing a
shared agenda. After resolving the maritime boundary dispute
in 2014 and the land boundary dispute in 2015, bilateral
relations have transformed considerably, and Bangladesh has
since become the largest overseas recipient of Indian state-
backed investments and a significant trade partner.[4]

Sri Lanka and the Maldives have never had quite the same
kind of relations with India as Nepal, Bhutan, and Bangladesh.
Both were administered separately during the later years of
British rule in India, and never had a protectorate relationship
similar to Nepal and Bhutan. Their maritime positions have
also made them more open to trade and political relations with
other parties. However, proximity and ethnic overlap have
necessitated close relations and periodic calls for assistance by
Colombo and Malé from New Delhi. India, Sri Lanka, and
the Maldives have participated in maritime security initiatives.
Cooperation Initiative to facilitate maritime domain awareness
in the busy sea lanes surrounding the three countries. While
Sri Lanka is not nearly as dependent on trade with India as
Nepal and Bhutan, it has become a major transhipment hub,

with India now a large export destination for the country. India has also been involved in post-civil conflict reconstruction in northern and eastern Sri Lanka, building housing for refugees, de-mining, and providing transportation equipment and infrastructure. It also provided its largest ever foreign financial loan to Sri Lanka following a major economic crisis in that country in the aftermath of the Covid-19 pandemic.

Despite their many differences, these five countries that constitute India's near neighbourhood—Bhutan, Nepal, Bangladesh, Sri Lanka, and the Maldives—have a few shared characteristics, with implications for their relations with India. One set of issues concerns physical and human geography. India enjoys a significant size disparity over all these neighbours. None are physically connected to each other, which means that regional integration is almost impossible without India. This also sometimes makes differences between these countries more difficult to resolve, such as the statelessness of Nepali-speaking communities who were expelled from Bhutan.[5] Furthermore, there are overlapping ethnic groups between these countries and India: Bengalis in Bangladesh, Tamils in Sri Lanka, and Madhesis in Nepal often have relatives on the Indian side of the border. The ethnic overlap can have domestic political implications in both India and its neighbours.

While these realities have been more or less constant, three major changes have been unfolding in India's near abroad. One is the gradual democratization of India's neighbourhood.[6] In the early 1990s, Bhutan was an absolute monarchy, Nepal was a constitutional monarchy under King Birendra, Bangladesh had semi-military rule under Hussain Muhammed Ershad, and the Maldives was under the rule of strongman Maumoon Abdul Gayoom. Sri Lanka, which after India had perhaps the strongest democratic institutions in the region, had witnessed the passage of a discriminatory Constitution, a three-decade long civil war, further rebellion in the south, and the regular assassination of political leaders between the 1970s and mid-1990s. But over the 1990s and 2000s, democratic rule and practices deepened in all these countries, although not always at the same pace and with occasional reversals. In time, Bhutan evolved into a constitutional monarchy. Nepal went further and became a republic with the abolition of its monarchy. Bangladesh eased into a partial democracy dominated by two major parties after the 1990s, despite concerns about the fairness of the electoral process. The Maldives saw democratic rule for the first time followed by a swift reversal into authoritarianism under Gayoom's half-brother Abdulla Yameen. Subsequent multi-party elections once again reversed this trend. In Sri Lanka, after the end of the civil war, the country has witnessed a number of peaceful transitions of power.

Two, while the region's ongoing political trajectory has been mostly positive, it has been accompanied by new challenges. India's neighbours are sovereign states and naturally sensitive to their sovereignty. As such, there are limitations as to what India can do in effecting preferable outcomes. The sovereignty and democratization of India's neighbours has in recent years been compounded by rising nationalism, sometimes directed against the region's big power: India. In Nepal, political elites often perceive India to be unnecessarily interventionist and supportive of certain factions.[7] Islamist groups in Bangladesh and their political affiliates similarly seek to resist the country's secularization and perceive India as supportive of such efforts. Even in Bhutan, opposition parties and bloggers sometimes speak out critically against the long-standing relationship with India. In Sri Lanka and the Maldives, authoritarian and democratically-elected leaders past and present have occasionally adopted positions that go against Indian preferences. New circumstances have also changed the orientations of various political actors in the neighbourhood: India often cooperated or engaged with the monarchy in Nepal in the 1950s, Tamil groups in Sri Lanka in the 1980s, and Maoist forces in Nepal in the 2000s. Yet, in many instances, these beneficiaries of Indian support subsequently adopted positions that opposed Indian interests. The interplay between international and domestic politics is never static.

Three, in addition to gradual democratization and growing nationalism, India's smaller neighbours now have viable alternative international partners to India, including in China. For decades, India resisted the more active role of major powers in what it perceived to be its immediate periphery. While India remains the primary external actor in its neighbourhood, and is unlikely to relinquish its position, China's role has certainly grown. The level and nature of China's influence differs from country to country. In Sri Lanka and the Maldives, it began as primarily economic, involving large-scale infrastructure investment, imports, and tourists. In Bangladesh, China enjoys longstanding defence relations, with Bangladesh having traditionally been the second-largest recipient of Chinese arms after Pakistan. In Nepal, Beijing plays an increasingly active political role, openly mediating between political parties and factions.[8] Chinese offers of overseas financing—whether aid or loans—have been used instrumentally in the Indian subcontinent, even if they have often contributed to economic distress or led to financially unviable projects.

While China's profile in India's neighbourhood is undoubtedly increasing, there is also a tendency on the part of some Indian observers to exaggerate it. In part, many Indians overlook the historical precedents. Nepal reached a border agreement with China in 1960. In the late 1980s, Kathmandu sought Chinese intelligence cooperation, military supplies, and project assistance in the Terai. Nepal was not alone in this respect. In the late 1970s, Beijing established regular military contacts with both Sri Lanka and Bangladesh and began to provide considerable military hardware to the latter. At the same time, many elements of India's relations with these countries— such as an open border with Nepal, defence arrangements with Bhutan, social links with Bangladesh, and aspects of trade with Sri Lanka—cannot be exactly replicated by China.

There are, of course, important Indian neighbours outside of China, Pakistan, and these five countries where India—while an important actor—is less omnipresent. One is Myanmar, with which India has a long land boundary. Burma, as it was formerly known, opted for self-isolation for long periods during its independent history. Even as India was the country's third-largest trade partner in the early 2000s, relations remained somewhat distant. At the same time, tactical security cooperation continued, as against insurgents on the shared border. Another neighbour is Afghanistan, which is separated from India by Pakistan-Occupied Kashmir. Afghanistan shares many features of India's neighbourhood relationships, including close economic and cultural ties. But the realities of physical separation and the active role of other external actors such as Pakistan, Iran, China, the United States, and Russia mean that the India–Afghanistan relationship is not entirely comparable to India's near neighbours.

In addition to Myanmar and Afghanistan, two small Indian Ocean island countries—Mauritius and the Seychelles—have certain privileged associations with New Delhi. Mauritius shares ethnic, linguistic, and religious links and is a major offshore financial centre for Indians. India also equips, trains, and helps staff the Mauritian maritime defence forces and its security apparatus. The Seychelles has a somewhat different relationship with India but has entered into military arrangements whereby the Indian Navy patrols its waters. It also receives military and other assistance from India.

India's political and military involvement in its neighbours during the 1970s and 1980s were often successful in ensuring narrow and immediate political objectives. But its political and, in some cases, military interventionism also sometimes contributed to friction and resentment against India. What was more, India's differences with these countries often had detrimental effects on its own domestic politics. For example, concerns about illegal migration involving Bangladesh, stemming in part from an unresolved boundary, resulted in tensions and occasional violence in West Bengal, Assam, and other eastern states. Political agitations among Madhesis in Nepal involved communities in India, particularly in neighbouring Bihar and Uttar Pradesh. The Sri Lankan civil war fanned Tamil nationalism in Tamil Nadu. Conflicts in Myanmar involving the Chin and Rohingya people threatened to spill over into India.

Stabilizing and integrating India's neighbourhood thus remains a priority. Changes to the international environment, and within many neighbouring states, mean that India has to find new ways to achieve its security objectives and manage domestic political implications. At a minimum, this will require India to do two things. One, it must give diplomatic priority and attention to the region while recasting regional institutions in a more productive light. Two, it must increase the amount and effectiveness of long-term aid, investment, and emergency assistance, and make conscientious efforts to improve connectivity and interdependence. This, in sum, is what India's 'Neighbourhood First' policy is about.

Priority 3. Prioritize Neighbourhood Diplomacy

For periods of time, India neglected developments in the neighbourhood at the highest levels. The mid-1980s to the late 1990s saw a flurry of regional diplomatic activity that was not subsequently matched by Indian leaders, although efforts belatedly picked up. This has helped create the perception that India places a low priority on its neighbourly relations and increases the possible involvement of external actors. One way of demonstrating sustained attention is through regular bilateral visits by senior Indian leaders, including the president, prime minister, and cabinet officials. This should not be unlike the frequent meetings of European leaders or Asian regional exchanges: for example, leaders of the European Union have met eight to ten times per year in recent years. Regular meetings between Indian and other regional leaders on the side lines of diplomatic summits, such as the UN General Assembly, help to show that India still prioritizes its neighbours even at global gatherings. Similarly, incoming visits by regional leaders for consultations should become more routine, while remaining focused on concrete deliverables and outcomes.

More than high level interactions, day-to-day diplomatic activity deserves a consistent priority. India already devotes a considerable share of its diplomatic resources to the neighbourhood: the Ministry of External Affairs has four specific divisions dedicated to bilateral diplomatic relations with neighbours and two further divisions working on regional multilateral institutions. Still, more could be done. While India has a handful of consulates in its neighbours, increasing its diplomatic footprint in Nepal, Bangladesh, and Sri Lanka to improve commercial and public diplomacy would be a natural progression of India's Neighbourhood First policy.

One way in which the neighbourhood is often overlooked by India is in terms of adequate intellectual capacity, including among the broader strategic community outside government. In addition to improving language capabilities (such as in Sinhala, Bhutanese, and Dhivehi) and engaging in Bengali, Tamil, and Nepali, a better understanding of the region by India will require greater scholarship on these countries' history, politics, and economics. While India has recently been devoting resources to develop a better understanding of China, including through Indian government-backed China studies centres, it could also consider encouraging country-specific policy centres for each of its neighbours. Such centres could also become valuable intellectual bridges between the policy communities of India and its regional partners.

Beyond bilateral relations, India has in recent years been forced to rethink its approach to regional institutions. For several decades, India's efforts were focused on the South Asian Association for Regional Cooperation (SAARC). Because of both Indian and Pakistani concerns about the organization being used against them, SAARC focused on less controversial issues. India did not want to be hemmed in by the organization while Pakistan harboured its own suspicions. There have been some benefits, including technical cooperation—for example on climate conditions—and the South Asia University in New Delhi. One way of reviving SAARC was to not always hold it to consensus, as had been past practice. A concrete example of this was the SAARC Satellite proposed by India in 2014 which was to include telecommunications, disaster management coordination, and mapping applications. While welcomed by most member countries, the initiative was blocked by Pakistan. Renamed the South Asia Satellite, the effort still went through, with the launch in 2017.

While continuing to pursue opportunities through SAARC, India has been seeking alternative institutional means of reviving regional cooperation. One such effort has involved the BIMSTEC. This organization was established in 1997 and headquartered in Dhaka. Membership initially included the Bay of Bengal countries of India, Bangladesh, Myanmar, Thailand, and Sri Lanka, and Nepal and Bhutan were subsequently added. As the membership includes much of South Asia, but not China and Pakistan, it opens avenues for Indian regional leadership and serves as a bridge to Southeast Asia.[9] A BIMSTEC Summit was held after many years in 2016 at India's initiation, on the side lines of the BRICS Summit in Goa. But while it has a large number of areas of work, it was for too long poorly resourced and received insufficient political investment. Recent efforts—including a revised charter in 2022—streamlined the group's areas of focus, and India has also increased its financial and diplomatic investment in the organization.[10]

Informal issue-specific networks might also be useful in the region. Cooperation on maritime domain awareness involving

India, Sri Lanka, and the Maldives has been ongoing, and now extended to other Indian Ocean countries. Similar cooperation could also extend to the four countries connected by land: India, Bangladesh, Nepal and Bhutan or BBIN. One such proposal involved a motor vehicle agreement (MVA). The proposal met with opposition in Bhutan, which was worried about the influx of Bangladeshi and Indian vehicles into the country. Nonetheless, the prospects of greater issue-specific cooperation among clusters of countries in South Asia needs to be more fully explored.[11]

Priority 4. Increase Assistance and Connectivity

Bilateral and multilateral diplomatic efforts will only go so far. Ultimately, India will also have to provide neighbours with attractive benefit whether in terms of economic or military assistance. Economic assistance can take several forms: grants, loans, lines of credit, and technical assistance. India's aid—which refers to grants or concessional loans—is already overwhelmingly devoted to its neighbourhood. Its five closest neighbours, along with Afghanistan, Myanmar, Mauritius, and Seychelles, receive the bulk of Indian grant assistance.[12] In addition to financial aid, India also provides various forms of technical assistance to its neighbours, whether satellite imagery, meteorological data, or hydrographical information, often through government-to-government partnerships or through regional institutional cooperation. India's assistance has also assumed a more strategic character, extending to issues of defence and security. This includes the provision of military and law enforcement equipment such as offshore patrol vessels, aircraft, and coastal radar systems as well as greater allotments to neighbouring countries in India's institutions of professional military education and training.

Lines of credit extended by the Export Import (EXIM) Bank of India and other financial mechanisms have increasingly been used for assistance that serves strategic purposes while remaining financially viable. Such efforts mitigate risk for private Indian actors to facilitate overseas exports, particularly to low-income countries. Like Indian aid, its lines of credit are also disproportionately allocated to the near abroad: Bangladesh, Sri Lanka, and Nepal have been among the largest recipients. Specific projects that have been approved in recent years include transportation and energy infrastructure in Bangladesh, railways in Sri Lanka, and hydropower initiatives and earthquake reconstruction in Nepal. Indian aid projects have often been criticized for lack of delivery, but recent steps have been taken to remedy that, including stronger and more regular oversight by senior officials, steps to ensure continuous financing, and better project design by including technical experts in the planning stages.[13]

Beyond aid and credit, India is also increasingly willing and able to provide humanitarian assistance and disaster relief (HADR). While the Indian armed services have conducted HADR operations farther afield—from Libya to Fiji—the majority of its recent overseas experience has been in the immediate neighbourhood, setting a strong precedent for India as a first responder in its region. For example, after Cyclone Sidr hit Bangladesh in November 2007, the Indian Navy used amphibious ships to deliver emergency food aid to Chittagong. In 2014, when an accident crippled the Maldives water supply, the Indian Air Force and Navy delivered fresh water. Following the devastating earthquake in Nepal in April 2015, India began to airlift relief materials within hours, and worked to evacuate Indian citizens and other foreign nationals. And in May 2017, when Sri Lanka experienced heavy flooding and deadly mudslides that left hundreds homeless, India diverted navy ships with relief assistance and provided divers and medical personnel.[14]

Many of India's efforts at increasing assistance—particularly long-term project financing—are intended to improve connectivity between India and its neighbours. This includes efforts to improve or facilitate the regulated flow of goods, capital, people, energy, and data across borders. It is often said that South Asia is the least connected region in the world. This is not entirely accurate. Although India is poorly integrated with Pakistan, its other relationships enjoy considerable and growing interconnectivity and interdependence. For example, Nepal and India enable visa-free travel and employment across their border. Bangladesh and India have seen increased cross-border road, rail, and electric grid connectivity. Direct flights between India and Sri Lanka have increased and the Maldives works closely with India on such matters as healthcare and emergency services. But further improving integration will require India to develop both the 'hardware' (roads, railways, ports, pipelines, electrical grids, satellites, inland waterways, and broadband cables) as well as the 'software' (customs facilities, consular arrangements, motor vehicle agreements, and common standards) of connectivity.[15]

Greater diplomatic attention, better functioning regional cooperation, increased economic, and humanitarian assistance, and improved regional connectivity are a bare minimum for India if it seeks to retain a leadership role in its neighbourhood. Even as India rises and its global ambitions increase, its immediate neighbours will remain a major priority—just as they were for other rising major powers. By contrast, neglecting the region could have important repercussions for Indian national security, which has long benefited from buffers to the north, manageable differences in the east, and an advantageous position in the Indian Ocean littoral. The growing influence and resources available to external actors, specifically China, have only increased Indian concerns, and forced it to improve upon its commitments and delivery. Given the structural factors at play, New Delhi must be prepared for cyclical ups and down in its neighbourhood relations, as political leaderships change due to factors outside of India's control. Mitigating differences while seizing positive signs of cooperation will gradually give the neighbourhood a stake in India's development—and vice versa. Ultimately, the future well-being of India's neighbourhood should matter far more to New Delhi than it does to any other major power.

8

Act East: Balancing
China in the Indo–Pacific

Background: China's Rise and the Indo–Pacific

In 1949, decades of civil war in China came to an end with
the victory of Communist forces under Mao Zedong and the
establishment of the People's Republic of China (PRC). The
previous Chinese government of the Kuomintang (KMT) fled
to the island of Formosa, today's Taiwan, where it continued
to claim legitimate rule over the entire country as the Republic
of China. By 1950, the PRC had not just annexed Tibet, but it
went to war with the United States and United Nations in Korea
and established a strong partnership with the Soviet Union
that extended to nuclear, scientific, economic and military
cooperation. But by the 1960s, fissures began to emerge between
Beijing and Moscow, leading eventually to a sharp border
conflict between the two nuclear-armed communist countries
in 1969. In the United States, President Richard Nixon and

his National Security Advisor Henry Kissinger sought to take advantage of the Sino–Soviet split. This was engineered during a secret visit to China by Kissinger (via Pakistan), and subsequently in an historic visit by Nixon to China. As part of this thaw, the United States recognized the PRC as a member of the United Nations (including as a permanent member of the Security Council), at the expense of Taiwan and established full diplomatic relations with Beijing a few years later.[1]

Throughout the 1970s and 1980s, the United States and China developed an increasingly close partnership, often directed against their common adversary, the Soviet Union. In the late 1970s, China underwent a messy leadership transition. But under Deng Xiaoping, who emerged as the country's leader, the communist country undertook economic reforms and established Special Economic Zones (SEZs) that enabled China to experiment with open trade and market economics.[2] US businesses and those of its allies, including Japan, pumped in investment, fuelling this initial growth of the Chinese economy, which also benefited from earlier Chinese investments in human capital, including in public health and primary education. Cooperation between Beijing and Washington also extended to the military and intelligence realms.[3]

China's crackdown against protestors in Beijing's Tiananmen Square in 1989, in the context of the PRC's second leadership transition, proved an inflection point.[4] By the late 1980s, single-party rule was already collapsing in the Soviet satellite states of Europe—including East Germany, Czechoslovakia, Poland, and Hungary. But rather than add to the pressure on China, the US government of George H.W. Bush opted to dilute sanctions and preserve good relations with Beijing. There were several reasons for this: commercial factors certainly contributed, as did lingering concerns about the necessity of the US–China partnership to balance the Soviet Union.[5] Although the US–China military relationship never recovered, economic ties only strengthened.

Throughout the 1990s and early 2000s, there were continuing reminders of the differences between the United States and China. These included the 1995–96 Taiwan Straits Crisis, the 1999 bombing by the United States of the Chinese Embassy in Belgrade, and the 2000 Hainan Island incident that saw the collision of military aircraft. Nonetheless, many in the United States were convinced that a stable political relationship with China and growing economic interdependence would advance American interests and lead to China's eventual political liberalization. This proved only partly correct: the United States was able to grow and prosper. But China benefited more, and in relative terms it managed to narrow the power gap with the United States. Moreover, the leadership of China seemed intent on displacing the United States as the world's premier power.[6]

China's rapid rise between 1980 and 2008—from Deng Xiaoping's economic reforms to the Beijing Olympics—was in many ways miraculous. In a single generation, it managed to pull the majority of its people out of poverty, urbanize at an unprecedented scale and rate, and become a world leader in manufacturing, exports, infrastructure, energy consumption, and emissions. But hopes that China would politically liberalize proved unfounded, particularly after the ascendance of Xi Jinping in 2012–2013 and his consolidation of power.

Over the decades, but particularly since the global financial crisis of 2008 and Xi's ascension to power, the rise of China has generated concern among countries surrounding its periphery.

There were several reasons for this. The first is that China retains a particular system of governance in which all political power is exercised by a single party: the Chinese Communist Party. All other political movements are considered illegal. Only a handful of other countries remain nominally one-party states. The level of centralized power in China, particularly given its global reach and influence, contributes to both opacity and uncertainty. This naturally produces greater anxiety in other countries about China as a global power.

A second cause for concern about China is that its economy still operates with close ties to the state. State-owned enterprises (SOEs) benefit from large state subsidies, giving them a competitive edge against private corporations in other global markets. The corporate governance of even nominally private Chinese corporations is often tied—directly or indirectly—to elements of the state. Furthermore, China's infrastructure spending and capital expenditure is not always driven by demand, resulting in overcapacity, dumping and other market distortions. The country has accumulated large amounts of debt, and its economic performance figures are often politically engineered.[7] And China also had a long record of stealing intellectual property, including through cyber theft, and reverse-engineering.[8] All of this has contributed to economic imbalances and contributed to suppressed growth and unemployment elsewhere.

A third reason is that while China is not alone in having territorial disputes with other countries, it has frequently engaged in territorial revisionism, either through infrastructure building or an advanced military presence, even while appearing to negotiate diplomatically. These activities have included frequent naval patrols in disputed areas and the extension of an Air Defence Identification Zone over the East China Sea around the Senkaku Islands controlled by Japan (which China calls the Diaoyu Islands). In the South China Sea, China has built artificial islands and imported military equipment—including surface-to-air missiles and electronic jammers—to stake claim to the surrounding international waters and airspace. It has used its maritime militia, coast guard, and navy to intimidate civilian and military vessels belonging to other claimant states, including the Philippines, Vietnam, and Malaysia.[9] In the Himalayas, infrastructure activity and encroachments by ground forces have represented attempts to expand Chinese control over territory it disputes with India and Bhutan. In short, despite claims of a peaceful rise, China's ascent as a global power has been accompanied by much more assertive behaviour, on its borders and beyond.[10]

A fourth reason to be concerned about China's rise is that it has frequently contravened certain established international norms. For example, prior to signing the nuclear Non-Proliferation Treaty (NPT), China transferred weapon-grade uranium and sensitive nuclear technology to Pakistan to build nuclear weapons. More recently, it provided Pakistan with nuclear reactors in violation of its Nuclear Suppliers Group (NSG) commitments. Similarly, China ignored international arbitration over its territorial claims in the South China Sea, despite falling within the jurisdiction of the ruling as a signatory of the United Nations Convention on the Law of the Sea (UNCLOS). It has tested the boundaries of the Antarctic Treaty system and conducted anti-satellite tests at low altitudes, contributing greatly to debris in space.[11] Obviously, China is not the only country to have flouted rules and norms. But the fact

that China is a rising global power means that its unwillingness
to abide by these international conventions represents a distinct
challenge to those countries—like India—that do broadly
ascribe to them.[12]

With Xi's ascent to the leadership of the Communist Party
and the Chinese presidency, there has been an exacerbation
along all of these trends. China's governance has become even
more centralized and opaque, the economy has become less
market-oriented and more state-controlled, territorial disputes
are being more forcefully dealt with, and international norms
are being more obviously trampled upon. Even as China
benefits from other countries' relatively open economies and
political systems, it places restrictions on businesses, educational
institutions, media distribution, and political engagement by
others in its own country.

Although these attributes have elicited broader concerns
about China's rise and behaviour, there are certain specific
reasons for India's heightened threat perception. In fact, it is
useful to think of India–China relations along four dimensions.
The first is bilateral security, mostly related to the border
dispute. China's ability to mobilize its military on the border
has improved significantly, and it has periodically attempted to
change the status quo as during the 1950s, the 1980s, and after
2013. When challenged by Indian patrols, Beijing selectively
interprets past legal treaties and agreements, conveniently
ignoring those that do not support its case. Its actions in
2020 violated almost three decades of written agreements
with India, severely setting back trust. The second element is
regional security, where the differences are even wider. India
harbours deep distrust of China's Belt and Road Initiative
(BRI), which it assesses to be a strategic project designed to

offer easy financing to vulnerable economies, with the resulting debt being leveraged for political or strategic gain. That the BRI is a unilateral project that also violates Indian territory (by traversing Pakistan-Occupied Kashmir) contributes to Indian resistance.[13] The third element concerns bilateral economic relations, where the trade deficit remained in China's favour. While previously optimistic about prospects of economic relations with China, Indian business is increasingly concerned that China does not offer a level playing field in areas where India enjoys comparative advantages. Furthermore, in many areas of emerging technology, the prospect of cooperation with China exposes India to critical vulnerabilities. The fourth area concerns global governance, where India and China have increasingly found themselves at loggerheads, whether it comes to terrorism, export control regimes, freedom of navigation, or UN Security Council reform.

While the boundary dispute and regional security differences have been long-standing concerns, bilateral economic ties and multilateral affairs until recently represented two areas of potential convergence and cooperation between New Delhi and Beijing. But in recent years, all four areas of India–China relations have witnessed a widening disparity in interests and perspectives. Due to geographic, historical, economic, and political factors, India is at the forefront in bearing the brunt of China's newfound assertiveness. There may continue to be issues on which both India and China find convergence, and there may also be times when both sides decide to tactically recalibrate the relationship. But unless China adopts a fundamentally different approach to its role in international affairs, New Delhi will have to continue to prepare for a much more competitive relationship with Beijing.

India's concerns about China have resulted in its Act East Policy in the Indo–Pacific. The Look East Policy, which began in the early 1990s, had a primarily economic focus. But in the mid-2000s—just as economic relations between India and China were taking off—renewed concerns about China began to feature as a bigger factor in India's eastward engagement.[14] As a result, relations with Southeast and North-East India became more comprehensive, with a more pronounced security focus. The geographical scope of India's eastward engagement also became wider, extending from the Indian Ocean to the Western and Southern Pacific, as China's own influence expanded. This in turn required India to imagine a larger neighbourhood: the Indo–Pacific. Third, increased urgency in responding to China's actions necessitated more activity, clearer deliverables, and shorter timelines. These three important features—a bigger security focus, larger geographical spread, and stronger delivery—resulted in a new name: Act East. If the original objective of the Look East Policy was primarily to accelerate India's economic development, the objective of Act East is to preserve a favourable balance of power in the Indo–Pacific.[15]

The transition from 'Look East' to 'Act East' required a change in India's strategic vocabulary, one that captured the wider geopolitical dynamics of play. Indian strategists began to discuss and debate the idea of the Indo–Pacific between 2007 and 2013.[16] The term already had currency in the biological sciences, referring to an ecologic zone of warm water spanning parts of both the Indian and Pacific Oceans. It also had historical antecedents in the ancient, medieval, and colonial periods, when the Indian and Pacific Oceans were linked through trade and cultural routes. But as a contemporary strategic concept, it gained ground after Japanese Prime Minister Shinzo Abe referred to the need to imagine a broader Asia as part of the 'confluence of the two seas'—the Indian and Pacific Oceans—in a speech to the Indian Parliament.[17]

After China began to assume a greater maritime presence in the Indian Ocean after 2008, Indian commentators such as C. Raja Mohan argued that 'the seas of the western Pacific and the Indian Ocean must be seen as a single integrated geopolitical theatre, the "Indo–Pacific"'.[18] The official adoption of the term in India and other countries followed suit, including in Australia's defence and foreign policy white papers and in various official articulations by Japan. Indian Prime Minister Manmohan Singh referenced the Indo–Pacific in a May 2013 speech in Tokyo. Subsequently, in a January 2017 address to the Raisina Dialogue, Prime Minister Narendra Modi said that India 'believe[s] that respecting freedom of navigation and adhering to international norms is essential for peace and economic growth in . . . the Indo–Pacific'.[19] Somewhat belatedly, in late 2017, the United States began to adopt the term and described the Indo–Pacific as a priority region in its 2017 National Security Strategy (NSS).[20] Modi elaborated upon the theme in a 2018 keynote address at the Shangri-la Dialogue in Singapore, where he emphasized that the Indo–Pacific was consistent with ASEAN centrality, allaying concerns in Southeast Asia about its use.[21] Thus, the Indo–Pacific gradually became part of the official strategic vocabulary of India, the United States, Japan, and several other countries.

Although the exact geographical definition may differ between various countries—in part, a reflection of their national interests and geographies—there are some conceptual overlaps. Perhaps most significantly, the Indo–Pacific signifies a single strategic arena encompassing parts of the Indian and Pacific Ocean basins. It highlights the importance of the maritime domain for both commercial cooperation and strategic competition, although not necessarily at the expense of the continental sphere as some imagine it. By highlighting the Indian Ocean and widening the regional scope, the Indo–Pacific also elevates the role of India and highlights the importance of the country in the regional balance of power. By its size and geographical location, India is a geopolitical keystone in the Indian Ocean and derives advantages from its economic weight, its long coastline, and its blue water navy.

In sum, India's Act East Policy reflects the growing importance of security, a wider geographical scope, and greater urgency on New Delhi's part, compared to the prior Look East Policy. It highlights startegic shifts, the importance of the maritime domain and the regional balance of power. In practice, Acting East will require at least four interlocking lines of effort. First, India must act to secure the Indian Ocean region where military competition risks escalation, particularly given the importance of regional chokepoints and the growing interests and involvement of the world's major powers. Second, India must begin to play the role of a balancer—even if it is unlikely to be *the* balancer—to China in Southeast Asia. This will require Indian political and security engagement and stronger diplomatic and economic connections with Southeast Asia. Third, India must deepen strategic partnerships with like-minded and capable maritime powers who share India's concerns about China's rise, particularly the United States, Japan, and Australia: the Quad. But it must not neglect other relationships important to the Indo–Pacific balance of power, including Russia, European powers, South Korea, Taiwan, and others with important roles and capabilities. And fourth, India must manage its long-term competition with China, preserving stability without yielding on core Indian interests.

Priority 5. Secure the Indian Ocean

As India becomes more integrated with the world, the role of the Indian Ocean assumes greater importance.[22] The ocean is a valuable conduit for global trade, including commercial shipping and especially energy, with significant amounts of the world's oil supply transported through its chokepoints. Its littoral is also densely populated, home to some two billion people. But while the Indian Ocean region links some of the fastest growing areas of the world—Southeast Asia, South Asia, and East Africa—it is also vulnerable to natural disasters. The 2004 Indian Ocean tsunami killed over 2,00,000 people and Cyclone Nargis is believed to have killed over 1,00,000 people in Myanmar in 2008. The ocean is naturally vital to Indian interests: most of India's trade by volume and a majority of its trade by value comes via the Indian Ocean.[23] Beyond that, the Indian Ocean plays a vital role as a source of fishing and mineral resources.

Apart from its growing importance, the Indian Ocean is distinguished by its politics. It has historically been less contested than the Pacific, and while relatively under-governed it is also more open. This inclusivity is reflected in India's vision for the Indian Ocean as laid out in a speech delivered by Modi in Mauritius in 2015.[24] The looser but more collaborative nature of governance in the Indian Ocean has presented complications in addressing issues such as piracy, which peaked in the Indian Ocean between 2005 and 2010 and cost the global shipping industry about $6 billion per year.[25] Countering piracy off the Somali coast and in the Gulf of Aden required naval operations by several countries, including India, and resulted in a drop in incidents after 2012. But another participant in counter-piracy operations during this period was China. And it was Beijing's entry into the Indian Ocean that began to generate renewed concerns about rising security competition.

China's activity in the Indian Ocean has generally assumed two forms. The first involves investments in infrastructure in several Indian Ocean countries. For example, many nominally civilian ports in the Indian Ocean littoral are of important strategic value and could conceivably be adapted to be used for military purposes. India feared that onerous debt related to the non-commercial nature of these port projects would be leveraged by Beijing to acquire equity and control, ensuring their future use for military or espionage purposes. The most obvious example was in Sri Lanka, where China invested in the port of Hambantota and having deepened its political influence, eventually docked a submarine in Colombo in 2014. After Sri Lankan elections, the new government assuaged Indian concerns but found it difficult to manage the rising debt owed to China. Eventually, as part of a debt write-off, a Chinese company acquired a stake in Hambantota.[26] Meanwhile, China did establish its first overseas military facility in 2016–17 in Djibouti, while the port of Gwadar in Pakistan became a Chinese-managed enclave. Several other commercial ports or infrastructure investments in the Indian Ocean remain points of concern for India, including in East Africa, Myanmar, Bangladesh, the Maldives, and West Asia.

The second concern about Chinese activity in the Indian Ocean relates to its growing naval presence in the region.

Other than its base in Djibouti, China's People's Liberation Army Navy (PLAN) has used ports such as Aden and Karachi for replenishment and made port visits to Sri Lanka and the Seychelles. In recent years, the PLAN presence in the Indian Ocean has included surface vessels but also submarines, which are harder to detect and have been active in the channels west of the Indian coast. As China undertakes one of the largest naval build-ups in history and develops aircraft carrier battle groups, it is only a matter of time before the PLAN begins to deploy a larger presence in the Indian Ocean, with significant implications for Chinese power projection and Indian security.[27]

India has been noting these developments, and it has not been inactive. It has increased naval deployments, built out civilian port and naval infrastructure on Indian and partner territory, increased maritime domain awareness efforts, provided military support, stepped up at regional institutions, and increased coordination with partner countries. Since 2017, the Indian Navy has begun to deploy permanently in several identified zones around the Indian Ocean, with vessels shortening their periods of maintenance and time in port. These include regions from the Gulf of Aden to the west to the Strait of Malacca in the east where the Indian Navy attempts to have at least one surface vessel, submarine or aircraft deployed any given time. Moreover, the Navy now operates at a higher state of readiness, with weapons and relief supplies. This has proved useful in contingencies such as anti-piracy operations and humanitarian disasters.[28]

Bilateral agreements for logistics—as with the United States, France, and Australia—and the establishment of operational turnaround points in arrangements with countries such as Oman and Indonesia, have helped extend the Navy's operational reach. In part, India has benefited from greater maritime domain awareness, the ability to track civilian, military and non-state vessels at sea. This includes surveillance through coastal radar networks extending across the Bay of Bengal and into the central Indian Ocean, as well as satellite capabilities. To integrate that information, India established an information fusion centre in Gurugram called the Information Fusion Centre – Indian Ocean Region (IFC-IOR), which hosts liaison officers from friendly partner countries. Several bilateral 'white shipping' agreements have helped to facilitate information sharing with partners as well. Cooperation on anti-submarine warfare remains sensitive but important, with considerable room for improvement.

While China has been investing in port infrastructure throughout the Indian Ocean region, India has invested in a parallel architecture, including civilian ports in Sittwe in Myanmar and a container port at Chabahar in Iran. It has also invested in maritime infrastructure in Sri Lanka, the Maldives, and Mauritius, while in other cases it has worked to ensure greater transparency and access to Chinese-financed facilities so as to ameliorate security concerns. In places like Mauritius and the Seychelles, India has tried to deepen its partnerships, supplying both with coast guard equipment (including aircraft and patrol vessels), patrolling their waters using ships and naval aircraft, and involving them in coast guard and maritime domain awareness efforts.[29] Using its newfound capabilities, partners and deployment patterns, India has also been playing a more active role in humanitarian assistance and disaster relief operation all around the Indian Ocean. Recent operations have extended to Indonesia, Sri Lanka, Yemen, Bangladesh, Myanmar, the Maldives, and East Africa. Finally, India has tried to lead regional institution-building at the Indian Ocean Rim Association (IORA) and increase naval transparency and goodwill through the Indian Ocean Naval Symposium (IONS). In 2019, India also announced an Indo–Pacific Oceans Initiative (IPOI) with seven pillars to facilitate international cooperation in a number of domains.

These initiatives, when taken together, are significant. But they still might not be enough. While India can certainly step up its own activities in the Indian Ocean, there are nonetheless limitations as to what it might be able to do, especially with respect to a country like Pakistan that also has an Indian Ocean coast. Thus, anticipating a larger Chinese naval presence, India should also be preparing for sea denial, and not just sea control. That will require much greater investments by the Indian Navy in its submarine fleet and in developing infrastructure on the Indian coast and its offshore islands (such as the Andaman and Nicobar Islands and Lakshadweep). India does hold several natural advantages in the Indian Ocean, including geography and political goodwill. The Chinese navy will also face significant technical and logistic difficulties in operating in the Indian Ocean.[30] The prospect of greater Sino–Indian competition in the Indian Ocean should therefore lead to neither panic nor complacency on New Delhi's part. But further steps—including greater investments in the Indian Navy and smart allocations within the naval budget—may well be required.

Priority 6. Connect with Southeast Asia

Southeast Asia—the region home to the member countries of the Association of Southeast Asian Nations (ASEAN)—will be the primary realm of geopolitical competition in

Asia for the foreseeable future. Asia features several major resident powers—large countries with sizeable economies and militaries—including the United States, China, India, Japan, and Russia. By contrast, Southeast Asia has in recent decades seen dampened security competition and cooperation through ASEAN. Proponents in the region trumpet the 'ASEAN Way' as an enlightened approach to managing the region through consensus. Critics, however, believe that such consensus has not been effective in managing serious disputes, as between China and several competing claimants in the South China Sea or civil conflict in Myanmar. Moreover, sceptics often question the wisdom and sustainability of the region's simultaneous economic dependence on China and military dependence on the United States.

In practice, India's engagement with Southeast Asia has often been led by relations with Singapore, which remains a critical node for regional engagement. The small but wealthy city-state has evolved into one of India's closest security partnerships and is a hub of trade, finance, business, education, and travel. At the same time, India's interactions with Southeast Asia have also been hampered by the self-isolation of Myanmar for many years. Despite that country's economic and political opening up after 2015, the coup and civil conflict after 2021 represents yet another complication for Indian attempts at physically integrating with Southeast Asia.

There is a widespread view in Southeast Asia that India's engagement with the region has been underwhelming. This overlooks the fact that India conducts more military exercises with Southeast Asian countries than any country after the United States, Japan, and Australia (including more than China).[31] It has among the largest number of visitors to Southeast Asia from outside the region (after the US and China) and has the third-largest trade deficit with ASEAN (after the US and European Union). This level of engagement is not necessarily reflected in public or elite opinion in Southeast Asia, in part because of a narrow definition of what many Southeast Asians consider a good partner, one that facilitates large-scale infrastructure financing and supply chain integration.[32]

Looking ahead, there are three elements to India's engagement with Southeast Asia. The first involves giving the region greater political and diplomatic priority, both at the bilateral and multilateral levels. The multilateral heavy lifting has largely been accomplished. Although India began to engage formally with ASEAN after 1992, it quickly became a member of the ASEAN Regional Forum (1994), the East Asia Summit (2005) and the Asian Defence Ministers Meeting-Plus (2010). The engagement with ASEAN-centred organizations has been complemented by renewed investments in BIMSTEC, which is meant to bridge South and Southeast Asia. The new level of diplomatic priority accorded the region has resulted in the creation of a separate Indian Ambassador to ASEAN, a dedicated division in India's Ministry of External Affairs and India-ASEAN Summits such as that held in 2018, in New Delhi, during which all ten Southeast Asian leaders appeared as chief guests for India's Republic Day celebrations.

A second element of India's relations with Southeast Asia—security—remains modest but has made some important strides in recent years. In relatively short order, India has strengthened its security relations with Singapore, Vietnam, Myanmar, Thailand, the Philippines, Indonesia, and Malaysia. With several of these countries, joint exercises and port visits have become routine. India conducts coordinated naval patrols and has provided technical assistance to several militaries, including Myanmar, with which counterterrorism cooperation remains important. Meanwhile, Singapore uses Indian territory to train its mechanized forces and artillery and Indian air space for air force drills. In 2017, India and Singapore also concluded a significant maritime agreement. With Vietnam, India is involved in training its air force combat pilots and submarine sailors. Since their origins in 1995, the MILAN maritime exercises represent an Indian effort at building naval cooperation and confidence with regional partners, including— but not limited to—the maritime forces of Southeast Asia. More recently, India has started to provide military equipment, including offshore patrol vessels to Vietnam, BrahMos cruise missiles to the Philippines, and a second-hand submarine to Myanmar.[33] India can still build upon these efforts to increase joint naval repair and maintenance facilities, and improve cooperative maritime surveillance and intelligence.

Perhaps the most challenging element of India's Southeast Asian engagement—rather ironically—was the original driver of relations: economic and commercial cooperation. In terms of trade, India is the seventh largest trade partner of ASEAN (if the EU is considered a single actor). But India's trade with ASEAN amounts to a small percentage of China's and is low given the size of its economy and geographical proximity. Although imports of manufactured goods from Vietnam and raw materials from Indonesia have grown, continuing sub-par trade is due in part to competition between India and Southeast Asian economies in critical manufacturing spheres. It has also been compounded by India believing that Southeast Asian countries have not been sensitive enough to its concerns about Chinese dumping while limiting labour mobility. Despite these differences, India can certainly be taking better advantage of its goodwill and cultural links by boosting educational exchanges for Southeast Asian students, promoting tourism from Southeast Asia, improving direct air connectivity, increasing cultural centres, and facilitating film distribution.

It does not help that physical connectivity between India and Southeast Asia has also been marred by traditionally poor Indian delivery and project management. Efforts have been made in recent years to try to rectify some of this. A few initiatives are of particular importance. The first is the India–Myanmar–Thailand (IMT) Trilateral Friendship Highway, meant to connect northeast Asia to Thailand. The second effort is the Kaladan Multi-Modal Transit Transport Project, which connects Sittwe on the Bay of Bengal coast in Myanmar with the Indian state of Mizoram. This project has struggled with poor cost estimates and implementation. Although severely complicated by the political and security situation in Myanmar, these efforts could increase trade and connectivity between India and Southeast Asia, and also better connect and develop India's North-East.[34] Beyond such specific efforts, attempts at improving connectivity will require better customs and immigration arrangements and regulatory harmonization.

On balance, much headway has been made with respect to diplomacy and institution building between India and Southeast Asia. From prior neglect and suspicion, important strides have been made over the past three decades on security cooperation with Singapore, Vietnam, Myanmar, Indonesia, Thailand, the Philippines and Malaysia, although there is room for considerable growth subject to the comfort levels of these countries. In part, Southeast Asian states may need to better communicate what kind of regional security cooperation they seek with India. Regarding connectivity with Southeast Asia, accelerating projects in India's North-East and improving the country's port and air infrastructure and connectivity still need to be higher priorities. However, all of these are subject to politics, sustainability and, most importantly, commercial viability. In Southeast Asia—a diverse and dynamic region abutting India—New Delhi is already doing a lot more than just looking east. But much work must still be done before India can play a sufficient balancing role.

Priority 7. Partner with the Quad and Others

India's challenges and obligations in the Indo–Pacific are already daunting, but particularly so given the power disparity between China and India. For this reason, partnerships with other balancing powers in the Indo–Pacific will be necessary. Because this will have to be limited to states that share similar concerns and worldviews as India and have sufficient military and economic capabilities, particularly in the maritime domain, the candidates are few. The most important and obvious is the United States. Another is Japan, which remains economically potent and, despite its traditionally pacifist orientation, has embarked upon significant defence reforms to enable it to play the role of a military balancer as well. Australia is also playing a more active role, and there is scope for India to partner with South Korea, Taiwan, France, the United Kingdom and others with a presence and influence in the Indo–Pacific. Equally, India will have to carefully manage its longstanding defence relationship with Russia in the light of closer China–Russia relations.

India does not seek a military alliance in the region. For some countries, notably the United States, an alliance is a specific agreement, normally ratified, which often commits the countries to mutual defence, joint command structures, and basing arrangements (or at least 'status of forces agreements' that give a legal structure to foreign military forces). Such agreements require a high level of interdependence, commitment, and seamlessness of operations. The US has five such treaty allies in the Indo–Pacific: Japan, South Korea, Australia, Thailand, and the Philippines. By contrast, India often seeks military partnership with many benefits but fewer dependencies and obligations. The benefits might include sharing of information such as strategic assessments, domain awareness, or intelligence; capacity-building through training, equipment sales, co-manufacturing, co-development or technological assistance; and increased interoperability through more complex and sophisticated military exercises, better communications integration, and coordinated operating procedures. Any kind of joint operations, if undertaken, are normally a political decision.

The United States is already India's most important security partner in the Indo–Pacific. The potential of this partnership began to be realized in the early 1990s, when initial military contacts began after the Cold War. After the 1998 nuclear tests, cooperation swiftly resumed. The administration of Bill Clinton lifted sanctions on India by October 1999, motivated by both commercial and strategic reasons, and for the first time the United States backed India in a crisis with Pakistan during the Kargil War of 1999. The George W. Bush administration was early to recognize the potential of India as a balancer, with his adviser Condoleezza Rice writing in 2000 that India could play a wider role in Asia.[35] In 2005, this was put into action with a senior official announcing that the United States' 'goal is to help India become a major world power in the 21st century . . . We understand fully the implications, including military implications of that statement'.[36] This meant an appreciation that, in the analyst Ashley Tellis's words, 'a strong, democratic, (even if perpetually) independent India [is] in American national interest'.[37] This eventually resulted in the civil nuclear agreement announced in July 2005, which bid to lift various technology export controls and political restraints on India. That agreement, finalized in 2008, culminated in a waiver by the Nuclear Suppliers Group, marking an effective end to India's nuclear isolation.

While it began its tenure by exploring avenues of cooperation with China, the Barack Obama administration eventually came to similar conclusions as its predecessors about India. In her 2011 essay that first explained the concept of the 'pivot' (or 'rebalance') to Asia, then-Secretary of State Hillary Clinton stated clearly that 'India's greater role on the world stage will enhance peace and security'.[38] It was during this period that India and the United States began an initial dialogue on East Asia. By the end of Obama's tenure, India and the United States agreed to a wide-ranging Joint Strategic Vision for the Asia-Pacific and Indian Ocean Region—which provided a strategic underpinning to the relationship—and India was elevated to a Major Defense Partner to enable defence cooperation on India's terms.[39] The Trump administration reinforced these commitments in bilateral statements with India and in its Free and Open Indo–Pacific Strategy unveiled over its first two years in office. With the conclusion of a host of foundational agreements between the United States and India to enable interoperability, the Biden administration built further on these efforts through a series of Quad working groups (including on maritime issues), elevated bilateral US–India defence and technology dialogues, greater defence industrial cooperation, more military liaisons, and operational cooperation, including as part of the Combined Maritime Forces (CMF).

Throughout this period, cooperation on information sharing—from intelligence to maritime domain awareness—has increased. India has benefited from US platforms including heavy lift, tactical transport and maritime reconnaissance aircraft, as well as helicopters, artillery, and drones. This equipment has facilitated India's ability to operate farther at sea, including in counter-piracy operations. In terms of interoperability, the two countries now conduct regular exercises involving all three military services. The Malabar exercises involving the navies is most evolved, and now includes Japan and Australia, with exercises alternating between the Indian and Pacific Oceans. The Indian and US armies take part in Yudh Abhyas and Vajra Prahar, involving special operations forces. The air forces conduct Cope India, with the Indian Air Force periodically participating in the United States' premier Red Flag exercises. A tri-service exercise called Tiger Triumph was also initiated. Despite a progressively deeper partnership in all these areas, efforts at facilitating defence technology transfers have struggled, requiring a change in course. In 2023, agreements on jet engines and drones, among others, were concluded and involved much higher rates of technology transfer. But they represent only a beginning of what could still be a much better developed defence–technological partnership.

Japan represents another important emerging security partnership for India in the Indo–Pacific. The two countries began to normalize relations in 2000 after India's nuclear tests.

Both New Delhi and Tokyo harboured similar concerns about China's rise and military assertiveness, and were equally worried about the future of the United States' security commitment to the region. For Tokyo, India is vital for securing sea lines of communications, upon which Japan's commercial interests and energy security are dependent. Due to the absence of historical baggage associated with Japan's role in World War II, India has been useful in helping to normalize Japan's military power and expanding its security role outside its immediate region. In the early 2000s, the two countries embarked upon some tentative anti-piracy operations and coast guard exercises. In 2001, a security dialogue was institutionalized and operational cooperation increased after the 2004 Indian Ocean tsunami.

India–Japan strategic relations took off in 2006 under the prime ministership of Shinzo Abe. In 2008, the two countries agreed to a Joint Declaration on Security Cooperation and initiated staff talks between the maritime forces. In 2010, a 2+2 dialogue involving the foreign and defence ministries was established. Bilateral naval exercises were held, somewhat belatedly, in 2012. Relations gradually extended to staff college talks, port calls, and participation in fleet reviews. In 2014, Abe was chief guest at India's Republic Day, which was significant in that the ceremony includes a military parade. Over the subsequent years under Abe and Modi, coordination on freedom of navigation in the South China Sea and on North Korea increased, Japan was permanently included in the Malabar naval exercises, a civilian nuclear agreement was signed and brought into force, and agreements were concluded to facilitate the sharing of classified information and defence technologies. Ground and air force exercises were also inaugurated. For Japan, India has emerged as among its most important security partners in the Indo–Pacific after the United States and Australia.[40]

For all the positive momentum, India–Japan relations will continue to have some obvious limitations. These include resource constraints in India and a still largely pacifist public opinion in Japan. Relations have often required top-down involvement, rather than an evolving into an organic partnership buttressed by business and societal connections. There are also structural constraints that will have to be worked around, including India's presence outside US alliance structures. This complicates some operational cooperation, including military communications and information sharing. Defence trade and technological cooperation has also not progressed, in part because of Japan's lack of experience with foreign sales and also due to questions of export controls and the management of classified information. Nonetheless, despite these evident limitations and concerns, the broader trajectory of India–Japan strategic relations has recently been positive.[41]

A third country that contributes significantly to the regional balance is Australia. India–Australia relations had previously been marked by differences, including on Pakistan, the Indian Ocean, China, and India's nuclear status. Some of that has been put to rest, including through a lifting of Australia's uranium ban on India and cooperation in forums such as IORA. Nonetheless, after several years of cautious engagement, India–Australia defence relations significantly increased after 2019 and in some areas surpassed India's relations with Japan. Military exercises, particularly by the navies, became more regular and complex. India also took part in Australia's Pitch Black air exercises, and they have engaged in official or semi-official trilateral dialogues involving Japan, Indonesia, and France. The two countries also established a 2+2 dialogue involving the foreign and defence ministers.[42]

The coming together of India, the United States, Japan, and Australia—or the Quad—was a natural progression of the strengthening bilateral relationships. The four countries initially coordinated in an ad hoc manner during relief operations following the 2004 Indian Ocean tsunami. In 2007, they held a one-off quadrilateral Malabar naval exercise, along with Singapore, and a working-level dialogue, before Australia withdrew in 2008. In 2017, the dialogue on the Indo–Pacific was restarted and the four met again in 2018 at a working level. This was upgraded initially to a foreign ministers' dialogue and in 2021 a leaders' level summit. While the four countries do military exercises—specifically, the Malabar naval exercise— much of their activities have been security adjacent. That is, they are led by the foreign or other ministries, but have indirect implications for security. The Quad's structure has been a suite of working groups, initially three on health, climate, and technology cooperation that subsequently proliferated to a large number that encompassed infrastructure, cyber security, maritime cooperation, space, and science and technology.[43] In part, the structure is intended to produce outcomes without the unnecessary bureaucracy of a secretariat. The Quad's issue set is meant to provide public goods in the Indo–Pacific that presents a viable alternative to China without exacerbating security competition, a concern of many partners in Southeast Asia and elsewhere. Still, the scope for broadening and widening the Quad's objectives—even if on a limited basis or set of issues— remains considerable.

Indian security partnerships to preserve a favourable balance in the Indo–Pacific should not be relegated to the states of the Indian Ocean, ASEAN, and the Quad. European states—and in particular France and Britain— retain a major footprint in the

Indo–Pacific. France has significant maritime territory in the southwest Indian Ocean and in the South Pacific, and resident populations there. It also has military facilities in Djibouti and the United Arab Emirates. The UK also has military assets in West Asia and South-east Asia. India has recognized their role, including through a logistics supply agreement with France. European Union member states such as Germany and the Netherlands and EU institutions have also been articulating Indo–Pacific strategies. Other Pacific countries, including South Korea and Taiwan, hold promise for defence, intelligence, and technological relations. South Korea has long had an active commercial relationship with India but is increasingly cooperating with India on defence and security. Taiwan's status is complex, but economic and technological relations have recently grown, including investments in electronics assembly and semiconductor supply chains. Along with some or all of its Quad partners, India has also occasionally participated in 'Quad-plus' exercises and activities, involving such countries as France, South Korea, the Philippines, Canada, and New Zealand.

Perhaps the trickiest balance that India will have to strike in the Indo–Pacific is with Russia. India has for many years been Russia's largest arms market, but concerns about a deepening China–Russia compact after the 2014 Crimea crisis and the Russia–Ukraine war after 2022 have exposed differences, including over Russia's nascent security relationship with Pakistan. India believes that positive relations with Russia will be vital to preserving a balance of power in Asia and it hopes to provide Moscow with options. For the near future, India will remain somewhat dependent on Russia for its military preparedness. It has benefited from advanced Russian technology (such as nuclear propulsion for leased submarines) and after 2022 has imported significant amounts of oil. At the same time, broader trade relations and people-to-people ties between India and Russia have struggled, and Western sanctions have complicated payment methods for trade. Despite criticism from the media and publics in the West, India has opted to continue investing in the relationship with Russia, which has rendered certain benefits for Indian security, economy, and foreign relations. One example is the sale of BrahMos cruise missiles—which were jointly developed by India and Russia—to the Philippines, in order to contribute to its security in the South China Sea. But the India–Russia relationship will be one that must be carefully managed in light of the changing geopolitics of the Indo–Pacific.

Equally, while the Indo–Pacific balance naturally has a maritime focus, there are important continental considerations at play. In addition to Russia, Indian outreach and engagement with the five Central Asian republics and Mongolia will remain important. To this end, India has been involved in the Shanghai Cooperation Organisation (SCO). New Delhi also hosted the five leaders of the Central Asian republics for Republic Day in 2022, during which agreements on investment, education, and health cooperation were announced. Meanwhile, Mongolia has been a major beneficiary of Indian project assistance and is among the largest recipients of Indian lines of credit. Cultural links, including Buddhism, are also potent. All told, it is only natural that Eurasia should also feature in India's Indo–Pacific calculations.

Priority 8. Manage Competition with China

India's Act East Policy—including efforts at securing the Indian Ocean region, connecting with Southeast Asia, and deepening partnerships with balancing partners such as the Quad—have their own value and purpose. But they assume greater importance and urgency as part of an effort to manage China's rise. This does not mean 'containing' China in the manner in which that term was used during the Cold War. The current era is far more globalized. Instead, it will require building strength and resilience, maintaining clarity on interests, and building coalitions that give Beijing incentives to be more transparent, engage in equitable and sustainable commercial interactions, peacefully manage territorial differences, and adhere to establish international norms. For India specifically, it is a way to help manage the boundary dispute, balance trade and economic ties, mitigate regional security competition, and advance Indian objectives at international institutions. It will require developing the power and having the political will to sometimes impose costs.

Among other steps, responding to China's rise will require overall improvements to India's military preparedness as China modernizes and reforms its own forces. Steps to this effect were taken beginning in the mid-2000s and included the raising of mountain divisions in the Indian Army and the transfer of frontline fighter aircraft to the eastern sector. The building of better logistical infrastructure such as forward positioned airfields and improved roads, enhanced intelligence (with support from satellites and unmanned aerial vehicles), and the acquisition of lightweight artillery and heavy-lift and high-altitude transport aircraft have all been part of the effort to improve defensive capabilities along the border. The experiences of Nathu La in 1967, Sumdorongchu in 1986–87, Doklam in 2017, and Ladakh after 2020 show that the application of military force along with complementary diplomatic efforts, can be used to counter Chinese military adventurism.

In its region, India will continue to face challenges. While India cannot always block Chinese investment in its neighbourhood, it can try to provide viable alternatives. This has involved stepping up aid and lending, including emergency financial resources and infrastructure investment. India has also pursued joint or coordinated projects with partners, including the United States and Japan, in South, Southeast, and West Asia.

Beyond arming, India will also have to play economic hardball, while advocating for reciprocal market access. While China dumps surplus materials in the Indian market, hurting Indian manufacturers, Indian firms have difficulty servicing Chinese companies, even in areas where they have comparative advantages. India will have to counter unfair Chinese trade practices, while continuing to advocate for greater and more equitable business opportunities. For example, in retaliation for China's actions on the border in 2020, India banned Chinese apps, screened Chinese involvement in public procurement, closely monitored Chinese investments, restricted Chinese media, and effectively disallowed Chinese vendors in 5G telecommunications infrastructure.[44] Indian concerns about China have also translated into digital and trade policies, including the notion of trusted geographies and complementary trade partners. Indeed, despite the large and continuing goods trade deficit, India may have done more than any other major economy to de-risk from China, particularly in critical and vulnerable sectors.

At the multilateral level, India and China have increasingly been competing or disagreeing at forums such as the United Nations and export control groups. Substantively, they have adopted different approaches to freedom of navigation and digital governance. India has joined China-led entities such as the Asian Infrastructure Investment Bank (AIIB), BRICS, and SCO, organizations that were established during at a more promising phase in India–China relations between 2009 and 2016. BRICS and the SCO remain useful talk shops with their own constraints while AIIB's lending has been limited. Despite its rapid expansion to include countries such as Egypt, Iran, Ethiopia, and the United Arab Emirates, BRICS has focused on safeguarding its members' sovereignty. In recent years, the agenda has focused on finding alternative mechanisms to the US dollar for trading. The SCO, meanwhile, remains a useful vehicle for India to engage the Central Asian Republics.

Despite the sharp and systemic differences, India can continue to work with Beijing when possibilities present themselves. One relatively recent example involved the Financial Action Task Force, where in 2018 China dropped its resistance to including Pakistan on a terrorism 'grey list' in exchange for Indian support for a leadership position for China in that international organization.[45] At other points, there may even be convergence on international issues. Engagement between the leaderships and business communities of the two largest countries in the world may still be both useful and necessary. But any such dialogue, especially if not conducted in the spirit of open-mindedness and mutual respect, is of limited value.

India cannot afford to delude itself into believing that the direct and indirect challenges associated with China's rise will disappear on their own. The consequences for India's security and territoriality, its economic well-being, and its overall rise in the international system would be far too great.

Working towards a healthy bilateral relationship with Beijing is necessary, but the odds of that will be greater only if India can increase its economic and military power, preserve a regional leadership role, and actively shape the balance of power in the Indo–Pacific.

9

Thinking West: Pakistan, Afghanistan, and West Asia

Background: Post-Islamist Openings

Independence and Partition disrupted India's long tradition of engagement to its west, the broad region ranging from Afghanistan and Iran to the Arabian Peninsula and North Africa. If India's renewed engagement with its east after 1991 was motivated primarily by economic opportunity, and subsequently assumed a stronger security-oriented character with China's rise, its engagement to its west moved in almost the opposite direction. For decades until the mid-2010s, India's westward relationships were often seen through a Pakistan prism. Competition with Islamabad for influence within the Arab and Islamic worlds predominated, and India's approach to Afghanistan from the late 1970s onwards was frequently an extension of its Pakistan policy. Such factors also imposed limitations on its relationship with Israel. In many ways, the regional dynamics were influenced by questions concerning Islamism.

It should be emphasized at the outset that Islamism is distinct from Islam. Broadly, Islamism is the idea that society should be ordered according to rules laid down in sharia, or Islamic religious law drawn from the Quran, the Hadith, and Islamic jurisprudence.[1] What makes Islamism distinct from many other forms of religiously-inspired politics is the alternate sense of international order that some of its adherents espouse: that is, the idea of a religious *ummah* (or 'community') that transcends national boundaries and—by some interpretations—transcends the very idea of the sovereign state. This is very different from, say, the Organisation of Islamic Cooperation, which is a community of mostly Muslim-majority member states. The notion of the ummah is an old idea, dating back to the foundation of Islam and its sudden spread from the Arabian Peninsula to Spain, North Africa, and Central Asia. Unlike some other major religions, Islam was political from the very beginning. (Under Islamic law, political entities were defined as Dar al-Islam, governed by norms of Islam; Dar al-Aman, non-Islamic regions where Muslims could live safely under agreement or treaty; and Dar al-Harb, where Islam was contested.)[2] But the idea of resurrecting the ummah as an alternate to prevailing notions of statehood through violent means captured the imagination of some adherents in the twentieth century, and especially after 1979.

Until the fall of the Ottoman Empire during World War I, Islamism had a notional political leader in the form of a Caliph. The Ottoman rulers claimed that title to establish their own legitimacy and draw a direct link from the Umayyad and Abbasid caliphates during the period of Islam's early political and religious expansion. In practice, Islam was never as politically unified as is sometimes believed. Very early on—just six decades after the Prophet Mohammed returned to Mecca from Medina—a schism erupted between Sunnis and Shi'as that exists to this day. Moreover, rival caliphates and autonomous emirs arose in Spain, North Africa, and elsewhere. After World War 1 and the collapse of the Ottoman Empire, most of the Muslim world found itself colonized by European powers: France, Britain, Russia, and others. Turkey, which inherited the remains of the Ottoman Empire, began a process of radical secularization under Kemal Ataturk. Eventually, however, the House of Saud inherited the mantle of protectors of the holy cities of Mecca and Medina and established the Kingdom of Saudi Arabia. After the World War II, the attention of much of the Islamic world focused on the creation of the State of Israel. This was a product of the Zionist movement that was supported by the Western powers following the horrors of the Holocaust in German-occupied Europe during World War II. From the 1940s to the 1980s, Arab nationalist states and monarchies of Egypt, Syria, Iraq, and Jordan led unsuccessful military efforts to defeat Israel. This resulted in a series of wars and crises that were primarily to Israel's benefit, but partly concluded with the Camp David Accords of 1978.[3]

The awakening of modern Islamism had its origins in the mid-twentieth century. The Indian-born Pakistani Abul Ala Maududi, founder of Jamaat-e-Islami, was among the first to articulate a vision for a modern political order based on Islamism, one that was distinct from both ethnic or linguistic nationalism and apolitical Islam.[4] In Egypt, Maududi's contemporary Sayyid Qutb—whose ideas led to the foundation of the Muslim Brotherhood—argued that the rejection of nationalism, socialism, secularism, and liberalism and the embrace of Islamism were the solutions to the moral and political decay of the Islamic world.[5] The Shi'a cleric Ayatollah Ruhollah Khomeini argued in a similar vein that '[W]e have set as our goal the world-wide spread of the influence of Islam . . . We wish . . . to destroy the systems which are based on [Zionism, capitalism, and Communism] and to promote the Islamic order of the Prophet.'[6] Khomeini also advanced the notion of the ummah by playing down differences between Shi'as and Sunnis.

The year 1979 proved a turning point for Islamism, a moment when many of its political objectives began to be realized and militarized. In Iran, Khomeini inspired a successful revolution against the corruption and authoritarianism of the Shah of Iran, resulting in the establishment of a revolutionary state.[7] Just as significantly, in Saudi Arabia, an uprising led by Mohammed Abdullah al-Qahtani—a self-proclaimed *mehdi* (or redeemer)—resulted in a takeover of Islam's holiest site at Mecca. While violently suppressed, the episode generated fears of a radical Islamist revolution in Saudi Arabia. It encouraged Saudi rulers to express a greater tolerance for extremist interpretations of Islamism within the country, and promote those ideas and beliefs abroad, including through generous financial support.[8] By the end of 1979, Islamist mujahideen had begun to organize to expel Soviet forces from Afghanistan, where they were supporting an embattled communist regime. These efforts were planned and supported by Pakistan, Saudi Arabia and the United States.[9] Thus it was in 1979 that Islamism moved from the ideological to the political and military realms, with the overt and covert backing of several states, including Iran, Saudi Arabia, and Pakistan.

After the defeat of the Soviet Union in Afghanistan in the late 1980s, the mujahideen's attention turned to other places including Kashmir and Chechnya. But another precipitating moment resulted from the first Gulf War of 1990–91, during which the United States ousted Saddam Hussein's Iraqi forces from Kuwait. The increased presence of US forces in West Asia—and especially in Saudi Arabia—after the Gulf War became a point of contention. It became a focus for Osama bin Laden, a wealthy Saudi who had been peripherally involved with the Afghan mujahideen and who founded an Islamist terrorist group known as al-Qaeda (or 'the base'). Expelled from Saudi Arabia for his opposition to the royal family, bin Laden went on to wage global jihad against the United States, Israel, and others from a haven in Sudan and later from Afghanistan.

What followed is well-known. After attacks against US embassies in Kenya and Tanzania in 1995, and an American naval vessel in Yemen in 2000, al-Qaeda used passenger airplanes to destroy the twin towers of the World Trade Center in New York and part of the Pentagon in Washington on 11 September 2001.[10] This was the most deadly attack on US soil after the World War II, and by hitting a major financial capital and nerve centre it affected citizens and interests of many other countries, including India. The United States announced a 'global war on terror' and by the end of the year had gone to war in Afghanistan, toppling the Taliban government that sheltered bin Laden and al-Qaeda. Al-Qaeda's leadership spent many years in hiding. In December 2001, an attack by Jaish-e-Mohammed on the Indian Parliament, and Pakistan's movement of forces from its western border to its east, facilitated bin Laden's to escape from Tora Bora in Afghanistan into Pakistan. He eventually made his way to the Pakistani town of Abbottabad, where a secure home was constructed for him. Finally, after the US intelligence agencies refocused on the hunt for bin Laden, his location was identified and in 2011, US special operations forces killed him in a daring raid.[11]

Although al-Qaeda remained the most high-profile international jihadist group in the years that followed, Islamist attacks continued to take place with alarming regularity around the world: Bali, Beslan, Madrid, London, Boston, Paris, Brussels, Dhaka, etc. India was not immune: major terrorist attacks on urban centres such as Delhi, Mumbai, and Bengaluru picked up after the 1990s, peaking after 2000 until the 26/11 attacks in 2008 in Mumbai. Another wave of attacks against urban civilian targets took place between about 2010 and 2013 before terrorists and their sponsors opted to focus their efforts on military and law enforcement targets in India. But throughout this period, the regular terrorist attacks in India were linked to a wide-ranging international terrorist infrastructure that encompassed training, recruitment, and financing networks. Pakistan and Afghanistan were an epicentre of such activity.[12]

Even before bin Laden's death, but especially in the years that followed, Islamism began to assume new forms. In 2010, a series of demonstrations across West Asia and North Africa against established dictatorships—known as the 'Arab Spring'—resulted in new governments in Tunisia and Egypt, and the outbreak of civil wars in Syria, Libya, and Yemen. While initially viewed in the West as a flourishing of democratic forces, the Arab Spring instead saw Islamists attempt to establish themselves in many Arab countries. In particular, the political turmoil in Egypt, where the Muslim Brotherhood briefly came to power, was viewed with alarm in many Middle Eastern capitals. Additionally, the Syrian Civil War and a vacuum of power in northern and western Iraq created the conditions for the rise of a new group, the Islamic State of Iraq and Syria (ISIS, also knowns as IS, ISIL, or Daesh). ISIS distinguished itself from other jihadist groups, including al-Qaeda, by its focus on creating a state with a defined territory.[13] In June 2014, ISIS leader Abu Bakr al-Baghdadi declared a new 'caliphate', claiming leadership of the global Islamist jihadist movement. Around the world, older Islamist movements such as Boko Haram in Nigeria and Abu Sayyaf in the Philippines pledged allegiance to the new 'caliphate' of ISIS.

For a time, ISIS was successful in establishing jurisdiction in Syria and Iraq and building its global presence online and through affiliations. A large number of foreign fighters joined the movement, from virtually every part of the world. ISIS developed many of the trappings of a state, including a revenue model, taxation system, social services, and a flag. But eventually, its efforts proved unsustainable, its two main capitals—Mosul in Iraq and Raqqa in Syria—fell in 2017, and al-Baghdadi was killed. Despite its military defeat and loss of territory, the widespread appeal of ISIS recruitment and the regularity of ISIS-inspired terrorist attacks around the world suggest that violent Islamist extremism retains its allure. The return of the Taliban in Afghanistan in 2021 may yet galvanize other violent Islamist groups and raises the prospect of renewed terrorism in the West, South, Southeast, and Central Asia.

Following the 'Arab Spring', India's approach to the broader region has altered significantly. Most importantly, it has led to several Arab countries—including in the Gulf—reconsidering their post-1979 relationships with Islamist groups and attempting to modernize their economies and societies. This has translated into greater counter-terrorism cooperation with countries like India and Israel, as well as a renewed appreciation for the economic value of these new partners.[14] Whereas the likes of the UAE and Saudi Arabia had once been supportive of and sympathetic to the Afghan Taliban and Pakistan's claims to Kashmir, recent developments have led to a readjustment in their positions on these and other issues. Meanwhile, some Gulf states, such as Qatar, as well as non-Arab regional powers such as Iran and Turkey have attempted to fill the void by propping up more conservative Islamist movements in the region.

Other long-term strategic, political, and economic factors are contributing to the restructuring of the regional architecture. The geopolitical rivalry between Saudi Arabia, and Iran continues to play out, including through proxies in Yemen and Lebanon. Saudi and Emirati frustrations with Pakistan, such as over the war in Yemen, have also added to the appreciation for better relations with India. There is a generational change underway, with new leaders in Saudi Arabia, the UAE, and Qatar who do not necessarily carry the baggage of their predecessors and are open to new possibilities. The Gulf economies are also beginning to plan for a post-fossil fuel future, using their oil and gas riches to invest in emerging technologies. When these trends are considered together, the post-'Arab Spring' environment has opened up the possibility of economic integration; robust trade, technology, and people-to-people ties; and security and intelligence cooperation between India and several regional partners.

For India, today, 'thinking West' will require at least three separate and interlocking lines of effort. With Pakistan, India's objective involves compelling a nuclear-armed revisionist state to abandon its longstanding policy of using terrorism for political objectives. This is a tall order, particularly given that

Pakistan's military leadership sees few incentives to change course. This will therefore require India to use all its available positive and negative leverage. A second, and related, effort will require India to continue engaging Afghanistan within its limited means and capabilities, so as to prevent it from becoming a haven for terrorist activity targeting India. Finally, in the broader West Asian region, India will have to continue to balance its diverse interests: with Israel on defence, technology and democracy; with Saudi Arabia, the United Arab Emirates and other Gulf Arab states on diaspora, energy, trade, investment, business, and counterterrorism interests; and with Iran on connectivity to Central Asia and Afghanistan. The Abraham Accords—the normalization between Israel, and several Arab states led by the United Arab Emirates—has opened room for India to invest in some of these relationships simultaneously. Moreover, the prospect of an India–Middle East–Europe Economic Corridor (IMEC) could increase connectivity and reshape the broader region in some fundamental ways by linking India with the Gulf, Israel and Mediterranean.

Priority 9. Compel Pakistan

The origins of India's problems with Pakistan are long and complex. Differences over territory and identity stemming from Partition remained, but areas of convergence and even cooperation could be found between 1948 and the early 1960s. Such cooperation extended to the division of financial and water resources, the peaceful resolution of some boundary differences, relatively normal diplomatic and cultural relations, and even discussion concerning defence cooperation against China.

At the same time, Pakistan's employment of non-state actors has a long history. It began with the use of tribal lashkars to invade Jammu and Kashmir in 1947. In the 1960s, Brigadier A.A.K. Niazi (who would later achieve notoriety for surrendering at Dhaka in 1971) wrote of 'battlefields of the future' requiring infiltration to cause maximum disorder among enemy forces, part of the Pakistani military establishment's long tradition of thinking systematically about asymmetric and covert warfare. The use of non-state militias continued: in addition to Operation Gibraltar in 1965, Pakistan employed state-supported Islamist proxies to suppress pro-Independence Bangladeshi forces in 1971. The use by Pakistan of non-state actors in Afghanistan similarly pre-dates the Soviet invasion of 1979.[15] But after that period, Pakistan's material and political support for terrorists targeting India—including Khalistani and Kashmiri separatists and members of criminal syndicates—increased dramatically.

In 1989, ISI officers informed Pakistan's new Prime Minister Benazir Bhutto that they would use covert jihad in Kashmir, as they had done to considerable success against Soviet forces in Afghanistan. The ISI's S-Wing—in charge of covert paramilitary operations—organized training camps for militants, where they were armed with Chinese-made weapons and often trained side-by-side with Arabs. After arming and training these and other militants, the ISI helped to infiltrate them into India across the Line of Control, including under covering fire provided by the Pakistan Army.[16] Among the groups supported by the Pakistan Army and ISI over the years are Lashkar-e-Taiba (LeT), Jaish-e-Mohammed (JeM), Hizbul Mujahideen, and the Haqqani Network. While many of these groups have been provided financing, arms, ammunition, other equipment (such as radio sets) and training by the Pakistani state security apparatus, they have also benefited from an enabling environment—a safe space—to organise, recruit, arm, train, and fundraise.[17]

The 1980s added a further element to Pakistan's asymmetric and sub-conventional warfare with India: a nuclear deterrent. From the 1970s, Pakistan benefited from Chinese bomb designs and fissile material, as well as A.Q. Khan's efforts, and had a working nuclear weapon capability by the mid-1980s. The prospect of a nuclear deterrent emboldened Pakistan's support for Kashmiri insurgents beginning in the late 1980s, for D-Company in the early 1990s, for an incursion in Kargil in 1999, for terrorists targeting major Indian urban centres in the 2000s, and most recently for attackers of Indian military facilities in Jammu and Kashmir and Punjab. As former Pakistani Ambassador Husain Haqqani has written, 'The possession of nuclear weapons . . . encouraged impunity in the ISI's clandestine operations in Afghanistan and Kashmir.'[18] Pakistan slowly increased its capacity to produce weapon-grade fissile material. It also worked to successfully develop plutonium-based weapons capable of miniaturization and invested in tactical ballistic missiles for use on the battlefield.

By the mid-2000s, US intelligence estimated that the ISI ran 128 training camps and facilities in Pakistan, with about 1,00,000 armed militants under their management and influence.[19] In November 2008, ten Pakistani men—who had been trained for three months at Lashkar camps in Karachi and Thatta in Sindh—killed 166 innocent civilians in Mumbai in perhaps the most dramatic televised terrorist attack since 9/11. In preparation for these attacks, ISI paid a Pakistani American, Daood Gilani (operating under the name David Headley), to

survey targets in Mumbai. The operation's planners coordinated
the attack via phone from Karachi.

In addition to India, Afghanistan has been another target
of Pakistan-sponsored terrorist groups. During the 1990s,
Pakistani military advisors were involved in training Taliban
fighters, and Pakistani nationals fought in the Taliban (in the
late 1990s, Pakistanis were estimated to have constituted about
20–40 per cent of Taliban forces).[20] In July 2008, a Pakistani
named Hamza Shahkoor—trained by Lashkar-e-Taiba and
assisted by the Haqqani Network—detonated a car bomb in
front of the Indian Embassy in Kabul, killing an Indian diplomat
among other victims. In 2010, Mullah Abdul Ghani Baradar, a
deputy to Afghan Taliban leader Mullah Omar, was arrested in
Karachi at the instruction of the United States, after which the
ISI refused to let him be interviewed alone by US intelligence
officers (presumably because he would have revealed too much
about their working relationship).[21]

Pakistani military and intelligence leaders have employed
a range of responses to charges of supporting terrorism. One
has been to flatly deny any links, as they did after the 2008
Indian Embassy bombing in Kabul and the 26/11 attacks
in Mumbai. Terrorism against targets in Afghanistan were
sometimes justified by the notion of 'strategic depth', a
somewhat preposterous idea that Pakistani forces can fall back
into Afghanistan in the event of an Indian invasion from the
east. Pakistani military and civilian leaders also complained
about Indian encirclement and long exaggerated India's
security presence in Afghanistan (for example, the media arm
of Pakistan's military propagated the notion that India was
running intelligence operations out of dozens of consulates in
Afghanistan, when in fact India never had more than four).

All of this has served to justify Pakistan's support for terrorist groups.

India has attempted to address this compound challenge from Pakistan through both negative and positive leverage: 'sticks' and 'carrots'. The sticks have included a military mobilization in 2001–02 after the attack on the Indian Parliament, known as Operation Parakram. More recently, in response to major terrorist attacks at Uri and Pulwama, India responded with ground based 'surgical strikes' across the Line of Control and air strikes on Balakot. The intention of these actions was to reduce predictability in India's responses. While continuing efforts will have to be made to increase India's punitive options against Pakistan—such as diplomatic efforts to isolate and condemn Pakistan and link economic assistance and benefits to its support for terrorism, such as through the Financial Action Task Force—it will be necessary to continuously develop military contingency plans.

Meanwhile, 'carrots' have consistently been rejected by Pakistan, such as Indian efforts to normalize trade relations and conclude a transit trade agreement with Afghanistan. Even efforts at improving diplomatic relations—from the Lahore summit of 1999 to President Asif Ali Zardari's outreach initiatives of 2008 and Prime Minister Narendra Modi's visit to Lahore in 2015—have been stymied by the Pakistani military establishment, which engineered or approved the Kargil incursion in 1999, the Mumbai terrorist attacks in 2008 and the Pathankot attack of 2015.

Continued Indian engagement with Pakistan, even if at a low level, is sometimes necessary to maintain direct channels of communication and prevent third-party mediation, which India believes could tilt outcomes in Pakistan's favour. The growing power disparity in India's favour helps it in the long run, whereas Pakistan has often sought to internationalize bilateral differences and use external mediators to pressure India into making greater concessions. Bilateral engagement will remain one way of forestalling that possibility and is a major reason for why every Indian prime minister since 1998 has made a concerted effort to engage with Pakistan. Continued outreach to civilian political leaders, the business community, and elements of Pakistan's civil society may still have some value for India, even if it is obvious that the Pakistan Army retains ultimate veto power on relations with India.

The reality is that India's efforts at compelling Pakistan using sticks and carrots will be a long-term effort—and will depend on a multitude of factors. The growing Pakistani dependence on China (as a consequence of the China Pakistan Economic Corridor or CPEC), a more contested Afghanistan, and a Pakistan in domestic political disarray make the prospects of compelling its Army more remote. By contrast, any durable solution from India's standpoint would benefit from a capable leader on the Pakistani side, the Pakistan Army's acquiescence, and Pakistan's relative international isolation. These are the conditions that would be more conducive to Pakistan abandoning its long-standing policy of supporting terrorism against India and Indian interests.

One reason for continuing pessimism remains the strategic culture of the Pakistan Army. The army sees its role as protecting the country's 'ideological frontiers' rather than its security. As C. Christine Fair concludes upon assessing the Pakistan Army's own writings, 'Pakistan will suffer any number of military defeats in its efforts to [undermine India's position], but it will not acquiesce to India. This, for the Pakistan Army, is genuine and total defeat.'[22] It is this worldview that largely explains Pakistan's repeated military overextension. It explains also Pakistan's propensity to paint India as a perpetual aggressor. The army's profitable role in Pakistan's economy accounts for some of its continued exaggeration of Indian belligerence; a constant external threat is a good way for the military to profit financially too.[23] For all these reasons, a nuclear-armed, terrorism-supporting, revisionist Pakistan is a problem to be managed by India over the medium-term, not necessarily one to be resolved.

Priority 10. Engage Afghanistan

The hijacking of an Indian Airlines plane to Taliban-controlled Kandahar in 1999—and the release by India of terrorists in its custody in exchange for the hostages—serves as a potent reminder of the imminent threat to India of an unstable Afghanistan.[24] Since the toppling of the Taliban by US-led forces in 2001, India attempted to help rebuild Afghanistan as the country tried to emerge from decades of terrible conflict. For India, this often required it to work against the preferences of the United States and its allies and despite the best efforts of Pakistan and its terrorist proxies.

India's contributions to Afghanistan's state-building efforts were significant. In terms of hard infrastructure, India provided assistance for the Salma Dam (renamed the Afghanistan India Friendship Dam), transmission lines, hospitals, highways, and the Parliament building. Overall, India was among the largest providers of aid to Afghanistan between 2001 and 2021. The development of human capital was just as important. India hosted a large number of Afghan students in India and provided training for officers of the Afghan National Security Forces (ANSF). India also attempted to incentivize trade. Following Pakistan's reluctance to facilitate transit trade between India and Afghanistan over land, India used an air freight corridor to become the largest destination for high-value Afghan exports. Although India, Iran, and Afghanistan agreed to a trilateral trade agreement, and India developed a port at Chabahar to help access Afghanistan, progress was slow due to a number of political and commercial factors in India, Iran, and the international environment.

The Taliban's sweeping return to power in 2021 initially placed India at a disadvantage. India had been excluded from dialogue by the United States and played a peripheral role in parallel discussions sponsored by Russia, in part due to Pakistan's necessary role in bringing the Taliban to the negotiating table. But despite Pakistani triumphalism, embodied in the appearance of the ISI chief in Kabul shortly after its takeover by the Taliban, cracks began to appear between the Taliban and Pakistan. India, despite supporting factions of the Northern Alliance in their escape to Tajikistan, sought to take advantage of these differences, and continue its engagement with Kabul under the new Taliban dispensation. It gradually reopened its embassy and continued providing technical assistance and food aid. Meanwhile, relations between Afghanistan and Pakistan deteriorated further, with firing across their border. Despite concerns about the Taliban's treatment of minorities and women, the lack of formal diplomatic recognition, and continuing security complications (which initially prevented India from issuing visas for Afghan refugees and students), India has found a way to engage the new leadership in Kabul.

Nonetheless, geography and other factors constrain the potential role that India can play in Afghanistan. Working to improve connectivity, particularly via Iran and Tajikistan, will be necessary. But the contours of Afghanistan's future are still very unclear. Divisions and factions remain within the Taliban, and the security situation is still precarious in places. Questions around the Taliban's diplomatic recognition, a new Constitution, and the status of minorities remain uncertain. Despite these complications, continuing Indian involvement to ensure that its larger security and regional objectives are met will remain important.

Priority 11. Reshape the Middle East

Beyond Pakistan and Afghanistan, there are larger and perhaps more important dynamics underway in West Asia, a region in which India has diverse interests. Traditionally, India's approach to the region has been based on safeguarding three issues of interest. This required India to maintain a careful balancing act between Israel, Iran, and the Gulf Arab states (including Saudi Arabia, the UAE, Qatar, Oman and others).

The first long-standing interest for India has been energy imports. India has been among the major economies most dependent on the region's oil and gas production. Oil was traditionally sourced from a variety of partners, including Iraq, Saudi Arabia, Kuwait, and the UAE. Qatar has emerged as a major natural gas provider, particularly after international sanctions on Iran led to an Indian reduction in imports from that country.

A second major preoccupation has involved the large Indian diaspora, primarily in the Gulf Arab states, from whom India receives significant remittances. There are over ten million Indian citizens in the Gulf and that number is only growing. The safety and security of Indian citizens in West Asia has required the Indian government to evacuate Indian nationals from the region in the event of conflicts, including from Iraq and Kuwait in 1990, from Lebanon in 2006, from Libya in 2011, from Yemen in 2015, and from Israel in 2023.

Third, India has developed important security relationships, particularly defence imports from Israel and intelligence cooperation with a variety of partners. After normalizing relations in the early 1990s, India and Israel developed a low-profile but cost-effective defence industrial relationship that involved sales of critical military supplies, upgrading older military platforms, and some nascent joint production. In time, India grew into one of the largest export destinations for Israel's defence industry. But India has vital security interests in the region beyond defence cooperation with Israel. This extends to intelligence cooperation with the United Arab Emirates and Saudi Arabia, coordination on Afghanistan with Iran, and port access and logistical cooperation with Oman.

Although diaspora, energy, and security have been the three major pillars of India's West Asian engagement, new opportunities have rapidly opened up. With Israel, for example, economic links have expanded to cover pharmaceuticals, technology, tourism, infrastructure, and especially agriculture and water management. With Saudi Arabia, concerted efforts have been made to diversify away from Indian migrant labour to other forms of people-to-people exchanges, including highly skilled workers and Indian students, who now account for a large number of overseas Indians in the country. Saudi Arabia's massive investments in universities, infrastructure, start-ups, and entertainment have significantly widened the potential for economic, business, and people-to-people cooperation with India. The United Arab Emirates has become a major hub in the region for Indian trade, travel, and finance, and is now one of India's most important partners. Sheikh Mohamed bin Zayed's visit to India in January 2017 can probably be identified as the critical turning point in India's relationship with the Gulf.

The development and consolidation of new regional partnerships is a natural progression, building upon the long-term changes underway in a post-'Arab Spring' region. After the Abraham Accords normalized relations between Israel, on the one hand, and the UAE, Bahrain, Morocco, and other Arab states on the other, India welcomed the move and established a dialogue focused on economic issues with the United States, Israel, and UAE, called I2U2.[25] Starting with specific projects focused on renewable energy and food security, the group has attempted to deepen their partnership by facilitating business contacts and cooperating on space and other technologies. A bigger bet involves the IMEC, which promises to develop port, rail, road, digital, and hydrogen infrastructure between India and Saudi Arabia, and eventually connect it to Israel and Europe.[26] This infrastructure could service key economies along the way, making it more sustainable than some other major connectivity initiatives. It would also build resilience given the vulnerabilities of regional chokepoints such as the Suez Canal and Bab-el-Mandeb.

While initiatives such as I2U2 and IMEC can be built upon further, potentially reshaping the region, India will have to remain cognizant of other important relationships. These will extend to Iran, which is functionally less useful, but still important given cultural connections and north–south connectivity (including from the Indian Ocean to Central Asia and beyond). Tactical cooperation, as on Afghanistan and Pakistan, is another reason for India to preserve positive relations with Iran. Among the Gulf Arab states, India has recently had more friction in its relations with Qatar and Kuwait. As with Saudi Arabia, the UAE and Bahrain, there is potential to further bolster these relationships, especially in terms of investment. Similarly, Turkey is an important regional power whose relationship with India has sometimes been held back by close Turkey–Pakistan ties. India has certainly made efforts at improving relations with Ankara, including through humanitarian efforts following the 2023 earthquake. Coordination at multilateral bodies, including the G20 and United Nations has also sometimes been fruitful. Widening security partners in the region, including countries with advantageous geographical positions such as Oman and Egypt, is another Indian imperative. Despite the growing relationship with Israel, India has sought to continue its diplomatic ties with the Palestinian Authority, including through humanitarian aid and support for a two-state solution.

The broader region to India's west is undergoing a sweeping transformation. India's approach, traditionally driven by energy security, diaspora relations, and competition with Pakistan, need no longer be limited or defensive. The potential for West Asia to become an important hub for trade, finance, education, technology, defence, business, and connectivity is immense, and indeed is already evident. But capitalizing on these regional transformations will require, among other things, continued efforts to compel Pakistan; engage Afghanistan; transform ties with Saudi Arabia, the UAE, Qatar, and Israel; invest in Oman, Jordan, and Egypt; manage relations with Iran, Turkey,

and the Palestinian Authority; and mitigate the fallout from
Syria and Yemen. Given the immense turbulence in the region,
this will require careful trade-offs and delicate diplomacy for
years to come.

10

A Leading Power: Shaping the International Order

Background: Global Misgovernance

A consistent challenge in international relations has involved efforts at governing the world. International politics has always been fundamentally different from national politics, in that it is characterized by 'anarchy' or the absence of an overarching ruler or government. Ancient literature reflects ideals that governed the rules of war and peace between sovereign entities, whether in the Iliad in Greece, the Mahabharata in India, or in literature from the Warring States Period in China. Large empires such as the Persians, Romans, and Mongols made efforts at establishing normative standards among their multicultural subjects and in their peripheries. Some cultures even attempted to derive power and legitimacy from a religious figure, such as the Pope in Western Christendom, the caliph in the Islamic world, or the 'Son of Heaven' under successive Chinese dynasties.

In practice, however, governance on a global scale was only seriously attempted by the colonial European powers after their imperial projects extended to the Americas, Asia, and Africa. The Congress of Vienna after the Napoleonic Wars, the Berlin Conference of 1884–85, the League of Nations after World War I, and the Washington Naval Conference of 1921–22 represented various attempts by the great powers to manage international conflict through a balance of power, colonial-era agreements, institution-building, and arms control. Although initially led by Western European colonial powers, they eventually involved others such as Russia, the United States, and Japan. But much of the rest of the world—including India—was systematically excluded.[1]

In the waning stages of World War II, the effort at governing the post-war world was led by the victorious allies, including the United States, United Kingdom, and (initially) the Soviet Union. These discussions between 1941 and 1949 produced the Bretton Woods institutions, the Atlantic Charter, the United Nations, and eventually the North Atlantic Treaty Organization. These institutions were meant to govern the post-war economy and trading order, support decolonization efforts, and manage security competition, although they quickly morphed into venues and instruments of Cold War competition.[2] Eventually, efforts such as the Nuclear Non-Proliferation Treaty (NPT) in the 1960s were advanced to manage nuclear weapon competition.

As a newly decolonized country, India was a partial beneficiary of this post-World War II order. It joined the Bretton Woods institutions and United Nations, although remained distrustful of early Cold War efforts such as NATO. It also perceived the NPT to be discriminatory and not serious

about its disarmament obligations, and thus India never signed
it. Later, India also did not support the Comprehensive Test
Ban Treaty (CTBT), which it felt would permanently have
frozen nuclear 'haves' and 'have nots'. But for the most part,
India voluntarily joined several multilateral institutions meant
to govern global and transnational challenges. When they
were not informal groupings or venues for coordination and
consultation—such as the Non-Aligned Movement—they
were sometimes treaty-based organizations with a governing
structure, voting shares, and international obligations.

In broad terms, the numerous international institutions,
agreements and arrangements that constitute modern global
governance generally attempt to do three things. First, the
international order helps to preserve peace between sovereign
states through confidence building measures, arms control
arrangements, dispute resolution mechanisms, information
sharing mechanisms, and alliances and coalitions that preserve
a balance of power. Indeed, matters of war and peace are what
laid the foundation for international order in the nineteenth
and early twentieth centuries. As a consequence, many
disputes that had previously led to military conflict—including
territorial disputes and even debt repayment—are now settled
through non-military means, including diplomacy and
international arbitration. The UN Security Council (UNSC)
has long been the premier forum for deliberating and deciding
important matters of peace and security, but its effectiveness
has grown more questionable due to its composition, its lack
of implementation, and the frequent use of the veto by three
of the five permanent members. Other institutions have grown
to complement the UNSC, from informal groups, regional
organizations, international legal and arbitration bodies, and

security groupings. India is party to several institutions and treaties that govern security matters, including the Conference on Disarmament, the Chemical and Biological Weapons Conventions (CWC and BWC), the Geneva Conventions that cover wartime acts, and the International Court of Justice.

For New Delhi, arms control measures have been a major preoccupation due to India's development of nuclear weapons. This placed India at odds with the institutional cornerstones of global non-proliferation. As India has begun to normalize its nuclear arsenal, including through a waiver by the Nuclear Suppliers Group that allowed other countries to engage in civilian nuclear commerce with India, it has gradually become incorporated into other arms control mechanisms and export control groups. These have included the Missile Technology Control Regime (MTCR), the Wassenaar Arrangement (that controls exports of conventional military and dual-use technologies), and the Australia Group (the controls exports of chemical and biological weapons). India's entry into the Nuclear Suppliers Group, which would give it a vote and voice in determining nuclear exports, has so far been blocked by China.

A second set of institutions and arrangements are responsible for managing the global commons. These include parts of the world that are ungoverned or ungovernable by sovereign states. By their very nature, global commons tend to be overused without any individual country bearing responsibility for upkeep and sustainability.[3] In practice, the global commons might include the oceans, outer space, polar regions, the atmosphere, and by some reckonings cyber space. Governance of the oceans is based on the United Nations Convention on the Law of the Sea (UNCLOS), which was agreed to in 1982 and came into force in 1994. UNCLOS demarcates twelve

nautical miles from a country's coast as territorial waters, a
further contiguous zone for hot pursuit, an exclusive economic
zone (EEZ) extending up to 200 nautical miles from the
coast for exploiting natural resources, and international waters
beyond that. In practice, these principles are fundamental to
the development of maritime economies, coastal security, and
freedom of commercial and military navigation. There are
even dispute resolution mechanisms, such as the International
Tribunal for the Law of the Sea (ITLOS) in Hamburg.
Although the United States has still not ratified the agreement,
China's territorial claims in the South China Sea and its refusal
in 2016 to accept international arbitration in a dispute with the
Philippines have further eroded the principles of UNCLOS.

Other mechanisms to govern the global commons include
the Outer Space Treaty of 1967, which bans weapons of mass
destruction and assigns responsibilities for objects launched
into space. But China's 2007 anti-satellite test, which created
considerable debris, and unsuccessful attempts at creating more
ambitious codes of conduct of space mean that the risks to safety,
management of space debris, and weaponization of outer space
remain priorities. The Antarctic Treaty System, where India
has consultative status, preserves that continent for scientific
research and bans military activity. However, there are concerns
that the limitations imposed by these arrangements are being
tested by some countries, including China. The Arctic has been
less well governed and has seen greater competition between
the eight Arctic states for resources and territory. In 2013, India
joined the Arctic Council—the primary international forum to
discuss Arctic issues—as an observer.[4]

The atmosphere and climate long proved a contentious
area to reach international agreement because of the potential

costs to industrialization and economic development. In the 1980s and 1990s, concerns increased that human activity resulting in the emissions of carbon dioxide and other gases would cause average atmospheric temperatures to rise more than 2°, temperatures never experienced in human history. While acknowledging the problem, developing countries such as India believed that they were being asked to bear the costs for greenhouse gas emissions by developed countries. Meanwhile, developed countries were reluctant to part with financing or technology to mitigate emissions in the developing world. Initial national commitments resulted in the Kyoto Protocol in the 1990s, which enshrined the principle of 'common but differentiated responsibilities' between developed and developing countries. After a near breakdown of talks on a successor mechanism at the Copenhagen Climate Summit in 2009, the United States, China, India, Brazil, and South Africa negotiated an agreement that kept alive the prospect of a binding accord to succeed the Kyoto Protocol. The 2015 Paris Summit proved more successful, with each country agreeing to meet voluntary targets or 'nationally determined contributions' (NDCs). Subsequent summits of the Conference of Parties (COP) of the UN Framework Convention on Climate Change (UNFCC) have built further on these developments. Paris is not the only significant international climate agreement: the Montreal Protocol and its subsequent revisions have made remarkable progress in eliminating halogenated hydrocarbons that were depleting the ozone layer.

Cyber space is in some ways a partial global common. Servers, routers, cables, and satellite communication systems are owned by private companies or governments and are subject to national laws. However, it is often difficult to ascribe responsibility, and many aspects of cyber space remain ungoverned or under-governed. While not subject to an international treaty, Internet governance has to date benefited from a 'multi-stakeholder' model that also involves non-governmental actors. This can be contrasted with a multilateral model in which only sovereign states govern the Internet. But in the absence of a global treaty and fast-changing technologies, the future of governance in cyber space will have to be continuously renegotiated.

A third function of multilateral institutions is to govern economic and social interactions across borders. This can extend potentially to such issues as trade, lending, monetary policy, development, and standards. Participating countries benefit by increasing market access, harmonizing regulations, coordinating monetary and other economic policies, securing financial flows, and facilitating lending. The traditional bases for the international economic order were the Bretton Woods institutions: the International Monetary Fund (IMF), World Bank and General Agreement on Tariffs and Trade (GATT) which evolved into the World Trade Organization (WTO). In recent years, the IMF and World Bank have been criticized for their dominance by Europe and the United States. For a time, India sought to work with other partners, including in the BRICS, to create alternate mechanisms. But after those institutions reached their own limitations, India sought to work more within existing structures to widen their mandate and improve their efficiency. Meanwhile, coordinating monetary policy after the global financial crisis of 2008–09 saw the elevation of the G-20 (along with the Basel III accord on banking supervision) as vehicles to manage international economic and financial matters.

Other important international agreements concern standards, which extend to such issues as telecommunications and air traffic control. To give but one example now often taken for granted, the International Organization for Standards (ISO)—a non-governmental entity that has been granted consultative status by the United Nations—created a global standard for shipping containers in 1968, known as ISO 668. This ensured that standard-sized containers could travel around the world via ship, train, or truck without being opened, thus bringing down the costs and inefficiencies of international commerce. Such containers now account for over 60 per cent of all sea-borne trade.[5]

The WTO, meanwhile, ran into its own problems during the so-called Doha Round of negotiations. Among other problems, India felt that its priorities, shared by some other developing countries, were often side lined—such as on food security. It thus sometimes wielded a veto on issues such as trade facilitation. But in recent years, broader questions about the further reduction of global trade barriers and setbacks to the WTO's arbitration mechanism have called the institution's effectiveness into question. Instead, trade and economic facilitation has assumed new forms, including bilateral and regional trade agreements, and supply chain arrangements. Beyond tariffs, such arrangements sometimes extend to trade facilitation, licensing, subsidies (especially in agriculture), trade in services, and regulatory restrictiveness.

As this brief overview illustrates, in many of these cases, legacy institutions governing the international security order, the governance of the global commons, and the international economic order are fraying or no longer always fit for purpose. This is often a result of their design or leadership, or in other cases simply a product of greater global contestation on important issues. For India, it is important to distinguish between these two causes of flailing multilateralism. In part, their ineffectiveness is due to traditional powers that lead and manage these institutions being unwilling to accommodate rising powers such as India. This has required India to either forge coalitions to advocate for institutional reform, such as the G-4 with Japan, Brazil, and Germany to advocate for the expansion of the UN Security Council, or back alternative institutions, such as the Asian Infrastructure Investment Bank (AIIB).

At the same time, India faces resistance at many organizations from revisionist states or other powers that seek to fundamentally overturn an institution and its objectives. For example, China has blocked India's entry to the Nuclear Suppliers Group (NSG), not supported it at the UN Security Council, and advanced international efforts such as the Belt and Road Initiative without stakeholder consultations. These two distinct causes for the vacuum in global governance today will require India to advocate for reforming institutions rather than overturning or undermining their purposes. In other words, India will often act as a reformist—but not a revisionist—power on matters of global governance.

In many respects, despite its frustrations with the unfairness of legacy institutions and agreements, India has much to gain from a well-functioning international order. Under the right circumstances, greater socialization among states and growing consent can help dilute adversarial competition and render considerable benefits. For all its shortcomings, the period between the end of the Cold War in 1991 and the onset of the global coronavirus pandemic in 2020 witnessed the largest drop in global poverty, global inequality (that is, between countries but not within countries), maternal and child mortality and illiteracy, and the sharpest rise in life expectancy around the world in history.[6] Despite the challenges of Covid-19, considerable progress was made in this period in combatting communicable diseases, including in eradicating smallpox and polio, and countering HIV/AIDS. Between the Congo wars in the mid-1990s and the Syrian civil war in 2011, international conflict became less common and less deadly.[7] Some of these trends are now witnessing reversals or are at grave risk of being overturned. It is all the more important that India lead efforts to rejuvenate multilateralism, create new institutions, and engage with a wider array of stakeholders from the developing world, many of whom share important aspects of India's concerns and outlook. Such efforts also advance Indian interests. They can enable India to favourably shape international rules and norms, advance preferred outcomes, and position itself as a leading power.

Priority 12. Revitalize Multilateral Institutions

In past eras, major conflicts such as world wars have represented opportunities to reset the institutions that represent the international order. For example, the Concert of Europe came out of the Napoleonic Wars, the League of Nations developed after World War I, and the United Nations after World War II. While fortunately the Cold War ended peacefully, there was no such opportunity to reset the fundamental terms of the international order. As such, the United Nations system and other international institutions have preserved, becoming increasingly outdated.

For all its limitations, the United Nations remains important. The UN General Assembly (UNGA) is by far the most representative international institution and thus an important forum for global discussions. In addition, it is also the basis for various economic and social agencies, the UNFCCC, and agreements such as the UN Convention on the Law of the Sea. But making the governance structures more representative and thus more effective ultimately requires UNSC reform. The UNSC features five permanent veto-wielding members—the United States, Russia, China, United Kingdom and France (or P-5)—representing the victors of World War II and their successor entities.

To this end, India has been consistently advocating for its own permanent membership in the UNSC as well as better representation overall for other countries, including those of the Global South. There are past precedents for UNSC reform, including the addition of non-permanent members in the 1960s as well as expansion of the UN Economic and Social Council. India has been part of the G-4 (along with Germany, Japan and Brazil) advocating for their group's permanent membership, as well as two more permanent members from Africa. This might initially involve membership for India without a veto, subject to a later review following a specific timeframe. India is also part of a group within the UN called the L.69 Group, involving mostly developing states, which has advocated for more radical reform.

But such efforts have faced resistance from many quarters. A group called United for Consensus (or informally the Coffee Club) includes Pakistan and resists expansion of permanent membership. The Africa Group at the UN remains hesitant about proposing how it would fill its seats should expansion of permanent members take place. Although four of P-5 have agreed in principle to new permanent and non-permanent members (while doing little to facilitate the process), China alone has not voiced support. Ironically, the greatest obstacle to better representation for Asia and the Global South at the UNSC comes from its sole Asian member. For all these reasons, the formal negotiations over the UNSC reform have stalled since 2015, with little movement on details, timeframes or record of proceedings.

India will have to continue advocating for representation and hold the process more to account, including by building the coalition for reform. Various compromises by the numerous negotiating parties might well be necessary, such as on geographical representation or the veto. But a formula could theoretically be worked out that would make the UNSC— and by extension UN governance—more representative and effective. An absence of such movement risks making the UN more irrelevant and unable to fulfil the obligation of its charter to shield future generations from the prospect of devastating war, ensure respect for treaties and international commitments, and promote social progress and human dignity. Not making the UN representative of the world of the twenty-first century would also grant more legitimacy to non-UN bodies, whether regional groupings or institutions such as the G-20.

The UN system is not the only multilateral body in dire need of reform, from India's standpoint. The United States and Europe have been reluctant to cede voting and other powers at the IMF and World Bank. While India sought alternatives to these bodies, it has also tried to use its G-20 presidency to reinvigorate the World Bank, in particular. By broadening that institution's mandate and enabling greater public–private financing potential, India has tried to support the World Bank's transition into a more effective body to achieve the development, technological, and sustainability objectives now needed.

India has been an active participant in the G-20 and tried to take the most advantage of its presidency in 2022–23 to ensure consensus among the world's leading economies on political and development issues. It also tried to highlight the value of digital public infrastructure and sustainable development, along with institutional reform. By working in the troika format, with the preceding and succeeding presidencies of Indonesia and Brazil, India has tried to embed these objectives as part of long-term efforts. In addition, India has been a frequent participant (although not a member) of G-7 discussions and at the Organisation for Economic Co-operation and Development. While these groups represent advanced economies, India has worked with the latter in particular on artificial intelligence (through the Global Partnership on Artificial Intelligence) and energy (by engaging with the International Energy Agency). Separately, India has also coordinated with the Club of Paris—a group of which it is not a member—on lending standards as a creditor.

There are also older entities related to export controls and weapons of mass destruction. Although India is unlikely to sign the Nuclear Non-Proliferation Treaty (NPT) except as a recognized nuclear weapon state, it has largely adhered to its principles. India is now a full member of most major export control regimes but will have to continue advocating for membership of the Nuclear Suppliers Group (NSG), which has been resisted by China. Finally, there is an opportunity for India to take a bigger leadership role at two legacy institutions: the Non-Aligned Movement (NAM) and the Commonwealth. Although their purpose and utility are increasingly in question,

India now presents the largest economy in both organizations. This presents it with an opportunity to repurpose these groupings to make them more relevant to the present day.

Priority 13. Build New Coalitions

While India can do its fair share to reform legacy multilateral entities, new issues also present an opportunity for India to take the lead in building coalitions. Some of these groupings are smaller and focused on specific issues and outcomes, reflecting varying degrees of formality and structure. For example, BRICS represented one early effort. In that case, it was a venue for non-western economies to advocate for better representation on international economic matters. The reluctance of established powers to make institutions more representative contributed to the creation of the BRICS New Development Bank (NDB). Although BRICS has expanded to include new members such the United Arab Emirates, Ethiopia, Iran, and Egypt, the agenda has diluted and focused on preserving member states' sovereignty. Although each member has different priorities when it comes to sovereignty, one area of convergence involves finding alternatives to the dollar for international trade. Over time, the NDB's limits also prompted China to establish the Asian Infrastructure Investment Bank (AIIB). India, recognizing the need for greater infrastructure financing and noting what were initially serious commitments by China to build accountable governance structures, has the second-largest voting share in that organization. Another China-led grouping of which India is a member is the Shanghai Cooperation Organisation (SCO), which has proved an important forum for India to engage with the Central Asian republics. Nonetheless, because of internal differences—particularly between India and China— these groupings have had only limited utility. The NDB and AIIB have not proved adequate replacements for the World Bank and other multilateral development banks. The BRICS and SCO have sometimes been useful talk shops on specific issues.

More recently, India has entered into a variety of minilateral groupings involving the United States. Chief among these is the Quad, along with Japan and Australia. These countries have similar outlooks to the Indo–Pacific and have established a range of working groups to deliver regional public goods, including on health, investment, green technologies, maritime domain awareness, training, telecommunications and infrastructure. Although the Quad is not yet a security grouping involving the defence ministries, the four countries do conduct regular naval exercises, and much of their agenda is on security-adjacent issues. In part, the grouping is attempting to address the demands and concerns of smaller Indo–Pacific countries without contributing to a regional arms race. Another emerging minilateral group involving India and the United States has been I2U2 with the UAE and Israel. This has focused on economic and technological issues, including food security, clean energy, space, and investment, with the expectation that such cooperation can facilitate closer strategic partnerships in the future.

Beyond these 'mini-laterals' (and regional groupings in which has assumed a leadership role such as BIMSTEC or IORA), India has recently experimented with creating a new category of India-led treaty-based international organizations. The first such effort involved the International Solar Alliance (ISA) headquartered in India. New Delhi has since tried to establish similar groupings such as the Centre for Disaster Resilient Infrastructure (CDRI). These efforts involve drafting a treaty, opening it up for membership, ensuring ratification, establishing and staffing a secretariat, and thereafter working towards effective outcomes.

As new issues and actors start shaping the global governance agenda and legacy institutions wither or stagnate, the demands for India to establish, consolidate, and lead more effective international groupings will increase. In some cases, small, nimble, and issue-specific coalitions will prove sufficient. This might extend to some areas of emerging technology—such as artificial intelligence and space—where only a few countries or groupings have significant capabilities. But in time, contributing to a parallel institutional architecture can advance Indian interests while contributing to an international order that manages conflict, improves global growth and development, and helps effectively govern the global commons.

Priority 14. Amplify the Global South

Finally, India's objectives of transforming the international order will require it to engage new stakeholders and widen its partnerships. In international politics, like in domestic electoral politics, there is strength in numbers. At a moment when many countries have genuine frustrations that they believe are being overlooked by the world's leading powers, it is India's interests to listen to and channel those frustrations, particularly when India's interests align with that agenda.

The Global South has long been used by historians and in the development community, but less so in international relations. At face value, the countries that constitute the Global South have little in common: no shared language, religion, culture, political system, or even economic profile. But they do have two shared features. One, they have historical experience with colonialism, even if in some cases—as in Latin America—that is two centuries old. Two, the countries of the Global South all developed belatedly after the 1960s if not later. As such, these are states that have been politically marginalized and underrepresented at international institutions.

The renewed Global South agenda was prompted by four recent trends. One, their lack of representation at international organizations was compounded by questions of international lending and debt sustainability. This made them vulnerable to established lenders in the developed world. But the alternatives that presented themselves—such as China—have also given little relief. In fact, in many instances, Chinese lending was linked to hidden strings and ungenerous refinancing terms. For the Global South, the challenges of sustainable financing were made worse by the global pandemic, geopolitical shocks, and little influence over major central banks' interest rates.

A further challenge relates to climate justice. The countries of the Global South are among the most vulnerable to climate change, being in tropical regions prone to heatwaves, tropical storms, droughts and floods. They include small island states for whom rising sea levels represent an existential threat. Many feel that the developed world has not been forthcoming with climate finance and technology sharing, has tried to walk back the notion of 'common but differentiated responsibility', and has downplayed adaptation efforts. Despite grand promises, successive Conferences of the Parties (COPs) of the UNFCCC have delivered less than many had hoped.

Three, many countries of the Global South proved particularly vulnerable to disrupted supply chains during the Covid-19 pandemic. They were often among the last to receive critical medical supplies, protective gear, medical devices, pharmaceuticals, and vaccines, with many developed and industrialized countries prioritizing their own domestic constituencies. Coordination among the Global South therefore assumed greater urgency.

Finally, the Russia–Ukraine war highlighted vulnerabilities in the Global South in terms of food and energy security. Energy prices spiked and impediments to the export of grain and fertilizer from Ukraine and Russia led to rising inflation and concerns about food availability in vulnerable countries. The strategic priorities of Russia, Europe, and the United States seemed to take precedence over these concerns.

Taken together, these trends have led to a renewed understanding that the Global South needs to coalesce and coordinate on these matters, despite their many other differences. India opted to take a role in channelling these concerns during its G20 presidency by holding a 'Voice of the Global South' virtual summit, inviting over 100 countries to participate. It also attempted to place food, energy, and health security, supply chains, sustainable lending, and climate justice more squarely on the G20 agenda and worked to permanently include the African Union in that grouping.

The Global South thus represents a strategic opportunity for India to advance its own development objectives along with global institutional reform. By amplifying the concerns of the Global South, India can advance both its interests and its values, in part because the shared agenda also serves India's interests. The Global South is also not necessarily an anti-western construct, as some imagine. But India believes its status as a developing country along with its capabilities in the aggregate enable it to serve as a bridging power between the West and the Global South.

In addition to global efforts, India has attempted to bolster its outreach to the Global South through regional conferences and engagements. This includes the India–ASEAN Summit, periodic India–Africa Summits, meetings with all five Central Asian leaders, the Forum on India and Pacific Island Countries (FIPIC), as well as lower-level engagement with the Caribbean Community (CARICOM) and Latin America. These should not simply be meetings held for symbolic purposes but offer concrete opportunities for cooperation between India and key regional blocs on trade, investment, loans, technical assistance, energy, and natural resources. Building goodwill among these constituencies also helps India advance its global governance agenda.

In conclusion, the world represents considerable opportunities and diverse challenges for a rising India. The outlines of its approach to international affairs are clear, involving enhancing its own power, security, and influence; managing its periphery; ensuring a stable regional balance of power; reshaping the difficult region to its west; and assuming a growing role in global governance. While remaining conscious of its resource advantages and limitations, India must focus on key priorities. For the growing cohort of practitioners and professionals in Indian foreign policy—both in and out of government—understanding those priorities amid changing global circumstances will be crucial. Equally, others—including observers outside the country—would benefit from appreciating India's evolving worldview in a rapidly changing world.

Select References & Further Reading

Pre-Independent India

Ali, M. Athar, ed. *Mughal India: Studies in Polity, Ideas, Society and Culture*. New Delhi: Oxford University Press, 2006

Bagchi, Prabodh Chandra. *India and China: A Thousand Years of Cultural Relations*, ed. Haraprasad Ray. New Delhi: Munshiram Manoharlal, 2008

Baruah, S.L. *Last Days of Ahom Monarchy: A History of Assam from 1769-1826*. New Delhi: Munshiram Manoharlal, 1993

Bowen, H.V. *The Business of Empire: The East India Company and Imperial Britain, 1756-1833*. Cambridge: Cambridge University Press, 2005

Chandra, Satish. *Medieval India: From Sultanat to the Mughals, Part One*. New Delhi: Har-Anand, 2012

Chaudhuri, K.N. *Trade and Civilisation in the Indian Ocean: An Economic History from the Rise of Islam to 1750*. Cambridge: Cambridge University Press, 1985

Cooper, Randolf G.S. *The Anglo-Maratha Campaigns and the Contest for India: The Struggle for Control of the South Asian Military Economy*. Cambridge: Cambridge University Press, 2003

Davis, Richard H. *Global India circa 100* CE*: South Asia in Early World History*. Ann Arbor: Association for Asian Studies, 2009

Eaton, Richard M. *India in the Persianate Age, 1000-1765*. Oakland: University of California Press, 2019

Flatt, Emma J. *The Courts of the Deccan Sultanates: Living Well in the Persian Cosmopolis*. Cambridge: Cambridge University Press, 2019

French, Patrick. *Younghusband: The Last Great Imperial Adventurer*. London: HarperCollins, 1994

Gole, Susan. *Indian Maps and Plans: From Earliest Times of the Advent of European Surveys*. New Delhi: Manohar, 1989

Gopal, Surendra. *Born to Trade: Indian Business Communities in Medieval and Early Modern Eurasia*. Abingdon: Routledge, 2017

Gordon, Stewart. *The New Cambridge History of India: The Marathas, 1600-1818*. Cambridge: Cambridge University Press, 1993

Grewal, J.S. *The New Cambridge History of India: The Sikhs of the Punjab*. Cambridge: Cambridge University Press, 1991

James, Lawrence. *Raj: The Making and Unmaking of British India*. London: Little, Brown, 2010

Kamal, Kajari. *Kautilya's Arthashastra: Strategic Cultural Roots of India's Contemporary Statecraft*. Abingdon: Routledge, 2022

Kamandakiya. *Nitisara or The Elements of Polity*, trans. Manmatha Nath Dutt, Calcutta: H.C. Dass, 1896

Karashima, Noburu, ed. *A Concise History of South India: Issues and Interpretations*. New Delhi: Oxford University Press, 2014

Kautilya. *The Arthashastra*, trans. L.N. Rangarajan. Gurugram: Penguin, 1992

Keay, John. *The Honourable Company: A History of the English East India Company*. London: HarperCollins, 1993

Kulke, Hermann, K. Kesavapany, and Vijay Sakhuja, eds. *Nagapattinam to Suvarnadwipa: Reflections on the Chola Naval Expeditions to Southeast Asia*. Singapore: ISEAS, 2009

Majumdar, R.C. *Ancient Indian Colonies in the Far East, Vol. II: Suvarnadvipa*. Dacca: Asoke Kumar Majumdar, 1937

Metcalf, Thomas R. *Imperial Connections: India in the Indian Ocean Arena, 1860-1920*. Berkeley: University of California Press, 2007

Namakkal, Jessica. *Unsettling Utopia: The Making and Unmaking of French India*. New York: Columbia University Press, 2021

Nag, Kalidas. 'Greater India: A Study in Indian Internationalism'. *Greater Indian Society Bulletin No. 1*, 1926

Nehru, Jawaharlal. *The Discovery of India*. New York: John Day, 1946

Olivelle, Patrick, trans. *The Law Code of Manu*. Oxford: Oxford University Press, 2004

Panikkar, K.M. *India and the Indian Ocean: An Essay on the Influence of Sea Power on Indian History*. London: Allen and Unwin, 1945

Pardesi, Manjeet S. 'Region, System, and Order: The Mughal Empire in Islamicate Asia', *Security Studies*, 26:2, 2017

Parker, Grant. *The Making of Roman India* Cambridge: Cambridge University Press, 2008

Possehl, Gregory L. *The Indus Civilization: A Contemporary Perspective*. Lanham: Rowman & Littlefield, 2012

Raghavan, Srinath. *India's War: The Making of Modern South Asia, 1939-1945*. Gurugram: Penguin Books, India, 2016

Raychaudhuri, Hemchandra. *Political History of Ancient India: From the Accession of Parikshit to the Extinction of the Gupta Dynasty*. Calcutta: University of Calcutta, 1923

Roy, Kaushik. *Warfare in Pre-British India, 1500 BCE to 1740 CE*. Abingdon: Routledge, 2015

Richards, John F. *The Mughal Empire*. Cambridge: Cambridge University Press, 1995

Rizvi, S.A.A. *The Wonder That Was India, Vol. II*. London: Picador, 2005

Rubiés, Joan-Pau. *Travel and Ethnology in the Renaissance: South India through European Eyes, 1250-1625*. Cambridge: Cambridge University Press, 2000

Saran, Shyam. ed. *Cultural and Civilisational Links between India and Southeast Asia: Historical and Contemporary Dimensions*. Singapore: Palgrave Macmillan, 2018

Sen, Tansen. *India, China, and the World: A Connected History.* New Delhi: Oxford University Press, 2018

————*Buddhism, Diplomacy, and Trade: The Realignment of India–China Relations, 600–1400.* Lanham: Rowman & Littlefield, 2016

Singh, Patwant and Jyoti M. Rai. *Empire of the Sikhs: The Life and Times of Maharaja Ranjit Singh.* London and Chicago: Peter Owen, 2008

Singh, Upinder. *A History of Ancient and Early Medieval India: India: From the Stone Age to the 12th Century.* New Delhi: Pearson Education India, 2009

———— *Political Violence in Ancient India.* Cambridge: Harvard University Press, 2017

Stein, Burton. *The New Cambridge History of India: Vijayanagara.* Cambridge: Cambridge University Press, 2005

Stoneman, Richard. *The Greek Experience of India: From Alexander to the Indo-Greeks.* Princeton: Princeton University Press, 2021

Subrahmanyam, Sanjay. *Europe's India: Worlds, People, Empires, 1500–1800.* Cambridge: Harvard University Press 2017

Tharoor, Shashi. *An Era of Darkness: The British Empire in India.* New Delhi: Aleph, 2016

Vivekanandan, Jayashree. *Interrogating International Relations: India's Strategic Practice and the Return of History.* New Delhi: Routledge, 2011

Independence and Integration

Austin, Granville. *The Constitution of India: Cornerstone of a Nation,* Oxford: Oxford University Press, 1999

Basu, Narayani. *V.P. Menon: The Unsung Architect of Modern India.* New Delhi: Simon & Schuster, 2020

French, Patrick. *Liberty or Death: India's Journey to Independence and Division.* London: HarperCollins, 1997

Hajari, Nisid. *Midnight's Furies: The Deadly Legacy of India's Partition.* Boston: Houghton Mifflin Harcourt, 2015

Menon, V.P. *Integration of the Indian States.* New Delhi: Orient Blackswan Private Limited, 1956

Khosla, Madhav. *India's Founding Moment: The Constitution of a Most Surprising Democracy*. Cambridge: Harvard University Press, 2020

Raghavan, Srinath. *War and Peace in Modern India: A Strategic History of the Nehru Years*. Ranikhet: Permanent Black, 2010

Sarila, Narendra Singh. *The Shadow of the Great Game: The Untold Story of India's Partition*. London: Constable, 2006

Shani, Ornit. *How India Became Democratic: Citizenship and the Making of the Universal Franchise*. Cambridge: Cambridge University Press, 2018

Singh, Raghvendra. *India's Lost Frontier: The Story of the North-West Frontier Province of Pakistan*. New Delhi: Rupa, 2020

von Tunzelmann, Alex. *Indian Summer: The Secret History of the End of an Empire*. New York: Picador, 2007

The Cold War

Bass, Gary J. *The Blood Telegram: Nixon, Kissinger, and a Forgotten Genocide*. New York: Knopf, 2013

Benvenuti, Andrea. *Nehru's Bandung: Non-Alignment and Regional Order in Indian Cold War Strategy*. London: Hurst, 2024

Bhagavan, Manu, ed. *India and the Cold War*. Chapel Hill: University of North Carolina Press, 2019

Daulet Singh, Zorawar. *Power & Diplomacy: India's Foreign Policies during the Cold War*. New Delhi: Oxford University Press, 2019

Dayal, Rajeshwar. *A Life of Our Times*. Hyderabad: Orient Longman, 1998

Dutt, Subimal. *With Nehru in the Foreign Office*. Calcutta: Minerva, 1977

Engerman, David C. *The Price of Aid: The Economic Cold War in India*. Cambridge: Harvard University Press, 2018

Frankel, Francine R. *India's Green Revolution: Economic Gains and Political Costs*. Princeton: Princeton University Press, 1971

———— *When Nehru Looked East: Origins of India-US Suspicion and India-China Rivalry*. Oxford: Oxford University Press, 2020

Guha, Ramachandra. *India After Gandhi*. New York: HarperCollins, 2007

Gundevia, Y.D. *Outside the Archives.* New Delhi: Sangam Books, 1984

Haksar, P.N. *India's Foreign Policy and its Problems.* New Delhi: Patriot Publishers, 1989

Logan, William A.T. *A Technological History of Cold-War India, 1947-1969.* New York: Springer, 2021

Madan, Tanvi. *Fateful Triangle: How China Shaped U.S.-India Relations during the Cold War.* Washington: Brookings Institution Press, 2020

Malhotra, Inder. *Indira Gandhi: A Personal and Political Biography.* London: Hodder and Stoughton, 1989

Mansingh, Surjit. *India's Search for Power: Indira Gandhi's Foreign Policy 1966-1982.* New Delhi: Sage, 1984

McGarr, Paul M. *The Cold War in South Asia: Britain, the United States and the Indian Subcontinent,* 1945-1965. Delhi: Cambridge University Press, 2013

McMahon, Robert J. *The Cold War on the Periphery: The United States, India, and Pakistan.* New York: Columbia University Press, 1996

Mehta, Jagat S. *Negotiating for India: Resolving Problems through Diplomacy.* Delhi: Manohar, 2006.

Merrill, Dennis. *Bread and the Ballot: The United States and India's Economic Development, 1947-1963.* Chapel Hill: University of North Carolina Press, 1990

Mirchandani, G.G. *India's Nuclear Dilemma.* New Delhi: Popular Book Services, 1968

Ramesh, Jairam. *Intertwined Lives: PN. Haksar and Indira Gandhi.* New Delhi: Simon & Schuster, 2018

———— *A Chequered Brilliance: The Many Lives of V.K. Krishna Menon.* New Delhi: Penguin Random House, 2019

Rasgotra, Maharajakrishna. *A Life in Diplomacy.* New Delhi: Penguin Random House, 2019.

Sharma, Shri Ram. *India-USSR Relations 1947-1971 From Ambivalence to Steadfastness Part I.* New Delhi: Discovery, 1999

———— *Indo-Soviet Relations 1972-1991 A Brief Survey Part II.* New Delhi: Discovery, 2003

Singh, S. N. *The Yogi and the Bear: Story of Indo-Soviet Relations*. London: Mansell, 1986

Srivastava, Renu. *India and the Non-Aligned Summits: Belgrade to Jakarta*. New Delhi: Northern Book Centre, 1995.

Westad, Odd Arne. *The Cold War: A World History*. New York: Basic Books, 2017

After the Cold War

Baru, Sanjaya. *The Accidental Prime Minister: The Making and Unmaking of Manmohan Singh*. Gurgaon: Penguin Viking, 2014

Dixit, J.N. *My South Block Years: Memoirs of a Foreign Secretary*. New Delhi: UBS Publishers, 1997

Hall, Ian. *Modi and the Reinvention of Indian Foreign Policy*. Bristol: Bristol University Press, 2019

Jaishankar, S. *The India Way: Strategies for an Uncertain World*. New Delhi: HarperCollins, 2020

——— *Why Bharat Matters*. New Delhi: Rupa, 2024

Khilnani, Sunil, Rajiv Kumar, Pratap Bhanu Mehta, Prakash Menon, Srinath Raghavan, Shyam Saran, Nandan Nilekani, and Siddharth Varadarajan, 'Nonalignment 2.0: A Foreign and Strategic Policy for India in the Twenty First Century'. Centre for Policy Research, 29 February 2012

Malone, David. *Does the Elephant Dance?: Contemporary Indian Foreign Policy*. Oxford: Oxford University Press, 2011

Menon, Shivshankar. *Choices: Inside the Making of India's Foreign Policy*. Washington DC: Brookings Institution Press, 2016

Mohan, C. Raja, *Crossing the Rubicon: The Shaping of India's New Foreign Policy*. New Delhi: Penguin, 2003

——— *Modi's World: Expanding India's Sphere of Influence*. Noida: HarperCollins India, 2015

Singh, Jaswant. *In Service of Emergent India: A Call to Honor*. Bloomington: Indiana University Press, 2007

Sinha, Shakti. *Vajpayee: The Years That Changed India*. Gurgaon: Penguin India, 2020

Sitapati, Vinay. *Half Lion: How P.V. Narasimha Rao Transformed India*. Gurugram: Penguin India, 2016

Subrahmanyam, K., and Arthur Monteiro. *Shedding Shibboleths: India's Evolving Strategic Outlook*. New Delhi: Wordsmiths, 2005

Relations with China

Ali, S. Mahmud. *Cold War in the High Himalayas: The USA, China and South Asia in the 1950s*. Abingdon: Routledge, 1999

Arpi, Claude. *Tibet: The Last Months of a Free Nation. India Tibet Relations 1947-1962, Part 1*. New Delhi: Vij Books, 2017

Bajpai, Kanti. *India versus China: Why They Are Not Friends*. New Delhi: Juggernaut, 2023

Bajpai, Kanti, Selina Ho, and Manjari Chatterjee Miller, eds. *Routledge Handbook on China-India Relations*. Abingdon: Routledge, 2020

Bhasin, Avtar Singh, ed. *India-China Relations 1947-2000: A Documentary Study, Vols. I-V*. New Delhi: Geetika Publishers, 2018

———— *Nehru, Tibet and China*. Gurugram: Penguin Random House, 2021

Dasgupta, Probal. *Watershed 1967: India's Forgotten Victory over China*. New Delhi, Juggernaut, 2020

Fravel, M. Taylor. *Strong Borders, Secure Nation: Cooperation and Conflict in China's Territorial Disputes*. Princeton: Princeton University Press, 2008

Gardner, Kyle J. *The Frontier Complex: Geopolitics and the Making of the India-China Border, 1846-1962*. Cambridge: Cambridge University Press, 2021

Gokhale, Vijay. *The Long Game: How the Chinese Negotiate with India*. Gurugram: Penguin Random House, 2021

———— *Crosswinds: Nehru, Zhou, and the Anglo-American Competition over China*. Gurugram: Penguin Random House, 2024

Krishnan, Ananth. *India's China Challenge: A Journey through China's Rise and What It Means for India*. Noida: HarperCollins, 2020

Lintner, Bertil. *China's India War: Collision Course on the Roof of the World*. New Delhi: Oxford University Press, 2018.

Mullik, B.N. *The Chinese Betrayal: My Years with Nehru*. Bombay: Allied Publishers, 1971

Pant, Harsh V. *The China Syndrome: Grappling with An Uneasy Relationship*. New Delhi: HarperCollins Publishers India, 2010

Rao, Nirupama. *The Fractured Himalaya: India, Tibet, China 1949-1962*. Gurugram: Penguin Random House, 2021

Saran, Samir, and Akhil Deo. *Pax Sinica: Implications for the Indian Dawn*. New Delhi: Rupa, 2019

Saran, Shyam. *How China Sees India and the World: The Authoritative Account of the India-China Relationship*. New Delhi: Juggernaut Books, 2022

Smith, Jeff M. *Cold Peace: China-India Rivalry in the Twenty-First Century*. Lanham: Lexington Books, 2014

Shakya, Tsering. *The Dragon in the Land of Snows: A History of Modern Tibet Since 1947*. New York: Penguin Compass, 2000

Relations with Pakistan

Ayoob, Mohammed and K. Subrahmanyam. *The Liberation War*. New Delhi: S. Chand, 1972

Bajpai, Kanti P., P.R. Chari, Pervaiz I. Cheema, Stephen P. Cohen, and Sumit Ganguly. *Brasstacks and Beyond: Perception and Management of Crisis in South Asia*. New Delhi: Manohar, 1995

Bajwa, Farooq. *From Kutch to Tashkent: The Indo-Pakistan War of 1965*. New Delhi: Pentagon Press, 2014

Behera, Navnita Chadha. *Demystifying Kashmir*. Washington: Brookings Institution Press, 2006

Bhasin, Avtar S. *India-Pakistan Relations 1947-2007: A Documentary Study*. New Delhi: Geetika Publishers, 2012

Bisaria, Ajay. *Anger Management: The Troubled Diplomatic Relationship between India and Pakistan*. New Delhi: Aleph, 2024

Chari, P.R., Pervaiz Iqbal Cheema, and Stephen P. Cohen. *Four Crises and a Peace Process: American Engagement in South Asia*. Washington: Brookings Institution Press, 2007

Coll, Steve. *Ghost Wars: The Secret History of the CIA, Afghanistan, and bin Laden, from the Soviet Invitation to September 10, 2001*. New York: Penguin Press, 2001

Dasgupta, Chandrashekhar. *India and the Bangladesh Liberation War*. New Delhi: Juggernaut, 2021

Devasher, Tilak. *Pakistan: Courting the Abyss*. Noida: HarperCollins, 2016

Dulat, A.S. *Kashmir: The Vajpayee Years*. Noida: HarperCollins, 2015

Fair, Christine C. *Fighting to the End: The Pakistan Army's Way of War*. New York: Oxford University Press, 2014

Ganguly, Sumit. *The Crisis in Kashmir: Portents of War, Hope of Peace*. Cambridge: Cambridge University Press, 1997

Gokhale, Nitin. *Beyond NJ 9842: The Siachen Saga*. New Delhi: Bloomsbury India, 2014

Haqqani, Husain. *Magnificent Delusions: Pakistan, the United States, and an Epic History of Misunderstanding*. New York: PublicAffairs, 2013

Hiro, Dilip. *The Longest August: The Unflinching Rivalry between India and Pakistan*. New York: Nation Books, 2015

Hussain, Ijaz. *Indus Waters Treaty: Political and Legal Dimensions*. Karachi: Oxford University Press, 2017

Jacob, Happymon. *Line on Fire: Ceasefire Violations and India-Pakistan Escalation Dynamics*. New Delhi: Oxford University Press, 2019

Khan, Feroz Hassan. *Eating Grass: Making of the Pakistani Bomb*, Stanford: Stanford University Press, 2012

Lambah, Satinder K. *In Pursuit of Peace: India-Pakistan Relations Under Six Prime Ministers*. New Delhi: India Viking, 2023

Raghavan, Pallavi. *Animosity at Bay: An Alternative History of the India-Pakistan Relationship, 1947-1952*. New York: Oxford University Press, 2020

Raghavan, Srinath. *1971: A Global History of the Creation of Bangladesh.* Cambridge: Harvard University Press, 2013

Raghavan, T.C.A. *The People Next Door: The Curious History of India's Relations with Pakistan.* Noida: HarperCollins, 2017

Siddiqa, Ayesha. *Military Inc.: Inside Pakistan's Military Economy*, 2nd Edition. London: Pluto Press, 2017

Small, Andrew. *The China-Pakistan Axis: Asia's New Geopolitics.* New York: Oxford University Press, 2015

Swami, Praveen. *India, Pakistan and the Secret Jihad. The Covert War in Kashmir, 1947-2004.* London: Routledge, 2007

Tankel, Stephen. *Storming the World Stage: The Story of Lashkar-e-Taiba.* New York: Oxford University Press, 2013

Relations with the Neighbourhood and Indian Ocean

Baruah, Darshana M. *The Contest for the Indian Ocean: And the Making of a New World Order.* New Haven: Yale University Press, 2024

Bhasin, Avtar S. *India-Bangladesh Relations 1971-2002 Documents.* New Delhi: Geetika Publishers, 2003

———— *India in Sri Lanka: Between Lion and the Tigers.* New Delhi: Manas Publications, 2004

———— *Nepal-India Nepal-China Relations 1947-June 2005.* New Delhi: Geetika Publishers, 2005

Brewster, David. *India's Ocean: The Story of India's Bid for Regional Leadership.* New York: Routledge, 2014

Brewster, David and Ranjit Rai. 'Operation Lal Dora: India's Aborted Military Intervention in Mauritius'. *Asian Security.* Vol. 9, Issue 1, 2013

———— 'Flowers Are Blooming: The Story of the India Navy's Secret Operation in the Seychelles'. *The Naval Review.* Vol. 99, No. 1, 2011

Chakma, Bhumitra. *South Asian Regionalism: The Limits of Cooperation.* Bristol: Bristol University Press, 2020

Chakravarty, Pinak Ranjan. *Transformation: Emergence of Bangladesh and Evolution of India-Bangladesh Ties.* New Delhi: KW Publishers, 2024

Das, Brajbir S. *Mission to Bhutan: A Nation in Transition.* New Delhi: Vikas Publishing House, 1995

Datta Ray, Sunanda K. *Smash and Grab: Annexation of Sikkim.* New Delhi: Vikas, 1984

Dixit, J.N. *Assignment Colombo.* New Delhi: Konark Publishers, 1998

Harrison, Selig S., and K. Subrahmanyam. *Superpower Rivalry in the Indian Ocean: Indian and American Perspectives.* New York: Oxford University Press, 1989

Jha, Prashant. *Battles of the New Republic: A Contemporary History of Nepal.* New Delhi: Aleph, 2014

Mulmi, Amish Raj. *All Roads Lead North: Nepal's Turn to China.* Chennai: Context, 2021

Muni, S. D. *India and Nepal: A Changing Relationship.* New Delhi: Konark Publishers, 1992

——— *India's Foreign Policy: The Democracy Dimension: With Special Reference to Neighbours.* New Delhi: Foundation Books, 2009

Paliwal, Avinash. *My Enemy's Enemy: India in Afghanistan from the Soviet Invasion to the US Withdrawal.* Noida: HarperCollins, 2017

———. *India's Near East: A New History.* London: Hurst, 2024

Rae, Ranjit. *Kathmandu Dilemma: Resetting India-Nepal Ties.* Gurugram: Penguin Random House India, 2022

Roy-Chaudhury, Shantanu. *The China Factor: Beijing's Expanding Engagement in Sri Lanka, Maldives, Bangladesh, and Myanmar.* Abingdon: Routledge, 2023

Singh, Sushant. *Mission Overseas: Daring Operations by the Indian Military.* New Delhi: Juggernaut, 2017

Sinha, A.C. *Himalayan Kingdom Bhutan: Tradition, Transition and Transformation.* New Delhi: Indus, 2004

van Schendel, Willem. *A History of Bangladesh.* Cambridge: Cambridge University Press, 2020

Relations with the United States

Acharya, Nish. *The India–US Partnership: $1 Trillion by 2030.* New Delhi: Oxford University Press, 2016

Ahamed, Meenakshi. *A Matter of Trust: India-US Relations from Truman to Trump*. Noida: HarperCollins India, 2021

Chari, P.R., ed. *Indo-US Nuclear Deal: Seeking Synergy in Bilateralism*. New Delhi, Routledge, 2009

Chaudhuri, Rudra. *Forged in Crisis: India and the United States since 1947*. Noida: HarperCollins India, 2014

George, Varghese K. *Open Embrace: India-US Ties in a Divided World*. New Delhi: India Viking, 2021

Kux, Dennis. *India and the United States: Estranged Democracies, 1941-1991*. Washington: National Defense University Press, 1992

Mistry, Dinshaw. *The US-India Nuclear Agreement: Diplomacy and Domestic Politics*. Delhi: Cambridge University Press, 2014

Mohan, C. Raja. *Impossible Allies: Nuclear India, United States, and the Global Order*. New Delhi: India Research Press, 2006

Pant, Harsh V. *The US-India Nuclear Pact: Policy, Process, and Great Power Politics*. New Delhi: Oxford University Press, 2011

Pant, Harsh V. and Yogesh Joshi. *The US Pivot and Indian Foreign Policy: Asia's Evolving Balance of Power*. London: Palgrave Macmillan, 2016

Talbott, Strobe. *Engaging India: Diplomacy, Democracy, and the Bomb*. Washington: Brookings Institution, 2004

Raghavan, Srinath. *The Most Dangerous Place: A History of the United States in South Asia*. New Delhi: Allen Lane, 2018.

Sirohi, Seema. *Friends with Benefits: The India-US Story*. Gurugram: HarperCollins Publishers India, 2023

Relations with Asia and the Indo–Pacific

Basrur, Rajesh and Sumitha Narayanan Kutty, eds. *India and Japan: Assessing the Strategic Partnership*. Singapore: Palgrave Macmillan, 2018

Chaulia, Sreeram. Modi Doctrine: The Foreign Policy of India's Prime Minister. New Delhi: Bloomsbury, 2016

Bhasin, Avtar S. *ASEAN-India Progress & Prosperity: Documents*. New Delhi: Geetika Publishers, 2012

Bhatia, Rajiv. *India-Myanmar Relations: Changing Contours*. New York: Routledge, 2016

Brewster, David, ed. *India & China at Sea: Competition for Naval Dominance in the Indian Ocean.* New Delhi: Oxford University Press, 2018

Datta, Sreeradha. *Act East Policy and Northeast India.* New Delhi: Vitasta Publishing, 2021

Datta-Ray, Sunanda K. *Looking East to Look West: Lee Kuan Yew's Mission India.* Singapore: ISEAS, 2009

Grare, Frederic. *India Turns East: International Engagement and US-China Rivalry.* Gurgaon: Penguin Random House, 2017

Jaishankar, Dhruva. 'Acting East: India in the Indo–Pacific'. Brookings India, 2019

Khurana, Gurpreet S. 'Security of Sea Lanes: Prospects for India-Japan Cooperation'. *Strategic Analysis.* Vol. 31, No. 1, 2007

Mattoo, Amitabh and Frederic Grare, Eds. *India and ASEAN: The Politics of India's Look East Policy.* New Delhi, Manohar, 2001

Menon, Shivshankar. *India and Asian Geopolitics: The Past, Present.* Washington: Brookings Institution Press, 2021

Medcalf, Rory. *Indo–Pacific Empire: China, America and the Contest for the World's Pivotal Region.* Manchester: Manchester University Press, 2020

Mohan, C. Raja. *Samudra Manthan: Sino-Indian Rivalry in the Indo–Pacific.* Washington: Carnegie Endowment for International Peace, 2012

Rehman, Iskander. 'India, China, and Differing Conceptions of the Maritime Order'. The Brookings Institution, 20 June 2017

Thant Myint-U. *Where China Meets India: Burma and the New Crossroads of Asia.* London: Faber & Faber, 2011

Relations with the Middle East, Europe, Africa, and Latin America

Bhatia, Rajiv. *India–Africa Relations: Changing Horizons.* Abingdon: Routledge, 2022

Bhojwani, Deepak. *Latin America, the Caribbean and India: Promise and Challenge.* New Delhi: Pentagon Press, 2015

Blarel, Nicolas. *The Evolution of India's Israel Policy: Continuity, Change, and compromise since 1922.* New Delhi: Oxford University Press, 2015

Dubey, Ajay K. *Indo-African Relations in the Post-Nehru era, 1965-1985.* New Delhi: Kalinga Publishers, 1990

Kumaraswamy, P.R. *India's Israel Policy.* New York: Columbia University Press, 2010

Mohan, Garima. 'The Evolution of Indian Foreign Policy Towards Europe'. *India Quarterly* 78, no. 2 (May 2022), 248–260

Mukherjee, Bhaswati. *India and EU: An Insider's View.* New Delhi: Vij Books, 2018

Singh, Gurjit, ed. *Opportunity Beckons: Adding Momentum to the Indo-German Partnership.* New Delhi: Rupa, 2017

Indian Foreign Policy

Abhyankar, Rajendra M. *Indian Diplomacy: Beyond Strategic Autonomy.* New York: Oxford University Press, 2019

Ayres, Alyssa. *Our Time Has Come: How India Is Making Its Place in the World.* New York: Oxford University Press, 2018

Bajpai, Kanti, Saira Basit, and V. Krishnappa, eds. *India's Grand Strategy: History, Theory, Cases.* New Delhi: Routledge, 2014

Basrur, Rajesh, and Kate Sullivan de Estrada. *Rising India: Status and Power.* Abingdon: Routledge, 2017

Chinoy, Sujan. *World Upside Down: India Recalibrates Its Geopolitics.* Gurugram: HarperCollins India, 2023

Dutt, V.P. *India's Foreign Policy in a Changing World.* Delhi: Vikas, 1999.

Malone, David M., C. Raja Mohan, and Srinath Raghavan, eds. *The Oxford Handbook of Indian Foreign Policy.* Oxford: Oxford University Press, 2015

Miller, Manjari Chatterjee. *Wronged by Empire: Post-Imperial Ideology and Foreign Policy in India and China.* Palo Alto: Stanford University Press, 2013

Mukherjee, Rohan. *Ascending Order: Rising Powers and the Politics of Status in International Institutions*. Cambridge: Cambridge University Press, 2022

Nayar, Baldev Raj and T.V. Paul. *India in the World Order: Searching for Major-Power Status*. Cambridge: Cambridge University Press, 2003

Pande, Aparna. *From Chanakya to Modi: The Evolution of India's Foreign Policy*. Noida: HarperCollins, 2017

————ed. *Routledge Handbook on South Asian Foreign Policy*. Abingdon: Routledge, 2022

Pant, Harsh V., ed. *Indian Foreign Policy in a Unipolar World*. New Delhi: Routledge, 2009

———— *Indian Foreign Policy: An Overview*. Manchester: Manchester University Press, 2016

Paul, T.V. *The Unfinished Quest: India's Search for Major Power Status from Nehru to Modi*. New York: Oxford University Press, 2024.

Saran, Shyam. *How India Sees the World: Kautilya to the 21st Century*. New Delhi: Juggernaut, 2017

Saran, Samir, and Shashi Tharoor. *The New World Disorder and the Indian Imperative*. New Delhi: Aleph, 2020

Schaffer, Teresita C., and Howard B. Schaffer. *India at the Global High Table: The Quest for Regional Primacy and Strategic Autonomy*. Washington: Brookings Institution Press, 2016

Tanham, George. 'Indian Strategic Thought: An Interpretive Essay,' Rand Corporation, 1992

Tharoor, Shashi. *Pax Indica: India and the World of the 21st Century*. New Delhi: Penguin India, 2011

Military and Intelligence

Ahuja, Amit and Devesh Kapur, eds. *Internal Security in India: Violence, Order, and the State*. New York: Oxford University Press, 2023

Cohen, Stephen P. *The Indian Army: Its Contribution to the Development of a Nation*. Berkeley, University of California Press, 1971

Cohen, Stephen P. and Sunil Dasgupta. *Arming Without Aiming: India's Military Modernization*. Washington: Brookings Institution Press, 2010

Gokhale, Nitin. *R.N. Kao: Gentleman Spymaster*. New Delhi: Bloomsbury India, 2019

Gupta, Arvind. *How India Manages Its National Security*. New Delhi: Viking, 2018

Kalyanaraman, S. *India's Military Strategy: Countering Pakistan's Challenge*. New Delhi: Bloomsbury, 2022

Kanwal, Gurmeet, and Neha Kohli, eds. *Defence Reforms: A National Imperative*. New Delhi: Pentagon Press, 2018

Kargil Review Committee. *From Surprise to Reckoning: The Kargil Review Committee Report* New Delhi: Sage Publications, 2000

Kavic, Lorne J. *India's Quest for Security: Defence Policies, 1947-1965*. Berkeley: University of California Press, 1967

Khera, P.N. *Operation Vijay: The Liberation of Goa and Other Portuguese Colonies in India (1961)* New Delhi: Ministry of Defense, 1974

Mukherjee, Anit. *The Absent Dialogue: Politicians, Bureaucrats, and the Military in India*. New Delhi: Oxford University Press, 2019

Mukherjee, Anit and C. Raja Mohan, eds. *India's Naval Strategy and Asian Security* Abingdon: Routledge, 2016

Nair, K. Sankaran. *Inside IB and RAW: The Rolling Stone that Gathered Moss*. New Delhi: Manas Publications, 2008

Pant, Harsh V., ed. *The Routledge Handbook of Indian Defence Policy*. New Delhi: Routledge, 2020

Rosen, Stephen P. *Societies & Military Power: India and Its Armies*. Ithaca: Cornell University Press, 1996

Subramaniam, Arjun. *India's Wars: A Military History, 1947-1971* (Noida: HarperCollins, 2016)

———*Full Spectrum: India's Wars, 1972-2020* (Noida: HarperCollins, 2022)

Thimayya, K.S. *Experiment in Neutrality*. New Delhi: Vision Books, 1981

Vaishnav, Milan, ed. *Institutional Roots of India's Security Policy*. Oxford: Oxford University Press, 2024.

Wilkinson, Steven I. *Army and Nation: The Military and Indian Democracy since Independence*. Cambridge: Harvard University Press, 2015

The Economy and Technology

Ahluwalia, Montek S. *Backstage: The Story Behind India's High Growth Years*. New Delhi: Rupa, 2019

Anderson, Robert S. *Nucleus and Nation: Scientists, International Networks, and Power in India*. Chicago: University of Chicago Press, 2010

Bhagwati, Jagdish N. *India in Transition: Freeing the Economy*. New York: Clarendon Press, 1993

Crabtree, James. *The Billionaire Raj: A Journey Through India's New Gilded Age*. London: OneWorld Publications, 2018

Dadabhoy, Bakhtiar K. *Homi J. Bhabha: A Life*. New Delhi: Rupa, 2023

Deaton, Angus. *The Great Escape: Health, Wealth, and the Origins of Inequality*. Princeton: Princeton University Press, 2013

Kelkar, Vijay and Ajay Shah. *In Service of the Republic: The Art and Science of Economic Policy*. Gurugram: Penguin Random House, 2019.

Kotasthane, Pranay and Abiram Manchi. *When the Chips are Down: A Deep Dive into a Global Crisis*. New Delhi: Bloomsbury India, 2023

Lele, Ajay. *Institutions that Shaped Modern India: ISRO*. New Delhi: Rupa, 2021

Mehra, Puja. *The Lost Decade (2008-18): How India's Growth Story Devolved into Growth Without a Story*. Gurugram: Penguin Random House, 2019

Mohan, Rakesh, ed. *India Transformed: 25 Years of Economic Reforms*, Gurgaon: Penguin Viking, 2017

Muralidharan, Karthik. *Accelerating India's Development: A State-Led Roadmap for Effective Governance*. Gurugram: Penguin Random House, 2024

Nilekani, Nandan and Viral Shah. *Rebooting India: Realizing a Billion Aspirations*. Gurgaon: Penguin, 2016

Panagariya, Arvind. *India: The Emerging Giant*. New York: Oxford University Press, 2010

Perkovich, George. *India's Nuclear Bomb: The Impact on Global Proliferation*. Berkeley: University of California Press, 1999

Ramachandran, M. *Metro Rail Projects in India: A Study in Project Planning*. Oxford: Oxford University Press, 2011

Rodrik, Dani and Arvind Subramanian. 'From "Hindu Growth" to Productivity Surge: The Mystery of the Indian Growth Transition'. IMF Staff Papers, Vol. 52, No. 2, September 2005

Seshadri, V.S. *Free Trade Agreements: India and the World*. Oxford: Oxford University Press, 2023

Sukumar, Arun. *Midnight's Machines: A Political History of Technology in India*. Gurugram: Penguin Viking, 2019

Suri, Anirudh. *The Great Tech Game: Shaping Geopolitics and the Destinies of Nations*. Noida: HarperCollins India, 2022

Tellis, Ashley J. *India's Emerging Nuclear Posture: Between Recessed Deterrent and Ready Arsenal*. Santa Monica: Rand Corporation, 2001

Tumbe, Chinmay. *India Moving: A History of Migration*. Gurugram: Penguin Random House, 2018

International Institutions

Jha, Vyoma. *The Making of the International Solar Alliance: India's Moment in the Sun*. Oxford: Oxford University Press, 2023

Kumar, Mohan. *Negotiation Dynamics of the WTO: An Insider's Account*. Basingstoke: Springer, 2018

Nachiappan, Karthik. *Does India Negotiate?* New Delhi: Oxford University Press, 2019

Puri, Hardeep Singh. *Perilous Interventions: The Security Council and the Politics of Chaos*. Noida: HarperCollins, 2016

Saez, Lawrence. *The South Asian Association for Regional Cooperation (SAARC): An Emerging Collaboration Architecture*. Abingdon: Routledge, 2011

Stuenkel, Oliver. *The BRICS and the Future of Global Order*. Lanham Md.: Lexington Books, 2020

Xavier, Constantino. 'Bridging the Bay of Bengal: Toward a Stronger BIMSTEC'. Carnegie India, February 2018

Acknowledgements

This book was a long time in the making. A very different version was originally composed between 2016 and 2018, but for various reasons I opted to pause, reconsider, and rewrite it almost entirely between 2021 and 2024. While writing was sometimes a lonely enterprise, it would not have been possible without a great deal of support from a great many people. I am indebted to Penguin Random House India, particularly Meru Gokhale who initially commissioned this work, Manasi Subramaniam for seeing it through to its conclusion, and Yash Daiv for his careful copy edits. I am also appreciative of several colleagues, assistants and interns who helped and provided constructive feedback over the years, especially Shruti Godbole, Nitika Nayar, and Ammar Nainar.

I owe much gratitude to my employers over the past two decades and others who gave me the professional space, time, and resources to think through the ideas in this book. Early in my career, I learned a lot from working with Edward Luttwak on how to think creatively through global and historical problems. The late Stephen P. Cohen, for whom I worked as a research assistant, was not only extraordinarily kind and generous but also introduced me to the complexities of security policy and India–Pakistan dynamics. I am grateful to Daniel Twining, Andrew Small and Craig Kennedy for supporting me at the German Marshall Fund from 2009 to 2016, and giving me considerable leeway, responsibilities and exposure to contemporary policy issues in such places as Europe, Southeast Asia and China. Rajesh Basrur and Sumitha Narayanan Kutty enabled a fellowship at the S. Rajaratnam School of International Studies in 2015 that allowed me to explore security relations between India and Japan. Additionally, Michael Fullilove at the Lowy Institute encouraged me to investigate growing India–Australia ties and invited me to be a non-resident fellow at his organization.

For my experiences at Brookings India between 2016 and 2019, when I initially conceived of and began writing this book, I am obliged to Vikram Singh Mehta, Harsha V. Singh, Rakesh Mohan, Shivshankar Menon, Shamika Ravi and Rahul Tongia. My perch in New Delhi in those years allowed me to traverse the length and breadth of India, interact with a variety of stakeholders and engage policymakers all over South and Southeast Asia. The sections on the Act East Policy, Indo–Pacific, Indian Ocean and India–US relations draw from some of my research during this time. Various colleagues at the Brookings Institution in Washington were also supportive of my efforts: Martin Indyk, Strobe Talbott and Bruce Jones encouraged me to write this book, and I am grateful to several anonymous reviewers of an earlier draft for their candid feedback.

After 2019, Samir Saran and Sunjoy Joshi gave me a chance at the Observer Research Foundation (ORF) to create a new institution, which became ORF America in Washington, D.C. The board of directors and my colleagues at ORF America have been extraordinarily supportive, but I want to single out Sharon Stirling, who helped tremendously in the organization's establishment and administration, thus giving me the time and space for creative and intellectual endeavours. Over many years, I drew inspiration from conversations with hundreds of policymakers, officials, and scholars from India and elsewhere. But I want to particularly acknowledge Tanvi Madan, Anit Mukherjee and Constantino Xavier for their many years of professional support and generous friendship.

Last, but not least, I want to thank my family. In their own ways, all four of my grandparents—Sulochana and K. Subrahmanyam and Lalita and K.S. Krishnan—and my late mother Shobha Jaishankar taught me a lot about India, its history, culture, and society. I remain in awe of their fierce intellects and rich perspectives. My immediate family— Kyoko and S. Jaishankar, Medha and Arjun—have been constant companions and sources of inspiration and humour. Most importantly, I want to express my immense gratitude to my wife, Cassandra, for her love, support, patience, and intellectual companionship. My children, Vivica and Darius, are everything to me. I hope this book and its contents prove a modest contribution to their ability to grow up in a more secure, prosperous, and knowledge-filled world.

Notes

Introduction

1   Data derived from 'World Economic Outlook Database', International Monetary Fund, April 2024; 'Energy Statistics Data Browser', International Energy Agency, 21 December 2023; 'World Bank Open Data', The World Bank, July 2024; 'SIPRI Arms Transfer Database', Stockholm International Peace Research Institute, 11 March 2024; 'Climate Watch Data', World Resources Institute, 2024; 'Global Migration Data Portal', International Organisation for Migration, 2021.

2   Ibid.

Chapter 1: Before Independence: Anarchy and Power

1   There was naturally much greater interest among leaders in newly independent India. See Jawaharlal Nehru, *The Discovery of India* (New York: John Day, 1946); K.M. Panikkar, *India and the Indian Ocean: An Essay on the Influence of Sea Power on Indian History* (London: Allen and Unwin, 1945).

2   Kalidas Nag, 'Greater India: A Study in Indian Internationalism',
     Greater Indian Society Bulletin No. 1, 1926, pp. 1–44; R.C.
     Majumdar, *Ancient Indian Colonies in the Far East, Vol. II*:
     Suvarnadvipa (Dacca: Asoke Kumar Majumdar, 1937).

3   Henry Kissinger, *White House Years* (Boston: Little, Brown, and
     Co., 1979), p. 842.

4   Upinder Singh, *A History of Ancient and Early Medieval India*:
     India: From the Stone Age to the 12th Century (New Delhi: Pearson
     Education India, 2009), pp. 163–169; See also Gregory L. Possehl,
     The Indus Civilization: A Contemporary Perspective (Lanham:
     Rowman & Littlefield, 2012).

5   Ralph T.H. Griffith, trans. *Hymns of the Rgveda Vols. 1 & 2* (New
     Delhi: Munshiram Manoharlal, 1999); Robert P. Goldman and
     Sally J. Sutherland Goldman, eds., *The Ramayana of Valmiki: The
     Complete English Translation* (Princeton and Oxford: Princeton
     University Press, 2021); Kisari Mohan Ganguli, trans., *The
     Mahabharata of Krishna-Dwaipayana Vyasa*, Vols. 1–18 (New
     Delhi: Munshiram Manoharlal, 1991); Hemchandra Raychauduri,
     *Political History of Ancient India: From the Accession of Parikshit to the
     Extinction of the Gupta Dynasty* (Calcutta: University of Calcutta,
     1923); for an example of the contemporary relevance of ancient
     Indian scriptures, see: Amrita Narlikar and Aruna Narlikar,
     Bargaining with a Rising India: Lessons from the Mahabharata
     (Oxford: Oxford University Press, 2014) and Swarna Rajagopalan,
     "'Grand Strategic Thought' in the Ramayana and Mahabharata,"
     in Kanti Bajpai, Saira Basit and V. Krishnappa, eds., *India's Grand
     Strategy: History, Theory, Cases* (New Delhi: Routledge, 2014).

6   Pierre Briant, *From Cyrus to Alexander: A History of the Persian Empire*,
     trans. Peter T. Daniels (University Park: Eisenbrauns, 2002); H.C.
     Rawlinson, *The Persian Cuneiform Inscriptions at Behistun, Decyphered
     and Translated* (London: Forgotten Books, 2017).

7   Peter Green, *Alexander of Macedon, 356–323 B.C.: A Historical
     Biography* (Berkeley: University of California Press, 1991),
     pp. 380–411.

8   Richard Stoneman, *The Greek Experience of India: From Alexander to the Indo-Greeks* (Princeton: Princeton University Press, 2021).

9   Upinder Singh, *Political Violence in Ancient India* (Cambridge: Harvard University Press, 2017), pp. 40–47, 480–482, fn. 72, 74.

10 Ibid. pp. 268–271.

11 N.A. Nikam and Richard McKeon eds., *The Edicts of Asoka* (Chicago: University of Chicago Press, 1959), p. 20.

12 Kautilya, *The Arthashastra*, trans. L.N. Rangarajan (Gurgaon: Penguin, 1992); Thomas R. Trautmann, *Artha Shastra: The Science of Wealth* (Gurgaon: Penguin, 2012).

13 Upinder Singh, *Political Violence in Ancient India*, pp. 166–170; John M. Rosenfield, *The Dynastic Arts of the Kushans* (Berkeley: University of California Press, 1967).

14 Patrick Olivelle, trans., *The Law Code of Manu* (Oxford: Oxford University Press, 2004).

15 Peter Frankopan, *The Silk Roads: A New History of the World* (New York: Vintage, 2017), pp. 17–20.

16 Anita G. Kunnappilly, 'The Trade of the Port of Muziris in Ancient Times', *International Journal of Maritime History*, Vol. 30, Issue 3, August 2018.

17 Grant Parker, *The Making of Roman India* (Cambridge: Cambridge University Press, 2008).

18 Wilfred H. Schoff, ed., *The Periplus of the Erythraean Sea: Travel and Trade in the Indian Ocean by a Merchant of the First Century* (Whitefish, Mont.: Kessinger Publishing, 2007).

19 Kamandakiya, *Nitisara or The Elements of Polity*, trans. Manmatha Nath Dutt (Calcutta: H.C. Dass, 1896).

20 Noburu Karashima, ed., *A Concise History of South India: Issues and Interpretations* (New Delhi: Oxford University Press, 2014).

21 Hermann Kulke, 'The Naval Expeditions of the Cholas in the Context of Asian History', in Hermann Kulke, K. Kesavapany, and Vijay Sakhuja, eds., *Nagapattinam to Suvarnadwipa: Reflections on the Chola Naval Expeditions to Southeast Asia* (Singapore: ISEAS, 2009).

22   David Schulman, *Tamil: A Biography* (Cambridge: Harvard University Press, 2016), pp. 150–155.

23   Susan Gole, *Indian Maps and Plans: From Earliest Times of the Advent of European Surveys* (New Delhi: Manohar, 1989), p. 17; Budhasvamin, *The Emperor of the Sorcerers, Vol. 1*, James Mallinson, trans. (New York: NYU Press, 2005).

24   Amitav Acharya, *Civilizations in Embrace: The Spread of Ideas and the Transformation of Power* (Singapore: ISEAS, 2013), p. 9.

25   Thomas Suarez, *Early Mapping of Southeast Asia: The Epic Story of Seafarers, Adventures, and Cartographers who First Mapped the Regions between China and India* (Hong Kong: Periplus Editions, 1999), pp. 24–25, 44–45.

26   Ed Douglas, *Himalaya: A Human History* (London: The Bodley Head, 2020), pp. 50–57, 85–90.

27   Shyam Saran, *How China Sees India and the World: The Authoritative Account of the India-China Relationship*, (New Delhi: Juggernaut, 2022), p. 74.

28   Mark Horton and John Middleton, *The Swahili: The Social Landscape of a Mercantile Society* (Oxford: Blackwell, 2000).

29   Edward Pollard and Okeny Charles Kinyera, 'The Swahili Coast and the Indian Ocean Trade Patterns in the 7th–10th Centuries CE', *Journal of Southern African Studies*, Vo. 43, No. 5, 2017, pp. 1–21.

30   Ewen Callaway, 'Ancient DNA Illuminates Swahili Culture's Origins', *Nature*, 31 March 2023.

31   Tansen Sen, *India, China, and the World: A Connected History* (New Delhi: Oxford University Press, 2018), pp. 29–110.

32   Prabodh Chandra Bagchi, *India and China: A Thousand Years of Cultural Relations*, ed. Haraprasad Ray (New Delhi: Munshiram Manoharlal, 2008), p. 31.

33   Richard H. Davis, *Global India circa 100 CE: South Asia in Early World History* (Ann Arbor: Association for Asian Studies, 2009), p. 24.

34   James Legge, *The Travels of Fa-hien: Fa-hien's Record of Buddhistic Kingdoms* (Delhi: Oriental Publishers, 1971), pp. 77–79.

35   Sen, *India, China, and the World*, p. 64.

36   Ibid. pp. 97–104.

37   S.A.A. Rizvi, *The Wonder That Was India*, Vol. II (London: Picador, 2005), pp. 12–24; Edward C. Sachau, *trans.*, *Alberuni's India: An Account of the Religion, Philosophy, Literature, Geography, Chronology, Astronomy, Customs, Laws and Astrology of India about AD 1030* (Cambridge: Cambridge University Press, 2012).

38   Richard M. Eaton, *India in the Persianate Age, 1000-1765* (Oakland: University of California Press, 2019), pp. 48–77.

39   Jack Weatherford, *Genghis Khan and the Making of the Modern World* (New York: Broadway Books, 2004), pp. 125–126.

40   S.A.A. Rizvi, *The Wonder That Was India, Vol. II* (London: Picador, 2005) pp. 8–28, 51–53.

41   Satish Chandra, *Medieval India: From Sultanat to the Mughals, Part One* (New Delhi: Har-Anand, 2012), p. 127.

42   Jayashree Vivekanandan, *Interrogating International Relations: India's Strategic Practice and the Return of History* (New Delhi: Routledge, 2011).

43   Rizvi, *The Wonder That Was India, Vol. II*, pp. 156–162.

44   Eaton, *India in the Persianate Age*, pp. 259–264.

45   K.N. Chaudhuri, *Trade and Civilisation in the Indian Ocean: An Economic History from the Rise of Islam to 1750* (Cambridge: Cambridge University Press, 1985).

46   Joefe B. Santarita, 'Panyupayana: The Emergence of Hindu Polities in the Pre-Islamic Philippines', in Shyam Saran, ed., *Cultural and Civilisational Links between India and Southeast Asia: Historical and Contemporary Dimensions* (Singapore: Palgrave Macmillan, 2018), pp. 93–106.

47   Surendra Gopal, *Born to Trade: Indian Business Communities in Medieval and Early Modern Eurasia* (Abingdon: Routledge, 2017), pp. 92–156.

48   Sanjay Subrahmanyam, *Europe's India: Worlds, People, Empires, 1500-1800* (Cambridge: Harvard University Press 2017), pp. 300–301.

49   M. Athar Ali, 'The Evolution of the Perception of India: Akbar and Abul Fazl', in M. Athar Ali, ed., *Mughal India: Studies in Polity, Ideas, Society and Culture* (New Delhi: Oxford University Press, 2006), p. 114.

50   Manjeet S. Pardesi, 'Region, System, and Order: The Mughal Empire in Islamicate Asia', *Security Studies*, 26:2, 2017, pp. 249–278.

51   Emma J. Flatt, *The Courts of the Deccan Sultanates: Living Well in the Persian Cosmopolis* (Cambridge: Cambridge University Press, 2019), p. 121.

52   Kaushik Roy, *Warfare in Pre-British India, 1500 BCE to 1740 CE* (Abingdon: Routledge, 2015), pp. 117–119.

53   Joan-Pau Rubiés, *Travel and Ethnology in the Renaissance: South India through European Eyes, 1250-1625* (Cambridge: Cambridge University Press, 2000), pp. 191–194.

54   Burton Stein, *The New Cambridge History of India: Vijayanagara* (Cambridge: Cambridge University Press, 2005).

55   Stewart Gordon, *The New Cambridge History of India: The Marathas, 1600-1818* (Cambridge: Cambridge University Press, 1993), pp. 160–162.

56   Randolf G.S. Cooper, *The Anglo-Maratha Campaigns and the Contest for India: The Struggle for Control of the South Asian Military Economy* (Cambridge: Cambridge University Press, 2003).

57   M.S. Naravane, *Battles of the Honourable East India Company: Making of the Raj* (New Delhi: APH Publishing, 2006).

58   John Sugden, *Nelson: A Dream of Glory, 1758-1797* (New York: Henry Holt, 2004), pp. 95–96.

59   J.S. Grewal, *The New Cambridge History of India: The Sikhs of the Punjab* (Cambridge: Cambridge University Press, 1991), pp. 42–91; Patwant Singh and Jyoti M. Rai, *Empire of the Sikhs: The Life and Times of Maharaja Ranjit Singh* (London and Chicago: Peter Owen, 2008).

60   Robert A. Huttenback, 'Gulab Singh and the Creation of the Dogra State of Jammu, Kashmir, and Ladakh', *The Journal of Asian Studies*, Vol. 20, No. 4, 1961, pp. 477–478.

61 S.L. Baruah, *Last Days of Ahom Monarchy: A History of Assam from 1769-1826* (New Delhi: Munshiram Manoharlal, 1993).

62 Subrahmanyam, *Europe's India*, pp. 17–21.

63 Eaton, *India in the Persianate Age*, p. 168.

64 Chandra, *Medieval India*, p. 202.

65 Subrahmanyam, *Europe's India*, pp. 4–5

66 John Keay, *The Honourable Company: A History of the English East India Company* (London: HarperCollins, 1993), p. 4.

67 Ranjit Sen, *Birth of a Colonial City: Calcutta* (Abingdon: Routledge, 2019).

68 John F. Richards, *The Mughal Empire* (Cambridge: Cambridge University Press, 1995).

69 G.J. Bryant, 'British Logistics and the Conduct of the Carnatic Wars (1746-1783)', *War in History*, Vol. 11, Issue 3, July 2004, pp. 278–306; French naval forces conducted significant campaigns in the Indian Ocean until the late 18th century. See: Alfred Thayer Mahan, *The Influence of Sea Power upon History (1660-1783)* (Overland Park: Digireads, 2020), pp. 324–364.

70 H.V. Bowen, *The Business of Empire: The East India Company and Imperial Britain, 1756-1833* (Cambridge: Cambridge University Press, 2005); C. Brad Faught, *Clive: Founder of British India* (Washington D.C.: Potomac Books, 2013).

71 Lawrence James, *Raj: The Making and Unmaking of British India* (London: Little, Brown Book Group, 2010); Ernest Llewellyn Woodward, *Oxford History of England : The Age of Reform, 1815-1870* (Oxford: Clarendon, 1962), p. 427; Stephen P. Cohen, *The Indian Army: Its Contribution to the Development of a Nation* (Berkeley, University of California Press, 1971).

72 William T. Rowe, *China's Last Empire: The Great Qing* (Cambridge, Harvard University Press, 2009), pp. 166–167.

73 Arthur Waley, *The Opium War Through Chinese Eyes* (London: George Allen & Unwin, 1958).

74 Pieter Emmer, 'The Great Escape: The Migration of Female Indentured Servants from British India to Surinam', in David

Richardson, ed., *Abolition and its Aftermath: The Historical Context, 1790-1916*, (London: Frank Cass, 1985).

75   Meilan Solly, 'Years After His Death, Abolitionist John Pierre Burr's Epitaph Updated to Include His Father, Aaron Burr', *Smithsonian Magazine*, 27 August 2019.

76   Srinath Raghavan, *The Most Dangerous Place: A History of the United States in South Asia* (Gurugram: Penguin Random House India, 2018), pp. 1–77; Kai Bird and Martin J. Sherwin, *American Prometheus: The Triumph and Tragedy of J. Robert Oppenheimer* (New York: Knopf, 2005), pp. 99–102.

77   Vikram Sampath, *Savarkar: Echoes from a Forgotten Past, 1883-1924* (Gurugram: Penguin Random House, 2019).

78   David J. Silbey, *The Boxer Rebellion and the Great Game in China: A History* (London: Farrar, Straus and Giroux, 2012).

79   Patrick French, *Younghusband: The Last Great Imperial Adventurer* (London: HarperCollins, 1994).

80   Srinath Raghavan, *India's War: The Making of Modern South Asia, 1939-1945* (Gurugram: Penguin Books India, 2016).

81   Joyce Chapman Lebra, *The Indian National Army and Japan* (Singapore: ISEAS, 2008); Nilanjana Sengupta, *A Gentleman's Word: The Legacy of Subhas Chandra Bose in Southeast Asia* (Singapore: ISEAS, 2012).

82   Narendra Singh Sarila, *The Shadow of the Great Game: The Untold Story of India's Partition* (London: Constable, 2006), pp. 125–133.

83   Andrew Porter, ed, *The Oxford History of the British Empire: Volume III: Nineteenth Century* (Oxford: Oxford University Press, 1999), p. 403.

84   Kyle J. Gardner, *The Frontier Complex: Geopolitics and the Making of the India-China Border, 1846-1962* (Cambridge: Cambridge University Press, 2021); Raghvendra Singh, *India's Lost Frontier: The Story of the North-West Frontier Province of Pakistan* (New Delhi: Rupa, 2020).

85   Cohen, *The Indian Army*.

86   Shashi Tharoor, *An Era of Darkness: The British Empire in India* (New Delhi: Aleph Book Company, 2016).

87   For assessments and critiques of realism in international politics among twentieth-century political scientists, see: Kenneth Waltz, *Theory of International Politics* (New York: McGraw Hill., 1979); Hans Morgenthau, *Scientific Man vs. Power Politics* (Chicago: University of Chicago Press, 1965); John H. Herz, *Political Realism and Political Idealism: A Study in Theories and Realities* (Chicago: University of Chicago Press, 1951); Stephen Walt, 'Alliance Formation and the Balance of World Power', *International Security*, Vol. 9, No. 4. Spring, 1985, pp. 3–43; Alexander Wendt, 'Anarchy Is What States Make of It', *International Organization*, Vol. 46, No. 2, Spring 1992, pp. 391–425.

Chapter 2: 1947–1971: Independence and Non-Alignment

1   Harold Henry Fisher, *The Communist Revolution: An Outline of Strategy and Tactics* (Stanford: Stanford University Press, 1955), p. 13.

2   Franklin D. Roosevelt, 'Annual Message to Congress on the State of the Union', 6 January 1941.

3   Tony Judt, *Postwar: A History of Europe since 1945* (New York: Penguin, 2005), pp. 88–99.

4   Odd Arne Westad, *The Cold War: A World History* (New York: Basic Books, 2017).

5   Alex von Tunzelmann, *Indian Summer: The Secret History of the End of an Empire* (New York: Picador, 2007), p. 3.

6   T.C.A. Raghavan, *The People Next Door: The Curious History of India's Relations with Pakistan* (Gurugram: HarperCollins, 2017), p. 18.

7   Tilak Devasher, *Pakistan: Courting the Abyss* (Noida: HarperCollins, 2016), pp. 3–26.

8   Ramachandra Guha, *India After Gandhi* (New York: HarperCollins, 2007), pp. 138–141.

9   Granville Austin, *The Constitution of India: Cornerstone of a Nation* (Oxford: Oxford University Press, 1999); Ornit Shani, *How India*

Became Democratic: Citizenship and the Making of the Universal Franchise (Cambridge: Cambridge University Press, 2018); Madhav Khosla, *India's Founding Moment: The Constitution of a Most Surprising Democracy* (Cambridge: Harvard University Press, 2020).

10   David C. Engerman, *The Price of Aid: The Economic Cold War in India* (Cambridge: Harvard University Press, 2018), p. 35.

11   Jawaharlal Nehru, 'The Interim National Government- Broadcast from New Delhi, September 7, 1946', *Jawaharlal Nehru's Speeches – Volume One,* (New Delhi: Government of India, Publications Division, 1949).

12   Ibid.

13   Jawaharlal Nehru, *India's Foreign Policy: Selected Speeches, September 1946-April 1961* (New Delhi: Ministry of Information & Broadcasting, 1961), pp. 24–28.

14   Avtar Singh Bhasin, ed., *India-China Relations 1947-2000: A Documentary Study, Vol. II.* (New Delhi: Geetika Publishers, 2018), pp. 441–447.

15   Francine R. Frankel, *When Nehru Looked East: Origins of India-US Suspicion and India-China Rivalry* (Oxford: Oxford University Press, 2020), p. 166.

16   Acharya J.B. Kripalani, 'For Principled Neutrality: A New Appraisal of Indian Foreign Policy', *Foreign Affairs*, October 1959; Rahul Sagar, "Jiski Lathi, Uski Bhains,': The Hindu Nationalist View of International Politics', in Kanti Bajpai, Saira Basit, and V. Krishnappa, eds., *India's Grand Strategy: History, Theory, Cases* (New Delhi: Routledge, 2014), pp. 234–257.

17   Narayani Basu, *V.P. Menon: The Unsung Architect of Modern India* (New Delhi: Simon & Schuster, 2020), pp. 253–329.

18   Srinath Raghavan, *War and Peace in Modern India: A Strategic History of the Nehru Years* (Ranikhet: Permanent Black, 2010), pp. 26–64.

19   Ibid., pp. 65–100.

20   Harbans Singh, *A Modern History of Jammu and Kashmir: The Troubled Years of Maharaja Hari Singh (1925-1949)* (New Delhi: Speaking Tiger Books, 2023).

21   Taraknath Das, 'The Kashmir Issue and the United Nations,'
     Political Science Quarterly, Vol. 65, No. 2, June 1950, pp. 264–282;
     Raghavan, *The People Next Door*, pp. 5–10; Arjun Subramaniam,
     India's Wars: A Military History, 1947-1971 (Noida: HarperCollins,
     2016), pp. 105–165.

22   Raghavan, *War and Peace in Modern India*, pp. 138–139.

23   Navnita Chadha Behera, *Demystifying Kashmir* (Washington:
     Brookings Institution Press, 2006), pp. 31–39; Das, 'The Kashmir
     Issue at the United Nations'.

24   Raghavan, *The People Next Door*, pp. 12–13.

25   R.V.R. Murthy, *Andaman and Nicobar Islands: A Geo-political and
     Strategic Perspective* (New Delhi: Northern Book Centre, 2007),
     p. 117.

26   'Treaty of Peace and Friendship between the Government of India
     and the Government of Nepal', Ministry of External Affairs, India,
     31 July 1950; 'Treaty of Perpetual Peace and Friendship between
     the Government of India and the Government of Bhutan,' Ministry
     of External Affairs, India, August 8, 1949; *Annual Report* (New
     Delhi: Ministry of External Affairs, 1951).

27   Shailendra Nath Sen, *Chandernagore: From Bondage to Freedom,
     1900-1955* (Delhi: Primus Books, 2012); Jessica Namakkal,
     Unsettling Utopia: The Making and Unmaking of French India (New
     York: Columbia University Press, 2021).

28   P.N. Khera, *Operation Vijay: The Liberation of Goa and Other
     Portuguese Colonies in India (1961)* (New Delhi: Ministry of
     Defense, 1974); Valmiki Faleiro, *Goa, 1961: The Complete Story of
     Nationalism and Integration* (Vintage, 2023).

29   Asoke Kumar Mukerji, 'The Challenges and Opportunities of a
     Rules-Based Order: India and the WTO', Ministry of External
     Affairs Distinguished Lecture at NLSIU, Bengaluru, July 22,
     2022.

30   Michele L. Louro, *Comrades against Imperialism: Nehru, India,
     and Interwar Internationalism* (Cambridge: Cambridge University
     Press, 2018), pp. 21–61; A.I. Yunel, 'Visit of Motilal and Jawaharlal

Nehru to the USSR in 1927', in Ilasai Manian and V. Rajesh, eds., *The Russian Revolution and India* (Abingdon: Routledge, 2020).

31   Paul M. McGarr, *The Cold War in South Asia: Britain, the United States and the Indian Subcontinent, 1945-1965* (Delhi: Cambridge University Press, 2013), pp. 30, 45.

32   Rudra Chaudhuri, *Forged in Crisis: India and the United States since 1947* (Noida: HarperCollins India, 2014), pp. 25–47; Tanvi Madan, *Fateful Triangle: How China Shaped U.S.-India Relations during the Cold War* (Washington: Brookings Institution Press, 2020), pp. 15–33; Meenakshi Ahamed, *A Matter of Trust: India-US Relations from Truman to Trump* (Gurugram,: HarperCollins India, 2021), pp. 59–83.

33   Ralph E. Goodwin, et al., eds., *Foreign Relations of the United States, 1947, The British Commonwealth; Europe Vol. III* (Washington: U.S. Government Printing Office, 1972).

34   Arun Sukumar, *Midnight's Machines: A Political History of Technology in India* (Gurugram: Penguin Viking, 2019), p. 10.

35   Chaudhuri, *Forged in Crisis*, p. 38.

36   Daniel Klingensmith, *'One Valley and a Thousand': Dams, Nationalism, and Development* (Oxford: Oxford University Press, 2007).

37   Madan, *Fateful Triangle*, pp. 15–33.

38   McGarr, *The Cold War in South Asia*, pp. 40–41.

39   K.S. Thimayya, *Experiment in Neutrality* (New Delhi: Vision Books, 1981); Sydney D. Bailey, *The Korea Armistice* (New York: Palgrave Macmillan, 1992).

40   Wiliam A.T. Logan, *A Technological History of Cold-War India, 1947-1969* (New York: Springer, 2021), pp. 75–89.

41   Sukumar, *Midnight's Machines*, pp. 23–45.

42   Swapna Kona Nayudu, 'The Soviet Peace Offensive and Nehru's India, 1953-1956', in Manu Bhagavan, ed., *India and the Cold War* (Chapel Hill: University of North Carolina Press, 2019), pp. 37–56; Engerman, *The Price of Aid*, pp. 81–143, 273–302; McGarr, *The Cold War in South Asia*, pp. 30–63.

43   Madan, *Fateful Triangle*, pp. 85–148; McGarr, *The Cold War in South Asia*, p. 33.

44   Michal Kalecki, *Selected Essays on the Economic Growth of the Socialist and the Mixed Economy* (Cambridge: Cambridge University Press, 1972), p. 167.

45   Davender Jain, *Making of the IIT Brand: Recounting the Journey of IIT's Alumni and its Growth to Fame* (Notion Press, 2022).

46   Ramachandra Guha, *India After Gandhi* (New York: HarperCollins, 2007), p. 174.

47   Bimal Prasad, ed., *Jayaprakash Narayan: Essential Writings: 1929-1979* (New Delhi: Konark, 2002), pp. 164–166.

48   Zorawar Daulet Singh, *Power & Diplomacy: India's Foreign Policies during the Cold War* (New Delhi: Oxford University Press, 2019), pp. 116–190; Vijay Gokhale, *Crosswinds: Nehru, Zhou, and the Anglo-American Competition over China* (Gurugram: Penguin Random House India, 2024).

49   S. Mahmud Ali, *Cold War in the High Himalayas: The USA, China and South Asia in the 1950s* (Abingdon: Routledge, 1999).

50   Engerman, *The Price of Aid*, pp. 163–170.

51   Westad, *The Cold War*, p. 429

52   Manmohan Singh, 'Export Strategy for the Take Off,' *Economic Weekly*, 1967.

53   'To Prosperity through Freedom: The Swatantra Party's Statement on Policy,' March 19-20, 1960; Guha, *India After Gandhi*, p. 303.

54   Robert S. Anderson, *Nucleus and Nation: Scientists, International Networks, and Power in India* (Chicago: University of Chicago Press, 2010), pp. 207–273.

55   George Perkovich, *India's Nuclear Bomb: The Impact on Global Proliferation* (Berkeley: University of California Press, 2002), p. 33.

56   G.G. Mirchandani, *India's Nuclear Dilemma* (New Delhi: Popular Book Services, 1968), pp. 5–6

57   Scott Kaufman, *Project Plowshare: The Peaceful Use of Nuclear Explosives in Cold War America* (Ithaca: Cornell University Press, 2013).

58   Bakthiar K. Dadabhoy, *Homi J. Bhabha: A Life* (New Delhi: Rupa, 2023), pp. 528–611.

59   A. Vinod Kumar, 'Between Idealism, Activism, and the Bomb: Why did India Reject the NPT?' in Roland Popp, Liviu Horovitz, and Andreas Wenger, eds., *Negotiating the Nuclear Non-Proliferation Treaty: Origins of the Nuclear Order* (London and New York: Routledge, 2017), pp. 137–160.

60   Perkovich, *India's Nuclear Bomb*, p. 127.

61   Rajeshwar Dayal, *A Life of Our Times* (Hyderabad: Orient Longman, 1998), pp. 394–463; Waheguru Pal Singh Sidhu, 'The Accidental Global Peacekeeper', in Bhagavan, ed., *India and the Cold War*, pp. 88–92.

62   K. Sankaran Nair, *Inside IB and RAW: The Rolling Stone that Gathered Moss* (New Delhi: Manas Publications, 2008), p. 123–144.

63   Ramachandra Guha, ed., *Makers of Modern India* (New Delhi: Viking, 2010), p. 341.

64   Philips Talbot, 'As the British Empire Was Falling Apart, Gandhi Gave This Advice to the Rest of Asia', *New Republic*, 28 April 1947.

65   William Stueck, *The Korean War: An International History* (Princeton: Princeton University Press, 1995), pp. 90–91; *Selected Diplomatic Papers of Zhou Enlai* (Beijing, Zhongyang Wenxian, 1990), pp. 25–27.

66   Zorawar Daulet Singh, *Power & Diplomacy*, pp. 113–142.

67   Vijay Gokhale, 'What Should India Do Before the Next Taiwan Strait Crisis?' Carnegie India, 17 April 2023.

68   Barbara Barnouin and Yu Changgen, *Zhou Enlai: A Political Life* (Hong Kong: The Chinese University Press, 2006), pp. 156–160

69   See Seng Tan and Amitav Acharya, eds., *Bandung Revisited: The Legacy of the 1955 Asian-African Conference for International Order* (Singapore: NUS Press, 2008).

70   Josef Purnama Widyatmadja, 'The Spirit of Bandung', *Yale Global Online*, 6 April 2005.

71 Tanvi Madan, *Fateful Triangle*, p. 134; Westad, *The Cold War*, p. 435.

72 Monika Chansoria, 'India's Refusal to Sign the 1951 San Francisco Peace Treaty: Revisiting the Motivations of the Decision and of Historical Reconciliation towards Japan', Policy Brief, The Japan Institute of International Affairs (JIIA), 2 June 2023.

73 Shinzo Abe, 'Two Democracies Meet at Sea: For a Better and Safer Asia', Indian Council of World Affairs and Japan Institute for National Fundamentals, September 20, 2011.

74 Constantino Xavier, 'Prudent Power: India's Democratic Realism in South Asia', Draft Manuscript, 2024.

75 Avtar Singh Bhasin, ed., *India-China Relations 1947-2000: A Documentary Study, Vol. III.* (New Delhi: Geetika Publishers, 2018), pp. 2611–2619.

76 Kyle J. Gardner, *The Frontier Complex: Geopolitics and the Making of the India-China Border, 1846-1962* (Cambridge: Cambridge University Press, 2021), pp. 26–91.

77 Avtar Singh Bhasin, ed., *India-China Relations 1947-2000: A Documentary Study, Vol. IV.* (New Delhi: Geetika Publishers, 2018), pp. 3477, 3480–84, 3491–3497.

78 *The Directory & Chronicle for China, Japan, Corea, Indo-China, Straits Settlements, Malay States, Sian, Netherlands India, Borneo, the Philippines, etc* (Hong Kong: Hongkong Daily Press Office, 1912), p. 71.

79 Rajiv Rai, *The State in the Colonial Periphery: A Study on Sikkim's Relation with Great Britain* (Gurugram: Partridge Publishing, 2015).

80 Avtar Singh Bhasin, ed., *India-China Relations 1947-2000: A Documentary Study, Vol. I.* (New Delhi: Geetika Publishers, 2018), pp. 2–10; Shivshankar Menon, *Choices: Inside the Making of India's Foreign Policy* (Washington DC: Brookings Institution Press, 2016), pp. 8–15.

81 John Garver, *Protracted Contest: Sino-Indian Rivalry in the Twentieth Century* (Seattle: University of Washington Press, 2001), pp. 32–37.

82   Dawa Norbu, *China's Tibet Policy* (Richmond, Surrey: Curzon Press, 2001), pp. 179–209.

83   Tsering Shakya, *The Dragon in the Land of Snows: A History of Modern Tibet Since 1947* (New York: Penguin Compass, 2000), pp. 23–25.

84   Avtar Singh Bhasin, ed., *India-China Relations 1947-2000: A Documentary Study, Vol. II.* (New Delhi: Geetika Publishers, 2018), pp. 441–447.

85   Ibid., pp. 458–463.

86   Nirupama Rao, *The Fractured Himalaya: India, Tibet, China 1949-1962* (Gurugram: Penguin Random House India, 2021), pp. 86–89.

87   B.N. Mullik, *The Chinese Betrayal: My Years with Nehru* (Bombay: Allied Publishers, 1971), pp. 148–149.

88   Avtar Singh Bhasin, ed., *India-China Relations 1947-2000: A Documentary Study, Vol. II.* (New Delhi: Geetika Publishers, 2018), pp. 1216–1217; *Important Documents on Relations between the People's Republic of China and the Republic of India* (Beijing, 2006), p. 26.

89   Mullik, *The Chinese Betrayal*, pp. 151–158.

90   Raghavan, *War and Peace in Modern India*, pp. 243–249

91   Shakya, *The Dragon in the Land of Snows*, p. 171.

92   Rao, *The Fractured Himalaya*, pp. 240–259.

93   Avtar Singh Bhasin, ed., *India-China Relations 1947-2000: A Documentary Study, Vol. II.* (New Delhi: Geetika Publishers, 2018), pp. 1748–1792.

94   Rao, *The Fractured Himalaya*, pp. 269–277.

95   Avtar Singh Bhasin, ed., *India-China Relations 1947-2000: A Documentary Study, Vol. III.* (New Delhi: Geetika Publishers, 2018), p. 1919.

96   Ibid., pp. 1929–1933.

97   Madan, *Fateful Triangle*, p. 122.

98   M. Taylor Fravel, *Strong Borders, Secure Nation* (Princeton: Princeton University Press, 2008), p. 194; John Garver, 'China's

Decision for War with India in 1962', in Alastair Iain Johnston and Robert S. Ross (eds) *New Directions in the Study of China's Foreign Policy* (Stanford: Stanford University Press, 2006), pp. 86–130.

99   Rao, *The Fractured Himalaya*, pp. 330–332.

100 Mullik, *The Chinese Betrayal*, p. 305.

101 Avtar Singh Bhasin, ed., *India-China Relations 1947-2000: A Documentary Study, Vol. III.* (New Delhi: Geetika Publishers, 2018), 2609–2619, 2982–2993.

102 Garver, *Protracted Contest,* pp. 100–102.

103 Rao, *The Fractured Himalaya*, pp. 330–332.

104 Mullik, *The Chinese Betrayal*, p. 309.

105 Raghavan, *War and Peace in Modern India*, p. 291; Avtar Singh Bhasin, ed., *India-China Relations 1947-2000: A Documentary Study, Vol. IV.* (New Delhi: Geetika Publishers, 2018), pp. 3774–3777.

106 Frankel, *When Nehru Looked East*, pp. 251–269.

107 Rao, *The Fractured Himalaya*, pp. 391–399; Bertil Lintner, *China's India War: Collision Course on the Roof of the World* (New Delhi: Oxford University Press, 2018), pp. 100–101.

108 Roderick MacFarquhar, *The Origins of the Cultural Revolution: Volume 3* (New York: Columbia University Press, 1999), p. 308.

109 'India: Subjects: Nehru Correspondence, November 1962: 11–19', Papers of John F. Kennedy Presidential Papers, National Security Files, John F. Kennedy Presidential Library and Museum, https://www.jfklibrary.org/Asset-Viewer/Archives/JFKNSF-111-016.aspx ; See also: Bruce Riedel, *JFK's Forgotten Crisis: Tibet, CIA, And the Sino-Indian War* (Washington: Brookings Institution Press, 2017).

110 Chaudhuri, *Forged in Crisis*, pp. 108–111.

111 Subramaniam, *India's Wars*, pp. 223–229, 253.

112 Sanakaran Nair, *Inside IB and RAW*, pp. 150–155.

113 Pallavi Raghavan, *Animosity at Bay: An Alternative History of the India-Pakistan Relationship, 1947-1952* (New York: Oxford University Press, 2020).

114 'Agreement between the Governments of India and Pakistan regarding Security and Rights of Minorities (Nehru–Liaquat Agreement)', Ministry of External Affairs, India, 8 April 1950.

115 Raghavan, *The People Next Door*, pp. 49–61.

116 Ijaz Hussain, *Indus Waters Treaty: Political and Legal Dimensions* (Karachi: Oxford University Press, 2017).

117 Raghavan, *War and Peace in Modern India*, p. 268; Sarvepalli Gopal, *Jawaharlal Nehru: A Biography Volume 3 1956-1964* (New Delhi: Random House, 2013), pp. 63–92.

118 Dayal, *A Life of Our Times,* p. 301.

119 Y.D. Gundevia, *Outside the Archives* (New Delhi: Sangam Books, 1984), p. 246

120 Farooq Bajwa, *From Kutch to Tashkent: The Indo–Pakistan War of 1965* (New Delhi: Pentagon Press, 2014), pp. 65–96.

121 Ibid., pp. 102–106.

122 Subramaniam, *India's Wars*, pp. 307–310.

123 Raghavan, *The People Next Door*, pp. 94–107.

124 Probal Dasgupta, *Watershed 1967: India's Forgotten Victory over China* (New Delhi, Juggernaut, 2020).

125 Rosemary Sullivan, *Stalin's Daughter: The Extraordinary and Tumultuous Life of Svetlana Alliluyeva* (New York: Harper, 2016).

126 Francine R. Frankel, *India's Green Revolution: Economic Gains and Political Costs* (Princeton: Princeton University Press, 1971); R. Douglas Hurt, *The Green Revolution in the Global South: Science, Politics, and Unintended Consequences* (Tuscaloosa: University of Alabama Press, 2020), pp. 44–73.

127 Inder Malhotra, *Indira Gandhi: A Personal and Political Biography* (London: Hodder and Stoughton, 1989).

Chapter 3: 1971–1991: Interventions and Alignment

1 McGarr, *The Cold War in South Asia*, pp. 63–65.

2 Surjit Mansingh, *India's Search for Power: Indira Gandhi's Foreign Policy 1966-1982* (New Delhi: Sage, 1984), pp. 163–179.

3   Maharajakrishna Rasgotra, *A Life in Diplomacy* (New Delhi: Penguin Random House, 2019).

4   Renu Srivastava, *India and the Non-Aligned Summits: Belgrade to Jakarta* (New Delhi: Northern Book Centre, 1995), pp. 84–108.

5   Ahamed, *A Matter of Trust*, pp. 337–355.

6   Mohammed Ayoob and K. Subrahmanyam. *The Liberation War* (New Delhi: S. Chand, 1972), pp. 112–150; 'Pakistan: Toppling Over the Brink', *Time*, 5 April 1971.

7   K. Subrahmanyam, 'Bangla Desh: Policy Options for India', Letter to Swaran Singh, P.N. Haksar, etc. P.N. Haksar Papers III, SF No. 276, Nehru Memorial Museum and Library, 4 April 1971.

8   Srinath Raghavan, *1971: A Global History of the Creation of Bangladesh* (Cambridge and London: Harvard University Press, 2013), pp. 211–213, 222; See also: Chandrashekhar Dasgupta, *India and the Bangladesh Liberation War* (New Delhi: Juggernaut, 2021).

9   Jairam Ramesh, *Intertwined Lives: PN. Haksar and Indira Gandhi* (New Delhi: Simon & Schuster, 2018), pp. 220–224.

10   Engerman, *The Price of Aid*, pp. 326.

11   Raghavan, *1971*, pp. 201–203.

12   Nicolas Blarel, *The Evolution of India's Israel Policy: Continuity, Change, and compromise since 1922* (New Delhi: Oxford University Press, 2015), pp. 186–187.

13   Gary J. Bass, *The Blood Telegram: Nixon, Kissinger, and a Forgotten Genocide* (New York: Knopf, 2013), pp. 211–213; Mohammad Delwar Hossain and James Aucoin, 'George Harrison and the Concert for Bangladesh: When Rock Music Forever Fused with Politics on a World Stage', in Uche Onyebadi, ed., *Music as a Platform for Political Communication* (Hershey, Penn.: IGI Global, 2017), pp. 149–163.

14   Subramaniam, *India's Wars*, pp. 381–390.

15   Bass, *The Blood Telegram*, pp. 310–319.

16   Raghavan, *1971*, pp. 259–260.

17   Zorawar Daulet Singh, 'The Puzzle of the 1972 Shimla Summit, or Why India Did Not Impose Its Will', *Wire*, 22 November 2017.

18   Raghavan, *The People Next Door,* p. 151.

19   Nitin Gokhale, *Beyond NJ 9842: The Siachen Saga* (New Delhi: Bloomsbury India, 2014), pp. 34, 79.

20   Hasan-Askari Rizvi, *Pakistan and the Geostrategic Environment: A Study of Foreign Policy* (London: Macmillan, 1993), p. 44.

21   Kanti P. Bajpai, P.R. Chari, Pervaiz Iqbal Cheema, Stephn P. Cohen, and Sumit Ganguly, *Brasstacks and Beyond: Perception and Management of Crisis in South Asia* (New Delhi: Manohar, 1997).

22   Perkovich, *India's Nuclear Bomb*, pp. 169–178.

23   Ibid., pp. 178–189.

24   Yogesh Joshi, 'Debating the Nuclear Legacy of India and One of Its Great Cold War Strategists', *War on the Rocks*, 27 March 2017.

25   Patrick Keatley, 'The Brown Bomb,' *Manchester Guardian*, 11 March 1965.

26   Feroz Hassan Khan, *Eating Grass: The Making of the Pakistani Bomb* (Stanford: Stanford University Press, 2012), pp. 109–128.

27   William Langewiesche, 'The Wrath of Khan', *The Atlantic*, November 2005.

28   Andrew Small, *The China-Pakistan Axis: Asia's New Geopolitics* (New York: Oxford University Press, 2015), pp. 27–46.

29   Khan, *Eating Grass*, pp. 157, 171, 187–190.

30   Husain Haqqani, *Magnificent Delusions: Pakistan, the United States, and an Epic History of Misunderstanding* (New York: PublicAffairs, 2013), p. 283.

31   Perkovich, *India's Nuclear Bomb,* pp. 242–274.

32   Gaurav Kampani, 'New Delhi's Long Nuclear Journey: How Secrecy and Institutional Roadblocks Delayed India's Weaponization', *International Security*, Vol. 38, Issue 4, Spring 2014.

33   Sunanda K. Datta-Ray, *Smash and Grab: Annexation of Sikkim*, (New Delhi: Vikas, 1984).

34   Garver, *Protracted Contest*, p. 94.

35   Shyam Saran. *How India Sees the World: Kautilya to the 21st Century* (New Delhi: Juggernaut, 2017), pp. 137–139.

36   Garver, *Protracted Contest*, p. 104.

37 Rishika Chauhan, 'Differences Not Disputes: India's view of the Border after 1962', in Kanti Bajpai, Selina Ho, and Manjari Chatterjee Miller, eds., *Routledge Handbook on China-India Relations* (Abingdon: Routledge, 2020).

38 C. Raja Mohan, *Samudra Manthan: Sino-Indian Rivalry in the Indo–Pacific* (New Delhi: Oxford University Press, 2013), pp 160–162; David Brewster, *India's Ocean: The Story of India's Bid for Regional Leadership* (New York: Routledge, 2014).

39 David Brewster and Ranjit Rai, 'Operation Lal Dora: India's Aborted Military Intervention in Mauritius', *Asian Security*, Vol. 9, Issue 1, 2013, pp. 62–74.

40 David Brewster and Ranjit Rai, 'Flowers Are Blooming: The Story of the India Navy's Secret Operation in the Seychelles', *The Naval Review*, Vol. 99, No. 1, 2011, pp. 58–62.

41 Sushant Singh, *Mission Overseas: Daring Operations by the Indian Military* (New Delhi: Juggernaut, 2017), pp. 13–76.

42 Steve Coll, *Ghost Wars: The Secret History of the CIA, Afghanistan, and bin Laden, from the Soviet Invitation to September 10, 2001* (New York: Penguin Press, 2001), pp. 333–335; Avinash Paliwal, *My Enemy's Enemy: India in Afghanistan from the Soviet Invasion to the US Withdrawal* (Noida: HarperCollins, 2017), pp. 47–78; For further background on the rise of the Taliban, see Ahmed Rashid, *Taliban: Militant Islam, Oil and Fundamentalism in Central Asia* (New Haven: Yale Nota Bene, 2001).

43 Prashant Jha, *Battles of the New Republic: A Contemporary History of Nepal* (New Delhi: Aleph, 2014), pp. 15–19; Garver, *Protracted Conflict*, pp. 131–163.

44 Menon, *Choices*, pp. 82–104.

45 Sushant Singh, *Mission Overseas*, pp. 79–148.

46 Arjun Subramaniam, *Full Spectrum: India's Wars, 1972-2020* (Gurugram: HarperCollins, 2022), pp. 164–209.

47 D.R. Kaarthikeyan and Radhavinod Raju, *The Rajiv Gandhi Assassination: The Investigation* (New Delhi: Sterling, 2004).

48 Garver, *Protracted Contest*, pp. 303–308.

49 Lawrence Saez, *The South Asian Association for Regional Cooperation (SAARC): An Emerging Collaboration Architecture* (Abingdon: Routledge, 2011), pp. 1–47.

50 'The Constitution (Forty-second Amendment) Act, 1976', Government of India, 28 August 1976.

51 Jagdish N. Bhagwati, *India in Transition: Freeing the Economy* (New York: Clarendon Press, 1993).

52 Guha, *India After Gandhi,* p. 683.

53 Ibid., pp. 506–507.

54 Dani Rodrik and Arvind Subramanian, 'From 'Hindu Growth' to Productivity Surge: The Mystery of the Indian Growth Transition', *IMF Staff Papers*, Vol. 52, No. 2, September 2005, p. 195.

55 Guha, *India After Gandhi*, pp. 580–583.

56 Arvind Panagariya, 'Growth and Reforms during 1980s and 1990s', *Economic and Political Weekly*, Vol. 39, Issue 25, 19 June 2004.

Chapter 4: 1991–2008: Liberalization and US Unipolarity

1 Vinay Sitapati, *Half Lion: How P.V. Narasimha Rao Transformed India*, (Gurgaon: Penguin India, 2016), pp. 84–106.

2 Coll, *Ghost Wars,* pp. 19–188.

3 Vladislav M. Zubok, *Collapse: The Fall of the Soviet Union* (New Haven: Yale University Press, 2021).

4 Marika Vicziany, 'Understanding the 1993 Mumbai Bombings: Madrassas and the Hierarchy of Terror' in P.R. Kumaraswamy and Ian Copland, eds., *South Asia: The Spectre of Terrorism* (New Delhi: Routledge India, 2009).

5 Montek Singh Ahluwalia, 'India's 1991 Reforms: A Retrospective Overview', in Rakesh Mohan, ed., *India Transformed: 25 Years of Economic Reforms* (Gurgaon: Penguin Viking, 2017), pp. 47–67.

6 Menon, *Choices,* p. 18.

7 Francis Fukuyama, *The End of History and the Last Man* (New York: Free Press, 1992). Samuel Huntington, *The Clash of Civilizations and the Remaking of World Order* (New York: Simon & Schuster,

1996); Benjamin Barber, *Jihad vs. McWorld: How Globalism and Tribalism Are Reshaping the World* (New York: Ballantine Books, 1996). Jean-Marie Guéhenno, *The End of the Nation-State* (Minneapolis: University of Minnesota Press, 1995); Paul Kennedy, *The Rise and Fall of the Great Powers: Economic Change and Military Conflict from 1500 to 2000* (New York: Random House, 1987). Andrew J. Bacevich, *American Empire* (Cambridge: Harvard University Press, 2002). John Mearsheimer, *The Tragedy of Great Power Politics* (New York: Norton, 2001).

8   Sunanda K. Datta-Ray, *Looking East to Look West: Lee Kuan Yew's Mission India* (Singapore: ISEAS, 2009); Frederic Grare, *India Turns East: International Engagement and US-China Rivalry* (Gurgaon: Penguin Random House India, 2017).

9   Blarel, *The Evolution of India's Israel Policy*; P.R. Kumaraswamy, *India's Israel Policy* (New York: Columbia University Press, 2010).

10 Blarel, *The Evolution of India's Israel Policy*, pp. 242–246.

11 Strobe Talbott, *Engaging India: Diplomacy, Democracy, and the Bomb* (Washington: Brookings Institution, 2004), p. 25.

12 Menon, *Choices*, pp. 17–21.

13 Tim Weiner, 'U.S. Suspects India Prepares to Conduct Nuclear Test', *New York Times*, 15 December 1995.

14 Sitapati, *Half Lion*, pp. 279–295.

15 Perkovich, *India's Nuclear Bomb*, pp. 353–377.

16 Praveen Swami, *India, Pakistan and the Secret Jihad. The Covert War in Kashmir, 1947-2004* (London: Routledge, 2007).

17 A.S. Dulat, *Kashmir: The Vajpayee Years* (Noida: HarperCollins, 2015), p. 59.

18 Bhabani Sen Gupta, 'Neither War, Nor Peace', *Far Eastern Economic Review*, 14 June 1990.

19 Raghavan, *The People Next Door*, pp. 187–212.

20 Sumit Ganguly, *The Crisis in Kashmir: Portents of War, Hopes of Peace* (Cambridge: Cambridge University Press, 1997), pp. 40–57.

21 Amit Ranjan, 'India's South Asia Policy: Changes, Continuity or Continuity with Changes', *The Round Table: The Commonwealth*

Journal of International Affairs, Vol. 108, Issue 3, 2019, pp. 259–274; Aneek Chatterjee, *International Relations Today: Concepts and Applications* (Delhi: Longman, 2010), p. 220.

22 Talbott, *Engaging India*, pp. 52–53, 96–97.

23 Ibid., pp. 142–143, 181–182.

24 Rajesh Basrur and Sumitha Narayanan Kutty, eds., *India and Japan: Assessing the Strategic Partnership* (Singapore: Palgrave Macmillan, 2018).

25 T.N. Ninan, 'The Political Economy of Reforms: The Art of the Possible', in Rakesh Mohan, ed., *India Transformed*, pp. 77–90.

26 Daniel Lak, *India Express: The Future of the New Superpower* (New York: Palgrave Macmillan, 2008).

27 Suzanne Goldenberg, 'Boom time in India as the millennium bug bites', *Guardian*, 30 December 1998.

28 Rone Tempest, 'India's Nuclear Tests Jolt Its Relations with China', *Los Angeles Times*, 11 June 1998.

29 China Welcomes Indian IT Venture, BBC News, 17 January 2002. http://news.bbc.co.uk/2/hi/ business/1765650.stm

30 Jaswant Singh, *In Service of Emergent India: A Call to Honor* (Bloomington: Indiana University Press, 2007), pp. 171–195.

31 Kargil Review Committee, *From Surprise to Reckoning: The Kargil Review Committee Report*, (New Delhi: Sage Publications, 2000), p. 109.

32 Talbott, *Engaging India*, pp. 159–169.

33 Paliwal, *My Enemy's Enemy*, pp. 130–138.

34 P.R. Chari, Pervaiz Iqbal Cheema, and Stephen P. Cohen, *Four Crises and a Peace Process: American Engagement in South Asia* (Washington: Brookings Institution Press, 2007); Steve Coll, *Directorate S: The C.I.A. and America's Secret Wars in Afghanistan and Pakistan, 2001-2016* (London: Allen Lane, 2018).

35 'Address by Shri Atal Bihari Vajpayee', Asia Society, New York, 7 September 2000; Chaudhuri, *Forged in Crisis*, pp. 190–211; C. Raja Mohan, *Crossing the Rubicon: The Shaping of India's New Foreign Policy* (New Delhi: Penguin, 2003), pp. 48–56.

36 S. Jaishankar, '2004 Tsunami Disaster: Consequences for Regional Cooperation', Presentation at the 26th Annual Pacific Symposium, Hawaii, 8–10 June 2005.

37 Dhruva Jaishankar, 'Chronicle of a Deal Foretold: Washington's Perspective on Negotiating the Indo-US Nuclear Agreement', in P.R. Chari ed., *Indo-US Nuclear Deal: Seeking Synergy in Bilateralism* (New Delhi, Routledge, 2009), pp. 99–122.

38 C. Raja Mohan, *Crossing the Rubicon*, pp. 109–115.

39 C. Raja Mohan, *Impossible Allies: Nuclear India, United States, and the Global Order* (New Delhi: India Research Press, 2006).

40 Harsh V. Pant, *The US-India Nuclear Pact: Policy, Process, and Great Power Politics* (New Delhi: Oxford University Press, 2011).

41 David M. Malone, C. Raja Mohan, and Srinath Raghavan, 'India and the World', in Malone, Mohan, and Raghavan, eds. *The Oxford Handbook of Indian Foreign Policy* (Oxford: Oxford University Press, 2015), pp. 15–16.

42 Tanvi Madan, 'The Rise, Fall, and Rebirth of the 'Quad", *War on the Rocks*, 16 November 2017.

43 Ashley J. Tellis, 'South Asian Seesaw: A New U.S. Policy on the Subcontinent', Policy Outlook, Carnegie Endowment for International Peace, 12 May 2005.

44 Daniel S. Markey, *No Exit from Pakistan: America's Tortured Relationship with Islamabad* (New York: Cambridge University Press, 2013), pp. 22–24, 136–169.

45 Jha, *Battles of the New Republic*, pp. 87–107; Saran, *How India Sees the World*, pp. 155–172.

46 Menon, *Choices*, pp. 82–104.

Chapter 5: 2008–2024: Opportunities and China's Rise

1 Menon, *Choices*, pp. 49–53.

2 Stephen Tankel, *Storming the World Stage: The Story of Lashkar-e-Taiba* (New York: Oxford University Press, 2013).

3   Adam Tooze, *Crashed: How a Decade of Financial Crises Changed the World* (New York: Penguin, 2018); Jean Pisani-Ferry, *The Euro Crisis and Its Aftermath* (New York: Oxford University Press, 2011).

4   Rory Medcalf, *Indo–Pacific Empire: China, America and the Contest for the World's Pivotal Region* (Manchester: Manchester University Press, 2020), pp. 85–102; Rush Doshi, *The Long Game: China's Grand Strategy to Displace American Order* (New York: Oxford University Press, 2021); James M. Goldgeier, 'The Future of NATO', Special Report No. 51, Council on Foreign Relations, February 2010, pp. 10-23; Svante E. Cornell & S. Frederick Starr, eds., *The Guns of August 2008: Russia's War in Georgia* (Abingdon: Routledge, 2015).

5   C. Fred Bersten, 'A Partnership of Equals: How Washington Should Respond to China's Economic Challenge', *Foreign Affairs*, July–August 2008; Zbigniew Brzezinski, 'The Group of Two That Could Change the World', *Financial Times*, 13 January 2009; George Packer, *Our Man: Richard Holbrooke and the End of the American Century* (New York: Vintage, 2019), pp. 450–543.

6   Oliver Stuenkel, *The BRICS and the Future of Global Order* (Lanham Md.: Lexington Books, 2020).

7   Hardeep Singh Puri, *Perilous Interventions: The Security Council and the Politics of Chaos* (Gurugram: HarperCollins, 2016).

8   V.S. Seshadri, *Free Trade Agreements: India and the World* (Oxford: Oxford University Press, 2023), pp. 114–149, 168–180; Rahul Nath Choudhury, 'What Went Wrong with India's FTAs?' *East Asia Forum*, 19 September 2023.

9   Sunil Khilnani, Rajiv Kumar, Pratap Bhanu Mehta, Prakash Menon, Srinath Raghavan, Shyam Saran, Nandan Nilekani, and Siddharth Varadarajan, 'Nonalignment 2.0: A Foreign and Strategic Policy for India in the Twenty First Century', Centre for Policy Research, 29 February 2012.

10   'The Civil Liability for Nuclear Damage Act, 2010', *Gazette of India*, 21 September 2010; Ahamed, *A Matter of Trust*, 459–461; *Lok Sabha Debates*, Lok Sabha Secretariat, Government of India, 2013, pp. 733.

11 Dilip Hiro, *The Longest August: The Unflinching Rivalry between India and Pakistan* (New York: Nation Books, 2015), pp. 358–359.

12 Sanjaya Baru, *The Accidental Prime Minister: The Making and Unmaking of Manmohan Singh* (Guragon: Penguin Viking, 2014), pp. 194–197.

13 Sumit Ganguly, 'India and Pakistan: An Elusive Peace', in Charles E. Howlett, Christian Philip Peterson, Deborah D. Buffton, and David L. Hostetter, *The Oxford Handbook of Peace History* (Oxford: Oxford University Press, 2023), p. 424.

14 'Reports of International Arbitral Awards: The Bay of Bengal Maritime Boundary Arbitration between the People's Republic of Bangladesh and the Republic of India, Award of 7 July 2014,' Vol. XXXIII, Office of Legal Affairs, United Nations, 2019.

15 Gareth Price, 'India's Support for Afghanistan's Reconstruction', in Adrenrele Awotona, ed., *Rebuilding Afghanistan in Times of Crisis: A Global Response* (Abingdon: Routledge, 2019).

16 Amish Raj Mulmi, *All Roads Lead North: Nepal's Turn to China* (Chennai: Context, 2021), pp. 159–162.

17 Andrew Small, *No Limits: The Inside Story of China's War with the West* (Brooklyn: Melville House, 2022), pp. 145–146.

18 Saneet Chakradeo, 'Neighbourhood First Responder: India's Humanitarian Assistance and Disaster Relief', Policy Brief, Brookings India, August 2020.

19 Constantino Xavier, 'Bridging the Bay of Bengal: Toward a Stronger BIMSTEC', Carnegie India, February 2018.

20 Prime Minister's Office, 'Text of the PM's Remarks on the Commissioning of Coast Ship Barracuda', Press Information Bureau, Government of India, 12 March 2015.

21 Ashley J. Tellis, 'Are India-Pakistan Peace Talks Worth a Damn?' Carnegie Endowment for International Peace, 20 September 2017.

22 Press Trust of India, 'Kartarpur Corridor is Army Chief Bajwa's Brainchild, Will Hurt India: Pakistan Minister', ThePrint, 30 November 2019.

23 Subramaniam, *Full Spectrum*, pp. 350–355.

24   'Official Spokesperson's Response to a Query on Participation of India in OBOR/BRI Forum,' Ministry of External Affairs, Government of India, 13 May 2017.

25   Ananth Krishnan, *India's China Challenge: A Journey through China's Rise and What It Means for India* (Noida: HarperCollins, 2020), pp. 182–193; Dhruva Jaishankar, 'Why are China and India in a Border Standoff?' *ChinaFile*, 8 August 2017.

26   Rudra Chaudhuri, 'Looking for Godot', *Indian Express*, 3 September 2017.

27   'U.S.-India Joint Strategic Vision for the Asia-Pacific and Indian Ocean Region', Office of the Press Secretary, The White House, 25 January 2015.

28   Medcalf, *Indo–Pacific Empire*, pp. 106–109; See also: Gurpreet S. Khurana, 'Security of Sea Lanes: Prospects for India-Japan Cooperation', *Strategic Analysis*, Vol. 31, No. 1, 2007; C. Raja Mohan, *Samudra Manthan: Sino-Indian Rivalry in the Indo–Pacific* (New Delhi: Oxford University Press, 2013); 'Confluence of the Two Seas: Speech by H.E. Mr. Shinzo Abe, Prime Minister of Japan at the Parliament of the Republic of India', (Provisional Translation), Ministry of Foreign Affairs of Japan, 22 August 2007.

29   'Defining Our Relationship with India for the Next Century: An Address by U.S. Secretary of State Rex Tillerson', Center for Strategic and International Studies, 18 October 2017; 'National Security Strategy of the United States of America', The White House, December 2017.

30   'Prime Minister's Keynote Address at Shangri La Dialogue', Ministry of External Affairs, Government of India, 1 June 2018.

31   'Secretary Michael R. Pompeo Opening Remarks at Quad Ministerial', US Department of State, 6 October 2020; Ministry of Defence, 'Malabar Naval Exercises' Press Information Bureau, Government of India, 8 February 2021.

32   Nandan Nilekani and Viral Shah, *Rebooting India: Realizing a Billion Aspirations* (Gurugram, Penguin, 2016).

33 'India-UAE Joint Statement during State Visit of Crown Prince of Abu Dhabi to India,' Ministry of External Affairs, Government of India, January 26, 2017; See also: P.R. Kumaraswamy, *The Arab-Israeli Conflict: A Ringside View* (Abingdon: Routledge, 2023).

34 Vyoma Jha, *The Making of the International Solar Alliance: India's Moment in the Sun* (Oxford: Oxford University Press, 2023).

35 Romila Thapar, N. Ram, Gautam Bhatia, and Gautam Patel, *On Citizenship* (New Delhi: Aleph, 2021).

36 'Official Spokesperson's Response to Media Queries Seeking Comments on the Statement Issues on 19 June by the Chinese Spokesperson the Events in the Galwan Valley Area', 20 June 2020.

37 Shiv Aroor, 'From Sky, See How China Builds Model of Indian Border 2400 km Away,' *Indian Express*, 5 August 2006.

38 'China Reveals Four Soldiers Killed in June 2020 Border Clash with India,' Reuters, 19 February 2021.

39 Ministry of Electronics & IT, 'Government Bans 59 Mobile Apps Which Are Prejudicial to Sovereignty and Integrity of India, Defence of India, Security of State and Public Order,' Press Information Bureau, 29 June 2020; Ministry of Finance, 'Restrictions on Public Procurement from Certain Countries,' Press Information Bureau, July 23, 2020; Ministry of Communications, 'Telecom Department Gives Go-Ahead for 5G Technology and Spectrum Trials,' Press Information Bureau, 4 May 2021.

40 'Joint Press Release of the 10th Round of China-India Corps Commander Level Meeting,' Ministry of External Affairs, Government of India, 21 February 2021.

41 'Official Spokesperson's Response to Media Queries on Disengagement at Area Gogra-Hot Springs (PP-15),' Ministry of External Affairs, Government of India, 9 September 2022.

42 Andrew Small and Dhruva Jaishankar, "For our Enemies, We Have Shotguns': Explaining China's New Assertiveness,' *War on the Rocks*, 20 July 2020.

43 'Joint Statement from Quad Leaders,' The White House, 24 September 2021.

44   Dhruva Jaishankar and Tanvi Madan, 'How the Quad Can Match the Hype,' *Foreign Affairs*, 15 April 2021.

45   'FACT SHEET: United States and India Elevate Strategic Partnership with the initiative on Critical and Emerging Technology (iCET),' The White House, 31 January 2023.

46   'Joint Statement from the United States and India,' The White House, June 22, 2023; Sameer P. Lalwani and Vikram J. Singh, 'What's the Deal with INDUS-X?' US Institute of Peace, 16 February 2024.

47   'Partnership for Peace, Progress and Prosperity. India-Russia Joint Statement following the visit of the President of the Russian Federation', The Kremlin, 6 December 2021.

48   'Joint Statement of the Russian Federation and the People's Republic of China on the International Relations Entering a New Era and the Global Sustainable Development', The Kremlin, 4 February 2022.

49   Rishabh Pratap, Larry Register and Heather Chen, 'Indian Leader Narendra Modi Tells Putin: Now Is Not the Time for War,' CNN.com, 17 September 2022.

50   Ministry of Commerce & Industry, 'Production Linked Incentive Schemes for 14 Key Sectors Aim to Enhance India's Manufacturing Capabilities and Exports,' Press Information Bureau, 2 August 2023.

51   '4. Indo–Pacific Economic Framework for Prosperity Agreement Relating to Supply Chain Resilience, done at San Francisco; November 14, 2023,' Office of Treaty Affairs, US Department of State, 24 February 2024.

52   Uditha Jayasinghe, 'India to Support Crisis-Hit Sri Lanka's Economic Recovery', Reuters, 23 June 2022.

53   'Joint Statement of the Leaders of India, Israel, United Arab Emirates, and the United States (I2U2)', The White House, 14 July 2022.

54   'Memorandum of Understanding on the Principles of an India Middle East Europe Economic Corridor', The White House, 9 September 2023.

55   Dhruva Jaishankar, 'A Common Agenda for the Global South', *Hindustan Times*, 5 April 2023.

56   Ammar Nainar, 'India's Foreign Assistance: Trends, Processes, and Priorities', Background Paper No. 25, Observer Research Foundation America, June 2024.

57   'English Translation of Prime Minister's Remarks at the G20 Summit Session 1,' Ministry of External Affairs, Government of India, 9 September 2023.

58   'G20 New Delhi Leaders' Declaration,' Ministry of External Affairs, Government of India, 9 September 2023.

59   'India to be world's third-largest economy by 2030—S&P Global Ratings,' Reuters, 5 December 2023.

Chapter 6: Atmanirbhar Bharat: Security and Prosperity

1   'Quarterly Fact Sheet: Fact Sheet on Foreign Direct Investment (FDI) Inflow', Department for Promotion of Industry and Internal Trade, Government of India, December 2023; 'Indian Petroleum & Natural Gas Statistics 2022-23', Economics and Statistics Division, Ministry of Petroleum and Natural Gas, 2024; 'Annexure-I to Rajya Sabha Unstarred Question No. 396: Data of Indian Students Studying Abroad', Ministry of External Affairs, 22 July 2021; Export-Import Data Bank, Department of Commerce, Ministry of Commerce and Industry, 11 May 2024.

2   William C. Hannas, James Mulvenon, and Anna B. Puglisi, *Chinese Industrial Espionage: Technology Acquisition and Military Modernization* (Abingdon: Routledge, 2013); Joachim Schild and Dirk H. Schmidt, EU and US Foreign Economic Policy Responses to China: The End of Naivety (Abingdon: Routledge, 2024), pp. 34–62.

3   Michael Pettis, *The Great Rebalancing: Trade, Conflict, and the Perilous Road Ahead for the World Economy* (Princeton: Princeton University Press, 2013).

4   Arvind Gupta, *How India Manages Its National Security* (Gurugram: Penguin Viking, 2018).

5   *SIPRI Yearbook: Armaments, Disarmament and International Security* (Oxford: Oxford University Press, 2023).

6   Amit Ahuja and Devesh Kapur, 'The State and Internal Security in India,' in Ahuja and Kapur, eds., *Internal Security in India: Violence, Order, and the State* (New York: Oxford University Press, 2023), pp. 6–19.

7   Ajey Lele and Parveen Bhardwaj, 'India's Nuclear Triad: A Net Assessment', IDSA Occasional Paper No. 31, Institute of Defence Studies and Analyses, April 2013.

8   Philip C. Saunders, Arthur S. Dingh, Andrew Scobell, Andrew N.D. Yang, and Joel Wuthnow, eds., *Chairman Xi Remakes the PLA: Assessing Chinese Military Reforms* (Washington, DC: NDU Press, 2019).

9   David Brewster, ed., *India & China at Sea: Competition for Naval Dominance in the Indian Ocean* (New Delhi: Oxford University Press, 2018).

10   Anit Mukherjee, *The Absent Dialogue: Politicians, Bureaucrats, and the Military in India* (New Delhi: Oxford University Press, 2019).

11   Ammar Nainar, 'The Evolution and Roles of India's National Security Council', Background Paper No. 7, Observer Research Foundation America, 25 February 2022.

12   Laxman Kumar Behera, 'Indian Defence Industry: Issues of Self Reliance', IDSA Monograph Series, No. 21, July 2013; Dhruva Jaishankar, 'The Indigenisation of India's Defence Industry', Brookings India, August 2019.

13   'India's Defence Exports Cross All-Time High of ₹21,000 crore: Rajnath,' *The Hindu*, 1 April 2024.

14   'FACT SHEET: United States and India Elevate Strategic Partnership with the initiative on Critical and Emerging Technology (iCET)', The White House, January 31, 2023; 'Joint Statement on the Establishment of the India-EU Trade and Technology Council', Ministry of External Affairs, February 6, 2023; 'Joint Statement of the Minerals Security Partnership', U.S.

Department of State, March 4, 2024; Ministry of Commerce & Industry, 'Indo–Pacific Economic Framework for Prosperity (IPEF) Supply Chain Agreement Signed by the 14 IPEF Partners', Press Information Bureau, 17 November 2023.

15   Rahul Nath Choudhury, 'What Went Wrong with India's FTAs?' *East Asia Forum*, 19 September 2023.

16   Samuel H. Preston, 'The Changing Relation between Mortality and Level of Economic Development', *Population Studies*, Vol. 29, No. 2, July 1975, pp. 231–248; Angus Deaton, *The Great Escape: Health, Wealth, and the Origins of Inequality* (Princeton: Princeton University Press, 2013), pp. 105–127.

17   Patrick French, *India: A Portrait* (New Delhi: Penguin, 2011), pp. 198–204.

18   M. Ramachandran, *Metro Rail Projects in India: A Study in Project Planning* (Oxford: Oxford University Press, 2011).

19   Jean Medawar and David Pyke, *Hitler's Gift: The True Story of the Scientists Expelled by the Nazi Regime* (New York: Simon & Schuster, 2000); Michael J. Neufeld, *Von Braun: Dreamer of Space, Engineer of War* (New York: Vintage Books, 2008).

20   Ian Grey, *Peter the Great: Emperor of All Russia* (Philadelphia: Lippincott, 1960); Pavel V. Oleynikov, 'German Scientists in the Soviet Atomic Project', *The Nonproliferation Review*, Summer 2000.

21   Ian Nish, ed., *The Iwakura Mission in American and Europe: A New Assessment* (London: Curzon Press, 1998).

22   Ibid.

23   Ezra Vogel, *Deng Xiaoping and the Transformation of China* (Cambridge: Harvard University Press, 2011), p. 303.

24   Ibid., pp. 377–594.

Chapter 7: Neighbourhood First: A Stable Periphery

1   'India-Bhutan Friendship Treaty', Ministry of External Affairs, 8 February 2007.

2   Vikrant Deshpande, 'Gorkhas of the Indian Army and India-Nepal Relations', Manohar Parrikar Institute for Defence Studies and Analyses, 17 February 2017.

3   Willem van Schendel, *A History of Bangladesh* (Cambridge: Cambridge University Press, 2020), pp. 217–255.

4   Pinak Ranjan Chakravarty, *Transformation: Emergence of Bangladesh and Evolution of India–Bangladesh Ties.* (New Delhi: KW Publishers, 2024).

5   A.C. Sinha, *Himalayan Kingdom Bhutan: Tradition, Transition and Transformation* (New Delhi: Indus, 2004), p. 230–232.

6   S.D. Muni, *India's Foreign Policy: The Democracy Dimension: With Special Reference to Neighbours* (New Delhi: Foundation Books, 2009).

7   Ranjit Rae, *Kathmandu Dilemma: Resetting India–Nepal Ties* (Gurugram: Penguin Random House India, 2022).

8   Shantanu Roy-Chaudhury, *The China Factor: Beijing's Expanding Engagement in Sri Lanka, Maldives, Bangladesh, and Myanmar* (Abingdon: Routledge, 2023); Monika Chansoria, *China: Military Modernisation and Strategy* (New Delhi: Centre for Land Warfare Studies, 2011); Amish Raj Mulmi, *All Roads Lead North: Nepal's Turn to China* (Chennai: Context, 2021).

9   Constantino Xavier, 'Bridging the Bay of Bengal: Toward a Stronger BIMSTEC,' Carnegie Endowment for International Peace, February 2018.

10   'BIMSTEC Charter,' Ministry of External Affairs, Government of India, March 30, 2022.

11   Bhumitra Chakma, *South Asian Regionalism: The Limits of Cooperation* (Bristol: Bristol University Press, 2020), pp. 122–129.

12   Ammar Nainar, 'India's Foreign Assistance: Trends, Processes, and Priorities', Observer Research Foundation America, June 2024.

13   Ibid.

14   Saneet Chakradeo, 'Neighbourhood First Responder: India's Humanitarian Assistance and Disaster Relief', Brookings India, August 2020.

15   Riya Sinha, 'Linking Land Borders: India's Integrated Check Posts', CSEP Working Paper No. 9, Centre for Social and Economic Progress, June 2021.

Chapter 8: Act East: Balancing China in the Indo–Pacific

1   Edgar Snow, *Red Star Over China: The Classic Account of the Birth of Chinese Communism* (New York: Grove, 1971); Sergey Radchenko, *Two Suns in the Heavens: The Sino-Soviet Struggle for Supremacy, 1962-1967* (Washington: Woodrow Wilson Center Press, 2009); Margaret MacMillan, *Nixon in China: The Week that Changed the World* (Toronto, Penguin, 2006).

2   Ezra F. Vogel, *Deng Xiaoping and the Transformation of China* (Cambridge: Harvard University Press, 2013).

3   Orville Schell, 'The Death of Engagement,' *The Wire China*, 7 June 2020.

4   Vijay Gokhale, *Tiananmen Square: The Making of a Protest* (Noida: HarperCollins, 2021).

5   David M. Lampton. *Same Bed, Different Dreams: Managing U.S.-China Relations, 1989-2000* (Berkeley: University of California Press, 2001), pp. 17–22.

6   Rush Doshi, *The Long Game: China's Grand Strategy to Displace American Order* (New York: Oxford University Press, 2021); Michael Pillsbury, The Hundred-Year marathon: China's Secret Strategy to Replace America as the Global Superpower (New York: Henry Holt, 2015).

7   Dinny McMahon, *Great Wall of Debt: Shadow Banks, Ghost Cities, Massive Loans, and the End of the Chinese Miracle* (New York: Houghton Mifflin, 2018).

8   William C. Hannas, James Mulvenon, and Anna B. Puglisi, *Chinese Industrial Espionage: Technology Acquisition and Military Modernization* (Abingdon: Routledge, 2013).

9   Bill Hayton, *The South China Sea: The Struggle for Power in Asia* (New Haven: Yale University Press, 2014); Monika Chansoria,

China, Japan, and Senkaku Islands: Conflict in the East China Sea amid an America Shadow (Abingdon: Routledge, 2018).

10 Andrew Small and Dhruva Jaishankar, '"For our Enemies, We Have Shotguns": Explaining China's New Assertiveness', *War on the Rocks*, 20 July 2020.

11 Bruce W. MacDonald, 'China, Space Weapons, and U.S. Security,' Council Special Report No. 38, Council on Foreign Relations, September 2008; Leslie Hook and Benedict Mander, 'The Fight to Own Antarctica,' *Financial Times*, 24 May 2018.

12 Iskander Rehman, 'India, China, and Differing Conceptions of the Maritime Order,' The Brookings Institution, 20 June 2017.

13 'Official Spokesperson's Response to a Query on Participation of India in OBOR/BRI Forum', Ministry of External Affairs, Government of India, 13 May 2017.

14 Frederic Grare, *India Turns East: International Engagement and US-China Rivalry* (Gurgaon: Penguin Random House, 2017).

15 Dhruva Jaishankar, 'Acting East: India in the Indo–Pacific', Brookings India, 2019.

16 Gurpreet S. Khurana, 'Security of Sea Lanes: Prospects for India-Japan Cooperation', *Strategic Analysis*, Vol. 31, No. 1, 2007; C. Raja Mohan, *Samudra Manthan: Sino-Indian Rivalry in the Indo–Pacific* (New Delhi: Oxford University Press, 2013).

17 'Confluence of the Two Seas: Speech by H.E. Mr. Shinzo Abe, Prime Minister of Japan at the Parliament of the Republic of India,' (Provisional Translation), Ministry of Foreign Affairs of Japan, 22 August 2007.

18 C. Raja Mohan, *Samudra Manthan: Sino-Indian Rivalry in the Indo–Pacific* (New Delhi: Oxford University Press, 2013), p. 212.

19 'Inaugural Address by Prime Minister at Second Raisina Dialogue', New Delhi, 17 January 2017.

20 'National Security Strategy of the United States of America', The White House, December 2017.

21 'Prime Minister's Keynote Address at Shangri La Dialogue', Ministry of External Affairs, Government of India, 1 June 2018.

22   Darshana M. Baruah, *The Contest for the Indian Ocean: And the Making of a New World Order* (New Haven: Yale University Press, 2024).

23   'Indian Maritime Security Strategy,' Indian Navy, Government of India, January 2016, p. 25.

24   'Text of PM's Address to the National Assembly of Mauritius,' Press Information Bureau, Government of India, 12 March 2015.

25   Jonathan Bellish, 'The Economic Cost of Somali Piracy 2012,' Oceans Beyond Piracy, April 2013.

26   Maria Abi-Habib, 'How China Got Sri Lanka to Cough Up a Port', *New York Times*, 25 June 2018.

27   Andrew S. Erickson, ed., *Chinese Naval Shipbuilding: An Ambitious and Uncertain Course* (Annapolis: Naval Institute Press, 2016).

28   Darshana M. Baruah, 'Maritime Competition in the Indian Ocean', Testimony before the U.S.-China Economic and Security Review Commission, 12 May 2022.

29   Jivanta Schottli, ed., *Maritime Governance and South Asia: Trade, Security and Sustainable Development in the Indian Ocean* (Singapore: World Scientific, 2018), pp. 10, 160, 217.

30   Raja Menon, 'Scenarios for China's Naval Deployment in the Indian Ocean and India's Naval Response', in David Brewster, ed., *India and China at Sea: Competition for Dominance in the Indian Ocean* (New Delhi: Oxford University Press, 2018).

31   Rahman Yaacob and Jack Sato, 'Southeast Asia's Preferred Military Exercise Partner', *Interpreter*, The Lowy Institute, 29 February 2024.

32   Sharon Seah et al., 'The State of Southeast Asia: 2024 Survey Report,' ISEAS-Yusof Ishak Institute, 2 April 2024.

33   Sanjeev Miglani, 'India to Supply Vietnam with Naval Vessels amid China Disputes,' Reuters, 28 October 2014; Ian Storey, 'Myanmar's Submarines: The Race Is on between China and Russia', *Fulcrum*, 4 January 2022; Dinakar Peri, 'India Delivers First Batch of BrahMos to Philippines,' *The Hindu*, 19 April 2024.

34   Prabir De, Sunetra Ghatak, and Durairaj Kumarasamy, 'Accessing Economic Impacts of Connectivity Corridors: An Empirical

Investigation', Research and Information System for Developing Countries (RIS), 2018.

35 Condoleeza Rice, 'Promoting the National Interest', *Foreign Affairs*, Vol. 79, No. 1, January–February 2000, pp. 45–62.

36 'Background Briefing by Administration Officials on U.S.-India Relations,' Office of the Spokesman, U.S. Department of State, 25 March 2005.

37 Ashley J. Tellis, 'The U.S.-India 'Global Partnership': How Significant for American Interests?' Testimony before U.S. House Committee on International Relations, 17 November 2005.

38 Hillary Clinton, 'America's Pacific Century', *Foreign Policy*, 11 October 2011.

39 'US–India Joint Strategic Vision for the Asia-Pacific and Indian Ocean Region', Ministry of External Affairs, Government of India, 25 January 2015.

40 Dhruva Jaishankar, 'A Confluence of Two Strategies: The Japan-India Security Partnership in the Indo–Pacific', in Rajesh Basrur and Sumitha Narayanan Kutty, eds., *India and Japan: Assessing the Strategic Partnership* (Singapore: Palgrave Pivot, 2018).

41 Ibid.

42 Dhruva Jaishankar, 'The Australia-India Strategic Partnership: Accelerating Security Cooperation in the Indo–Pacific', The Lowy Institute, 16 September 2020.

43 Tanvi Madan, 'The Rise, Fall, and Rebirth of the "Quad"', *War on the Rocks*, 16 November 2017; Dhruva Jaishankar and Tanvi Madan, 'How the Quad Can Match the Hype', *Foreign Affairs*, 15 April 2021.

44 Ministry of Electronics & IT, 'Government Bans 59 Mobile Apps Which Are Prejudicial to Sovereignty and Integrity of India, Defence of India, Security of State and Public Order', Press Information Bureau, 29 June 2020; Ministry of Finance, 'Restrictions on Public Procurement from Certain Countries,' Press Information Bureau, 23 July 2020; Ministry of Communications, 'Telecom Department Gives Go-Ahead for 5G Technology and Spectrum Trials', Press Information Bureau, 4 May 2021.

45   Adnan Aamir, 'The Grey List: More Trouble for Pakistan's Economy', *Interpreter*, The Lowy Institute, 18 July 2018.

Chapter 9: Thinking West: Pakistan, Afghanistan, and West Asia

1   Rached Ghannouchi, 'From Political Islam to Muslim Democracy', *Foreign Affairs*, September/October 2016; Shadi Hamid, *Islamic Exceptionalism: How the Struggle Over Islam is Shaping the World* (New York: St. Martin's Press, 2016).

2   I.K. Khan, *Islam in Modern Asia* (New Delhi: MD Publications, 2006), p. 344.

3   Mark Tessler, *A History of the Israeli-Palestinian Conflict*, 2nd Ed. (Bloomington: Indiana University Press, 2009).

4   Sayyid Abul A' La Maududi, *Islamic Law and Constitution*, trans. Khurshid Ahmad (Lahore: Islamic Publications, 1960).

5   Sayyid Qutb, *In the Shade of the Qur'an: Vol. 1*, trans. Adil Salahi (Markfield, UK: Islamic Foundation, 2015).

6   Zhand Shakibi, *Khatami and Gorbachev: Politics of Change in the Islamic Republic of Iran and the USSR* (London and New York: I.B. Tauris, 2010), p. 84.

7   Said Amir Arjomand, *The Turban for the Crown: The Islamic Revolution in Iran* (New York: Oxford University Press, 1988).

8   Pascal Ménoret, 'Fighting for the Holy Mosque: The 1979 Mecca Insurgency', in *Treading on Hallowed Ground*, eds. C. Christine Fair and Sumit Ganguly (New York: Oxford University Press, 2008).

9   Steve Coll, *Ghost Wars: The Secret History of the CIA, Afghanistan, and bin Laden, from the Soviet Invitation to September 10, 2001* (New York: Penguin Press, 2001).

10   *The 9/11 Commission Report: Final Report of the National Commission on Terrorist Attacks Upon the United States* (New York: W.W. Norton, 2011).

11   Mark Bowden, *The Finish: The Killing of Osama bin Laden* (New York: Atlantic Monthly Press, 2012).

12   Stephen Tankel, *Storming the World Stage: The Story of Lashkar-e-Taiba* (New York: Oxford University Press, 2013).

13   Will McCants, *The ISIS Apocalypse: The History, Strategy, and Doomsday Vision of the Islamic State* (New York: Palgrave Macmillan, 2015).

14   Rama Lakshmi, 'Saudi Arabia's Policy Shift toward India Helps Nab Terror Suspects,' *Washington Post*, 6 July 2012.

15   C. Christine Fair, *Fighting to the End: The Pakistan Army's Way of War* (New York: Oxford University Press, 2014), p. 226–251.

16   Steve Coll, *Directorate S: The C.I.A. and America's Secret Wars in Afghanistan and Pakistan, 2001-2016* (London: Allen Lane, 2018), p. 45.

17   Praveen Swami, *India, Pakistan and the Secret Jihad: The Covet War in Kashmir, 1947-2004* (New York: Routledge, 2007).

18   Husain Haqqani, *Magnificent Delusions: Pakistan, the United States, and an Epic History of Misunderstanding* (New York: PublicAffairs, 2013), p. 297.

19   Coll, *Directorate S*, pp. 345–346.

20   Haqqani, *Magnificent Delusions*, p. 297; Coll, *Ghost Wars*, p. 221.

21   Coll, *Directorate S*, pp. 444, 460.

22   Fair, *Fighting to the End*, p. 4.

23   Ayesha Siddiqa, *Military Inc.: Inside Pakistan's Military Economy*, 2nd Edition (London: Pluto Press, 2017).

24   Avinash Paliwal, *My Enemy's Enemy: India in Afghanistan from the Soviet Invasion to the US Withdrawal* (Noida: HarperCollins, 2017), pp. 122–137.

25   'Joint Statement of the Leaders of India, Israel, United Arab Emirates, and United States (I2U2),' The White House, 14 July 2022.

26   'Memorandum of Understanding on the Principles of an India-Middle East-Europe Economic Corridor', The White House, 9 September 2023.

Chapter 10: A Leading Power: Shaping the International Order

1 Mark Mazower, *Governing the World: The History of an Idea, 1815 to Present* (New York: Penguin, 2013).

2 Benn Steil, *The Marshall Plan: Dawn of the Cold War* (Oxford: Oxford University Press, 2018), pp. 2–13.

3 Garrett Hardin, 'The Tragedy of the Commons', *Science*, Vol. 162, 1968, pp. 1243–1248; See also Elinor Ostrom et al., 'Revisiting the Commons: Local Lessons, Global Challenges', *Science*, Vol. 284, 1999, pp. 278–282.

4 Kabir Taneja, 'India Arrives at the Arctic,' *New York Times*, 20 May 2013; Leslie Hook and Benedict Mander, 'The Fight to Own Antarctica', *Financial Times*, 24 May 2018.

5 Costas Paris, Thomas Di Fonzo, and Liliana Llamas, 'A Brief History of Shipping', *Wall Street Journal*, 24 January 2018.

6 Christoph Lakner and Branko Milanovic, 'Global Income Distribution: From the Fall of the Berlin Wall to the Great Recession', Policy Research Working Paper, No. WPS 6719, World Bank Group, 1 December 2013; Joe Hasell, Max Roser, Esteban Ortiz-Ospina, and Pablo Arriagada, 'Poverty', *Our World in Data*, 2022, https://ourworldindata.org/poverty; Saloni Dattani, Finoa Spooner, Hannah Ritchie, and Max Roser, 'Child and Infant Mortality', *Our World in Data*, 2023, https://ourworldindata.org/child-mortality; Max Roser and Esteban Ortiz-Ospina, 'Literacy', *Our World in Data*, 2018, https://ourworldindata.org/literacy; Saloni Dattani, Lucas Rodes-Guirao, Hannah Ritchie, Esteban Ortiz-Ospina, and Max Roser, 'Life Expectancy,' *Our World in Data*, 2023, https://ourworldindata.org/life-expectancy.

7 Bastian Herre, Lucas Rodes-Guirao, Max Roser, Joe Hasell, and Bobbie Macdonald, 'War and Peace', *Our World in Data*, 2024, https://ourworldindata.org/war-and-peace.

Index